MONEY MORONS

THEIR CAUSES & CURES

Mark DiGiovanni

iUniverse books may be ordered through booksellers or by contacting:

iUniverse
1663 Liberty Drive
Bloomington, IN 47403
www.iuniverse.com
1-800-Authors (1-800-288-4677)

ISBN: 978-1-4401-4281-9 (sc)
ISBN: 978-1-4401-4282-6 (ebook)

Printed in the United States of America

iUniverse rev. date: 10/5/2009

This book is dedicated to those who have entrusted me with their financial future. You honor me more than words can say.

Contents

▪ Page 7......**Introduction**

▪ Page 12....**Money – What It Isn't & What It Is**
Considering the time we spend earning it, spending it, and trying to accumulate it, we are remarkably uninformed about money and its role in our lives.

▪ Page 30....**You're Human – But That's No Excuse**
Along with understanding money, we need to understand ourselves and all the things we do to sabotage ourselves when it comes to money.

▪ Page 58....**Death By Debt**
The Bible says that the borrower is slave to the lender, but the Bible is soft-pedaling the danger that debt poses to those who dare mistreat it.

▪ Page 84....**Champions Start With Defense**
Protection against catastrophe is boring and a waste of money, right up to the moment catastrophe strikes and it saves your life.

▪ Page 114...**Money At Work**
You're not getting to where you want to go without money doing most of the driving, so you better know how to give it directions.

▪ Page 156...**A Home First – A House Second**
If you think your house is your biggest single investment, you're overlooking those who reside there with you.

▪ Page 174...**The $2,000,000 BMW**
The reason the last quarter of your life may be spent in abject poverty and misery may be sitting in your driveway.

▪ Page 192...**Money Morons – The Next Generation**
American youth today have more money, more access to money, and less knowledge about money than any group of people in history – that's not good.

▪ Page 210...**You – At 82**
You're either going to die young or grow old, and since most people prefer the latter, you need to know how to get ready for your personal fourth quarter.

▪ Page 246...**Don't Make This Journey Alone**
Just as Lewis and Clark had Sacajawea to safely guide them, you are more likely to get where you want to go with a trusted competent advisor by your side.

▪ Page 256...**Miscellaneous Money Musings**
Words of wisdom from people much smarter than the author.

▪ Page 260...**Appreciations**

Page 261...**References**

INTRODUCTION

You owe it all to Croesus.

You owe him your job, your paycheck, your house, your mortgage, your car, your credit cards, all your assets and all your liabilities. Without Croesus, your wealth would consist only of what you could produce with your bare hands and could swap with someone else for what they produce. The previous list is a lot to owe to someone you probably never heard of. Not to worry, though. Croesus has been dead for over 2,500 years, so he won't be coming to collect.

Croesus (pronounced CREE-suss) was the King of Lydia from 560 to 546 B.C. Lydia was a small kingdom in what is today western Turkey. While the Lydians were known for producing perfume and cosmetics, that wasn't their source of greatness. Croesus is credited with the production of the first gold and silver coins to be used in trade; in essence, he invented money as we know it today. The widespread use of coins as a medium of exchange enabled Lydia to become the first society to become wealthy from trade and not conquest. The durability of coins enabled wealth to be accumulated for future use in a way that commodities like grain and cattle could not. The desirability and familiarity of gold and silver to the world at large enabled coins minted from these metals to be accepted as a unit of account and as a medium of exchange by almost everyone, everywhere.

Other cultures had come up with methods of facilitating trade before Croesus, but they had severe limitations. For example, the ancient Aztecs used cacao (from which chocolate is made) to make up the difference when a barter transaction wasn't even. Commodity money like cacao made more trading possible, and commodity money like cacao, tobacco or deerskins (the original *buck*) had uses all on their own. But such commodities had a limited shelf life, and were not always accepted in trade.

It's interesting to see how humans revert back to commodity money when traditional money stops being useful. Zimbabwe, with an inflation rate in the neighborhood of 11 million percent (which is not a misprint) is now a barter economy. During communist rule in Romania, cigarettes were the currency of choice, much as they are in prisons. If money becomes worthless because the government prints too much of it (Zimbabwe), if the money is useless because there's nothing to buy (Romania), or if a commodity like cigarettes is a more useful medium of exchange (prisons), then traditional money loses its influence. But these are the exceptions. Money exists simply because it is more useful than the alternatives.

MONEY MORONS

Money connected humans in greater numbers than anything before or since its creation. Although the breadth of relationships widened because of money, the depth of relationships narrowed. Money weakened connections that had been based on family, tribe, religion and nationality. Money enabled the establishment of the bottom line, and the bottom line began to dominate more and more human actions. Money became the measure of the value of work, of time, and even of human life itself. Slaves were first brought to the new world to work the mines to fill the coffers of the European powers with gold and silver.

Money has also been a great democratizing force in history. The ancient Greeks were one of history's greatest cultures, but they didn't have great armies; they couldn't even organize into a single state. Greece became great because of trade made possible by money, which they copied from the Lydians. Money helped the Greeks democratize, and made possible a society that could produce people like Plato and Aristotle. Even the word *economics* comes from Greek, and means skilled in managing an estate. Money enabled Greek society to more fully tap its potential.

The Roman Empire was actually organized around money. Prior empires favored government as the center of organization, but the Romans realized they could extend their empire further, incorporate conquered peoples into the Roman mindset, and facilitate trade within all parts of the empire with a standardized monetary system. It is said that the coins used to flow from the Roman mint in a constant stream. The Latin word *currere*, which means to flow, was used to describe the stream. Our word *currency* comes from it.

With the collapse of the Roman Empire around 500 A.D., a thousand years of money's predominance ended. Almost another thousand years would pass before money would reemerge as an economic factor. And it was the rebirth of money in new and different forms that promoted advances in human achievement that continue to this day.

Up until the last hundred years or so, common people only borrowed money out of desperation. To charge interest on loaned money was the sin of usury, and the Christian Church had strict laws forbidding it. What little money lending there was at the time was often handled by Jews, who were not subject to the constraints of the church. But the laws against usury applied to loans; if some other method, like a contract was used to transfer money, the restrictions on usury could be bypassed without risking excommunication. Around 1300, some clever Italian merchants figured out this loophole.

In the early 14th century, the church's power was in decline, and no state powers could yet fill the vacuum. The Knights Templar (see *The Da Vinci Code*) had been the de facto bankers of Europe with endorsement by the

Pope until King Philip IV of France crushed them to obtain their wealth in 1314.

A handful of wealthy families in northern Italy stepped in to fill the void left by the destruction of the Knights Templar. These families had a slightly different business model than the knights. These new financiers served everyone, not just the nobility. And they weren't doing it for God; they were doing it for profit.

The word *bank* is derived from the Italian for *bench*, and these families started modestly by operating from a bench or table at fairs in their hometowns. To avoid accusations of usury from charging interest on a loan, the Italian merchants created and traded bills of exchange, which were written documents that ordered a specific payment in gold or silver to a specific person at a specific place and time. The person writing the bill of exchange acted as an intermediary between someone needing money and someone with the means to provide it, and they collected a fee for their services.

Bills of exchange were a boon to finance. They were much easier to transport than comparable amounts of gold or silver. If a bill of exchange was lost or stolen, it could not be redeemed by another. They were harder to counterfeit than coins because only literates could counterfeit a bill of exchange, and literates were few and far between and occupied the upper most rungs of society.

Bills of exchange had the effect of increasing the amount of money in circulation as well as the speed of circulation. Money was now liberated from the physical limitations imposed by scarce and cumbersome coins and a primitive transportation system. The checks and paper money we use today are the descendents of these early bills of exchange.

Even though bills of exchange greatly improved the circulation of money, they ultimately had to be paid in precious metal. The amount of money in circulation, and the ability of an economy to grow were dependent on the amount of gold and silver. This constant need for more gold and silver was the reason for the discovery and colonization of the Americas. Between 1500 and 1800, an estimated 2,800 tons of gold and 155,000 tons of silver were extracted and shipped from Spanish and Portuguese colonies in the Americas to Europe. Because of this influx of gold and silver, money was being produced faster than were goods to buy, leading to history's first inflationary economies.

As economies grew in size and complexity, so did governments. These governments, whether Chinese, Italian, American or other, saw the issuance of paper money as a way of gaining greater control of the money supply and of their economy. Paper money as we think of it today was the creation of Benjamin Franklin who was among other things, a printer. The success of the American Revolution (as well as the subsequent success of America itself) was made possible by paper money. It was the first war financed in such a manner. Of course, the paper money was in effect deficit spending, and created horrible inflation during the revolution and immediately after. Americans were so disgusted with the economic effects of paper money (despite the fact that it financed their independence), paper money would virtually disappear from the scene until the Civil War.

As long as paper money was redeemable in silver or gold, the amount that could be circulated was limited. Paper money was a very practical incarnation, but it could not exist separate from gold or silver backing it, without creating problems of inflation and public skepticism about its value. Fiscal conservatives had preferred a gold-only standard because its supply now and in the future was more predictable. People needing a larger and looser money supply, farmers in particular, wanted a bi-metal standard of gold and silver. Farmers borrowed regularly, and more money also meant cheaper money in the form of lower interest rates. This conflict between eastern bankers and western farmers was captured in *The Wizard of Oz*, published in 1900. Dorothy and her companions represent the farmers. The counterfeit wizard represents the eastern bankers. (Dorothy's magical slippers are silver in the book; ruby looked better for a color movie.)

World economies spent much of the twentieth century extricating themselves from the gold standard, so that no major world currency is now backed by gold. The great benefit to this change is that economies are no longer limited in size by the amount of gold their governments hold. The risk is that governments will finance expenditures by simply printing more money, which they find preferable to raising taxes. This can lead to inflation, as money in circulation increases faster than goods or services available for purchase.

A nation's currency is only as stable as its government's discipline in issuing it. The Treaty of Versailles that ended World War I required Germany to pay reparations totaling some $33 billion, or twice the total annual GDP of the country. As Germany printed more money to meet reparation payments, inflation raged. What had cost one German mark at war's end cost 700 billion marks four years later. The chaos and humiliation this hyperinflation created in Germany was a catalyst for Hitler's rise to power a few years later. Currently, Zimbabwe's disastrous land reform program has had similar results. Over a six-month period in 2008, a loaf of bread went from 200,000 to 1,600,000,000,000 (1.6 trillion) Zimbabwean dollars.

Money has continuously become less constrained over time. First, it no longer had to be in the form of gold or silver coin. Then it no longer had to even be backed by gold or silver. A banking and checking system meant that money was seen less and less frequently in the form of cash. Today, with electronic deposit, automated bill pay and credit cards, the vast majority of the world's money is nothing more than electronic blips. Someone making $100,000 this year is likely to see less than $2,000 of that in the form of cash. The rest is out there in cyberspace.

As money has become less constrained, its control has become decentralized. Money now moves more from bottom-up than from top-down. Financial institutions don't have to create currency to create money. They don't need printing presses or armored cars to generate and transport capital all over the globe. When you can buy stock on the Tokyo Exchange or transfer funds to the Bank of Dubai with the click of a mouse, Fort Knox becomes an anachronism. Individuals and institutions are replacing governments as the real controllers of money supply and movement.

Money now moves at the speed of light. It also moves at the speed of thought, which makes careful thought more necessary than ever when it comes to decisions about money. Shrinking attention spans and thousands of daily distractions make it hard to give money decisions a proper gestation period. The ability to send your money to anyone anywhere on a whim and a mouse click only compounds the risk of sending your money to a place from whence it ne'er shall return.

Money of today not only has the ability to move from anywhere to anywhere, money of today has an unprecedented ability to be created from the money of tomorrow. Governments can create more money today, but its value today comes in part from its diminished capacity tomorrow, as inflation whittles away its purchasing power in the future. Individuals can transform the money of tomorrow into the money of today with the swipe of a credit card. The problem with moving money from the future to the present is you will then spend the future paying for the past.

Money is easily one of man's most wonderful and powerful inventions. Such an invention, be it money, language, or nuclear fission requires a thorough understanding of it in order to obtain its benefits while at the same time avoiding disaster. Let the understanding of money begin.

MONEY:

WHAT IT ISN'T
&
WHAT IT IS

Before we can understand what money is, it is necessary to get an understanding of what money is not. By clearing away some of the misconceptions we have about money, by realizing that money isn't many of the things we think it is, we can then get a clearer understanding of what money really is. Once we get a better understanding of what money is and isn't, we can then give money the appropriate place in our lives, and use it properly.

Money Isn't the Cause

You're going to spend some 100,000 hours training for and working at your work. I know you work to get paid, and you work harder in the hopes of getting paid more. So how can I say that money isn't the cause of all that effort?

You aren't working for the money. You are working (hopefully) for two reasons: to give meaning to your life by making a contribution to society, by providing your fellow man with needed goods and services. And you are working to provide you and your family with all of the necessities and a few of the luxuries of life. Money has nothing to do with the first reason for working. (If you are getting none of the first reason out of your work, no amount of money can make up for that absence.) As for the second reason, money is a medium of exchange that enables you to efficiently convert your work into those necessities and luxuries that are the actual cause of your work. Never confuse money as the cause of what you do with the real cause of what you do. The real cause is what you use the money for. The rest of this chapter discusses some of the intangibles that we seek to acquire through money.

If money is acquired through an illegal or immoral process, its use will be tainted by the method of obtainment, regardless of the morality of its use. Money legally acquired that is used for an illegal or immoral purpose is similarly tainted. Both the method of acquiring money and its use must be legal and moral to prevent either being corrupted.

If the cause is the acquisition of money, albeit legally, and the only purpose of that money is its acquisition and accumulation, then the cause is itself bankrupt. The cause of money acquisition must always be something larger than acquisition as its own end. The cause may be providing shelter, saving for old age, helping a destitute stranger, or merely the purchase of an interesting knick-knack. Even a frivolous reason for acquiring money is better than having no reason at all.

Money should never be the end, only the means to an end.

Money Isn't (a) God

When money is desired only for money's sake, it is the beginning of the worship of money. It is not accidental that the Bible mentions money more than any other topic, which is in large part because we are more likely to use money more than anything else in this world as a substitute for the Almighty.

A couple of biblical passages are especially relevant in this conversation. The first is "The love of money is the root of all evil." Many people abbreviate this phrase to "Money is the root of all evil." Such editing creates an entirely different and incorrect meaning. Saying that money is the root of evil is to blame money for the evil. But it is the love of money, not the money that is the problem. And the love of money comes from within us, and it is our fault if we allow it to develop. Saying that money is the root of all evil is to try to shift the blame for our weakness to an inanimate object. It is like blaming heroin addiction not on the user or the dealer, but on the heroin itself. It is absolving, it is easy, and it is wrong.

The other biblical passage of note is "Render unto Caesar that which is Caesar's, and unto God that which is God's." Our life is spent walking a tightrope between the material world and the spiritual world. Part of awareness involves understanding the relative position of these two worlds and reconciling them to each other. What Jesus is trying to tell us in that passage is to not let the material world dominate the spiritual world, and that money is insignificant in comparison to one's relationship with God.

The amassing of wealth can give us the illusion of self-sufficiency, which is a delusion. This delusion makes us believe we don't need other people, and that we don't need God. Such pride was considered a sin in times past, and weakened the bonds of a society, and weakened the bonds between individuals and God. The material world is not evil; it is merely secondary to the spiritual world. When we allow ourselves to forget that and make the material world primary, evil actions are an almost inevitable result.

The less the role of God in your life, the more likely you are to ask money to fill that void. This substitution does not mean that material wealth and spiritual well-being are mutually exclusive. Many people with a strong spiritual side become very rich, but they do so because they understand money's secondary role in their life. Those who do not seek to worship a higher being are doomed to worship something of this earth, and money is almost always the default god of choice.

If you need confirmation that money is not a god, look at your money. It says "In God We Trust". It does not say "In This We Trust". Even money itself understands its subordinate role in our lives.

Money Isn't Power

If you read *The Millionaire Next Door*, you get an interesting and surprising portrait of the American millionaire. Millionaires are typically male, have a college degree, are in their mid-50's, own their own business, have been married only once, live well below their means, are actively involved in their community, and are first-generation wealthy. In short, their status as millionaires is not the result of a love of money; it is the result of extraordinary self-discipline.

It is easy to think that money is power because we often see people with money exerting influence on those without money. We conclude that money is the most obvious difference between the parties, so money must be the reason for the difference in power. What we tend to ignore is the self-discipline and strength of character of the person with money. A person with such traits is able to exert enormous influence over people, without the introduction of personal wealth. History is full of such people: Martin Luther King, Jr., Gandhi, Abraham Lincoln, Joan of Arc, Jesus.

Exerting influence is not the same as exerting power. Influence involves persuasion and leading people in a direction they want to move to, but may not have the knowledge or courage to do so. Power involves using negative reinforcement to compel someone to do something they would not do without the threat of harm - physical, financial or otherwise. You use influence on your allies; you use power against your enemies.

People who have accumulated money through hard work, self-discipline and honesty have few, if any, enemies. When we see someone using money to compel others to act against their own self-interest, it is likely the person with money did not obtain it with integrity. If their money had been acquired through hard work, self-discipline and honesty, they would have more respect for that money, and would use it more carefully. People who misuse money in such a manner eventually have it taken away from them. Their character flaws make it almost impossible to control such a valuable asset for a long time. Their ability to control money is undermined by their inability to control themselves.

America has a lot of wealthy people in it, and there are certainly many wealthy people who equate their money with power; this equation is a primary reason they wanted to acquire wealth. Such people are weak, and they equate money with power because they equate a lack of money with weakness. The ability to be ruled by people with money is first and foremost the result of an inability to rule money in one's own life. Someone with an understanding of money and a self-discipline about money is immune from anyone attempting to use money to get them to act against their own self-interest.

Money is power against you only if you are under the power of money.

Money Isn't a Weapon

Let's first clarify what a weapon is. A weapon is a device used to harm another person. If a weapon is used for offensive purposes, its use assumes the desire to harm the other person in some way. Even when a weapon is used for defensive purposes, its effectiveness is based on deterrence backed by the threat of harm. The greater the ability to harm someone, the more effective is the weapon. An arrow isn't much of a weapon until you match it with a bow. Some items, like a frying pan or money, were not designed to be weapons, but do get used as such on occasion.

With true weapons, it is their use against the other person that creates harm to that person. It would be difficult to argue that discharging money at someone would be harmful. If you gave $1,000 to a heroin addict, it is possible they may use that money to inject a fatal overdose. But the addict used free will to decide what to do with the money. Money was not the instrument of destruction here.

When people attempt to use money as a weapon, it is usually done by withholding money, not by providing it. A couple going through a bitter divorce may use the withholding of money to extract concessions from the other side. The federal government routinely threatens to withhold funds to compel state and local governments to meet various requirements, from clean air standards to test scores in schools. Going back to the addict analogy, it isn't the supplying of the drug that frightens the addict; it is the withholding of the drug that frightens the addict.

To be vulnerable to money being used as a weapon against you, you have to have put yourself in a position similar to the addict. You have to need an inflow of money to the extent that any disruption of that inflow is extremely harmful. (We're all vulnerable to some degree.) More important, you have to be dependent on others providing you with your money "fix." I'm not talking about depending on your employer for your paycheck. You earn that paycheck through a fair and voluntary exchange of labor for it. If you lose your job, you can still get another. I'm talking about the person who receives money from others without giving something in return. Whether the money comes from a government program or a domineering parent, the person who accepts it runs the risk of being coerced into behaviors they object to, because that seems less repugnant than the loss of funding.

Someone attempting to use money as a weapon runs the risk of unintended consequences. Using money as a weapon is guaranteed to destroy relationships and create enemies. Rarely does someone use money to harm others without harming themselves as well. Money makes a poor weapon in part because it almost always backfires on its user.

Money Isn't Character

"Just because you are a character doesn't mean that you have character." opines Winston Wolfe in *Pulp Fiction.* To extend Mr. Wolfe's line of thought further, just because you have money doesn't mean you have character. Character in this sense refers to moral or ethical strength, integrity, fortitude.

In America we admire wealth to such a degree that we often assume the people who have wealth are admirable as well. At the same time, there can be a certain envy of the wealthy, which can make us think less of them because of their wealth. What is your reaction to the name Donald Trump? For most people, there is a definite reaction, either positive or negative. A Donald Trump is either admired as a person for his financial success or reviled because he seems to rub everyone's nose in it. What is your reaction to the name Warren Buffett? I'm guessing it's a more muted reaction. Although Warren Buffett's net worth is at least fifteen times Donald Trump's, Buffett doesn't elicit many negative reactions. This juxtaposition is due in large part to people's perceptions that Warren Buffett does not seek the spotlight and does not seem to be purposely reminding us of his wealth and success.

In truth, most people of wealth are also people of high character. Since most wealthy people in this country made it through hard work and sacrifice (Buffett and Trump included), it is safe to assume their character is an asset to them, and a large reason for their financial success. Very few of the wealthy are known by the general public. I recognize only a few names on the Forbes 400 list of richest Americans. You probably know a millionaire or three. There's a good chance you don't know they are wealthy, though. Most people who accumulate wealth are discreet about their wealth. The guy you know that flaunts his "wealth" is likely one missed paycheck away from bankruptcy. When you've got it, you don't need to flaunt it.

A person of high character possesses the traits that make them immune to the negative aspects of money. A person possessing loyalty, integrity, discipline, honesty and generosity instinctively knows the limitations of money. A person of high character does not expect money to provide human qualities that can only be generated from within. If you are a person of high character, you can't be bought, and you would never "sell out" someone else, or yourself.

Money isn't character, but it can reveal character. How someone earns money and how he spends it reveals his priorities, and priorities reveal character. Someone of high character will earn money honestly, save it seriously, spend it carefully, and give it generously. Man makes the money; money doesn't make the man (or woman).

Money Isn't Happiness

If you ever doubt the uniqueness or greatness of the United States, remember these words, *the pursuit of happiness*. No other nation in the history of the world has ever embedded an individual's pursuit of happiness as a national right.

Success is getting what you want. Happiness is wanting what you get. It is easy to assume that with success comes happiness. For success to also bring happiness, the goal one is seeking must be correctly perceived. One of the worst feelings a person can experience is, after achieving success with great effort, they end up thinking, "This isn't what I thought it would be."

The dictionary uses the words *well-adapted*, *appropriate* and *felicitous* when defining *happiness*. Just as it is important not to equate success with happiness, it is also important not to confuse happiness with pleasure. The dictionary uses the words *sensation*, *amusement*, *diversion* and *indulgence* when defining *pleasure*. Pleasure usually involves an external stimulus, is mostly physical in nature, and is short-lived. Happiness involves thoughts and emotions, and is generated internally, not externally. The act of procreation (generally) gives pleasure. Holding your newborn child in your arms brings happiness.

Money can buy pleasure, but not happiness, in the same way that money can buy books, but not wisdom. Pleasure involves receiving. Happiness involves giving. It is not only more blessed to give than receive, it also brings greater happiness. In remembering my fifty-something Christmases, I can tell you that the pleasure I enjoyed as a child opening my gifts was dwarfed by the happiness I enjoyed as a parent watching my child open her gifts.

Money can bring pleasure in its accumulation, but it can bring happiness only through its distribution. I don't mean distribution to a car payment, medical bill or tax liability. I mean distribution to someone or something that benefits others, and not you, and that is made voluntarily. I mean charity.

Several studies over several decades have confirmed certain correlations between money and happiness. First, it's harder to be happy when you're poor. Your ability to give is hampered, and you are focused on survival. Once basic needs are met, more money barely moves the happiness meter. Buying more stuff brings short-lived pleasure, then disappointment. The disappointment of no happiness is compounded by the disappointment of less money. Finally, avarice, an extreme desire for wealth, is a cause of great unhappiness. The pursuit of money for money's sake becomes all-consuming, and gives nothing in return.

Happiness comes from the inside out, and money can create happiness only if it moves the same way. Happiness for yourself is the product of creating happiness for others. It's a never-ending upward spiral.

Money Isn't Human

With the invention of money, we created the ability to quantify almost every aspect of life. Money grew beyond its traditional roles as a store of value, a medium of exchange, and a unit of account to become the measuring stick for almost every activity in our lives. Unfortunately, using money as a measurement has also led to money being used as a replacement for human activities, interactions, emotions and affections.

Money is easily the most powerful secular force in the world. I can think of only four motivators to Americans that might be stronger than money – they are God, family, country and sex. For the great majority of Americans, at least one of these four trumps money in importance. But that still leaves money as a powerful influence on a large number of people, here and around the world.

Even for these four strong motivators, money is a factor. We may prefer to give God our treasure, instead of our time or our talent, because it's easier. Much, often too much of the family dynamic revolves around money. We love our country, but that doesn't stop us from fudging on our taxes. And money-for-sex isn't the world's oldest profession by accident. Money is our main method of contact with the outside world. Money enables us to have greater contact with the outside world, although it is largely on a superficial transaction basis. When money starts being used as a substitute in our closest relationships, we risk becoming less human.

We don't give of ourselves if it's easier to give money. We don't owe gratitude; we just owe money. Money greatly enabled and simplified transactions, but a consequence of that is we tend to think of relationships as transactions. Mutually beneficial relationships are based on reciprocity, but reciprocity can be difficult to measure, and the people in the relationship may have vastly differing perceptions of the equality of the reciprocity. The natural inclination is to revert to money to settle any disputes of inequality.

When we use money to substitute for the giving of ourselves, we devalue that which wasn't given. By putting a dollar figure on that which each of us can uniquely offer from our hearts, we take something that was priceless and make it almost worthless.

The worst use of money is when we attempt to measure our humanity with money. Faith, love, kindness and loyalty can not be measured or demonstrated by money, or at least not by money alone. To use money in such a manner debases the giver, and insults the receiver. Money can be used to enhance our humanity, enabling us to reach out to more people. It should never be used to enable us to reach out less.

Money Is the Effect

In addition to leading to financial ruin for many families, easy credit has also created a distortion in our understanding of the real cause-and-effect relationship of money. Our ability to acquire almost anything now and pay for it later violates the natural order of the world. Such violations were never possible before the introduction of money and its demented offspring, debt.

Our Cro-Magnon forebears had nothing resembling money, yet they understood the concept of pay-as-you-go. Their environment might have been more accurately described as pay-before-you-go. Their needs were extremely basic: food, clothing and shelter sufficient to keep them alive through the current season. Two and sometimes all three of these needs could be supplied by what they hunted. But they got nothing until they killed an animal that was highly likely to kill them too in self-defense. There was no deviation from pay-before-you-go, even if it meant starvation. Such an environment was a great catalyst for initiative, teamwork, and thrift.

Fast-forward to the 21st century A.D. Governments, corporations and individuals have collectively spent to date some four years of future production. In Cro-Magnon terms, settling that debt would require killing four years' worth of meat before you saw your next meal.

Because we have become so accustomed to spending money we haven't yet earned, we have developed a tendency to see money as cause, rather than as effect. It is hard to see money as the effect of our work, when the money is spent years before the work to earn it is performed. Money-in-the-present is seen as the motivator to produce more in the future, rather than seeing it in its correct place, as the reward for having produced more in the past. On the job, this misperception creates the mindset that, if my boss would only pay me more, I would be a more productive worker, which is backward. First you create higher value; then you receive higher value. To see money as the cause is akin to standing in front of your fireplace and declaring, "OK, fireplace, give me some heat, and I'll give you some wood." You'll freeze to death while you're waiting.

Compensation that's disconnected from performance invites complacency and mediocrity. With guaranteed contracts in professional sports, there is little correlation between a team's payroll and its place in the standings. As evidence, three of the top four baseball teams with the highest payrolls didn't make the playoffs in 2008. The team that did make it, the Boston Red Sox, lost to Tampa Bay, which had a payroll one-third the size of Boston's.

Money Is a Tool

As a former Industrial Arts teacher, I know a little about tools. As a teacher-in-training, and later as teacher, the first emphasis was always on the proper and safe use of any tool. Lack of proper instruction on safety could lead to misuse of a tool, which typically leads to accidents. Any intentional misuse of a tool would earn you a permanent ban from my shop.

Money that is used to destroy is a weapon, and you know my position on that. Money that is used to build is a tool - the greatest building tool ever devised. To misuse such an incredible tool as a dangerous weapon warrants a lifetime ban on its future use, if only such a ban could be enforced.

For safety reasons, and to avoid lawsuits, tools have all kinds of safety warnings on them. Money, in none of its myriad forms carries any such safety warning. When determining whether you are using money properly, I recommend referring back to the Golden Rule – would you want to be on the receiving end of someone using money in the same way you're using it? If your answer is no, then you're not using money properly.

There is an old shop teacher saying – when your only tool is a hammer, every problem is a nail. Money's ability to be used now and in the future, to solve enormously varied problems, and to seize equally varied opportunities makes it the best single tool to possess. Money has flexibility of use that puts a Swiss army knife to shame.

And what money is best at building is a future. When used properly, money does not deteriorate over time like most things we build. When properly used and managed, money becomes bigger and better over time, enabling the building of bigger dreams in the future than can be built today. Money creates its own new-and-improved version as it moves forward. It never becomes obsolete. With apologies to Gershwin, in time the Rockies may crumble, Gibraltar may tumble, but money can still be on the job.

I used to know some Industrial Arts teachers who were reluctant to use the tools in their shops. They liked to see them all shiny and clean and in their proper place. Letting a bunch of kids use them would mess them up, so they were parsimonious in their use. I could never understand this logic. What else were these tools for? The gain from their use more than offset the wear and tear. Money should never be a tool that sits unused. It should always be building something – a worry-free retirement, a Ph.D. for a grandchild, protection from catastrophe, whatever is needed and important. It's too great a tool to sit idle.

Money Is Dignity

It's no secret that status is highly correlated with money. The list of wealthiest people and the list of highest incomes in America are studied each year with great interest. They are the American version of a register of royalty. But the status that money may create is not the same as dignity.

Status is something that is conveyed by other people unto an individual. Dignity is something that individuals convey unto themselves. Dignity is a measure of your self-respect. It must be earned for yourself, and it can't be taken away by others.

Few things generate self-respect like a dollar earned through honest labor. Fewer teens have jobs now than when I was young. I don't refer here to child labor, which is exploitation. You don't see young people delivering newspapers, shoveling driveways or mowing lawns like they did back in the day. As a result, today's youth don't have the experience of earning money on their own, and they don't have the opportunity to earn that self-respect. When humans, especially the young, don't sacrifice for the money they get, they respect the money less and themselves as well.

The ability to accumulate money out of earnings is a great source of dignity. There are many, many people in this country who make fantastic incomes, but have little or nothing saved. Whether or not people save out of their earnings can be very telling. People who save regularly show discipline and foresight. The increasing value of their savings is a double source of pride – they have earned the money, and they haven't spent the money. People with little savings, especially if they make a good income, are reminded by their low savings balance that they have failed to exercise self-discipline. In the end, true self-respect is the product of self-discipline.

Earning money is also the world's way of saying your work is valued. The world at large can be a cold, calculating place. The only consistent way a complex environment like the modern world can tell people thank you for their efforts is to give them money. A paycheck is the world's most popular thank-you note.

It is important not to place too much emphasis on the size of the paycheck when it comes to assessing your self-worth. Several hedge fund managers "earned" over a billion dollars each in 2007. What compensated one fund manager would have compensated 20,000 teachers. No one, not even the hedge fund manager, is stupid enough to think that those compensation figures accurately reflect the relative contributions of these two jobs to society. Any one of those 20,000 teachers has earned as much dignity as the hedge fund manager, even if they didn't earn as much money.

Money Is Freedom

I doubt there is a single worker in the U.S. over the age of thirty who at some point on the job hasn't been tempted to tell the boss to go to hell. Many have acted on that urge, most to their regret later on. There are usually several reasons why it is best to hold your tongue when such an urge comes over you, but the biggest reason for discretion is the loss of income if you express your true feelings and get canned.

Even the self-employed get the urge to chuck it all from time to time. A recent survey of doctors showed more than half of them would like to quit the medical profession, mostly because of the aggravation of dealing with insurance companies and other bureaucrats. Almost none of them do quit, because almost none of them could match the income they make as doctors in any other field, and because they are spending all of their income now. They are shackled to their current jobs by its high income.

Money spent can be a prison, but money saved can be freedom. The smaller your financial liabilities and the larger your financial assets, the greater is your freedom. One of the advantages of living well below your means is that jobs that pay less than you currently make are a viable alternative, because you can make that change without hurting your standard of living. Those unhappy doctors have limited their options in as much as they have not limited their spending.

Money can enable you to change jobs when the situation warrants it, and money can create opportunities that only money can create. One of the best examples is starting your own business. Such a big step may require money up front, but often it requires only the ability to reduce your income while the new business gets on its feet. I was able to leave a salaried position with an insurance company and go on my own as a financial planner because we lived below our means and had established a financial reserve for just such an opportunity.

Lastly, money that generates an income can free you of the burden of generating an income. Money's ability to make money is greater than yours. The day may come when you don't want to work. The day will almost certainly come when you can't work. Money can give you the freedom to stop working when the time comes. Just as important, money enables you to have the dignity of leaving on your own terms. One of my great concerns for my fellow baby-boomers is they have spent almost all their productive years spending and not saving. The time will come when a lot of the 75,000,000 boomers can't keep their old jobs, but will still need a paycheck. And there just aren't 75,000,000 Wal-Mart greeter positions available.

Money Is Hope

"Hope is a good thing; maybe the best of things. And no good thing ever dies." writes Andy Dufresne in *The Shawshank Redemption*, probably the greatest movie about hope ever made. Andy's friend Red, who is finally released after forty years of hopeless incarceration, ends the movie with the words, "I hope." Hope is the fuel of all progress, of all success, and of all happiness. It is impossible to be optimistic without hope in your heart.

In addition to freedom, the other ingredient that turned Andy and Red's hopes into reality was money. Without money, the happy ending wouldn't have happened. Without money, many of our hopes for the future get compromised, or crushed altogether. In addition to hard work, sacrifice, determination and optimism, many dreams require money to motivate the outside world to assist in making those dreams a reality.

One of the most fundamental of human hopes is that your children will enjoy greater opportunity than you had. One of the best ways to increase your child's opportunities is to make sure they get a good education. At the very least, that means a four-year college degree with a $20,000 price tag for tuition alone. Without the ability to pay for it, hopes for a college degree and the opportunities the degree will afford may soon be crushed. Paying for college is just the most common example of how money affects the hopes we have for our children.

Money also affects our hopes for our own future. We hope our investments will do what they're supposed to do so we can retire as planned. We hope that raise comes through so we can get a new car. We hope we don't get laid off and have to sell our house. We hope our parents don't have to go to a nursing home, because we'll have to pay for it, dashing our hopes for a lot of our future plans.

The one type of hope that is counterproductive is hoping for a longshot. When it comes to money, such false hope includes any kind of gambling, but especially long chance games like the lottery. The money spent on such activities is no longer available for more productive uses, and hoping for such a payoff is likely to keep you from devoting time and money to those activities that can actually pay off. Money is hope, which is very different than hoping for money.

Hope is the ultimate motivator. Hope enables us to work hard, delay gratification, set priorities, and remain disciplined. Money can help us realize our hopes, but it is hope itself that motivates us to act in ways that enable us to accumulate wealth. Hope leads to actions that lead to money that leads to the realization of hopes.

Money Is a Legacy

The Nobel Prize has been awarded annually since 1901 for work in the areas of medicine, physics, economics, literature, chemistry and peace. Among the over 800 recipients are Jimmy Carter, Winston Churchill, Marie Curie, Albert Einstein, Martin Luther King, Jr., Nelson Mandela, Theodore Roosevelt, and Mother Teresa. The Nobel Prize is arguably the most well-known and prestigious award in the world.

Alfred Nobel is known for the prize that bears his name. He funded the Nobel Foundation in the late 1800's with the equivalent of $190 million in today's money. Nobel amassed his great fortune primarily through his invention of dynamite. Wishing to make some kind of atonement for the damage caused by dynamite's use in weapons, he amended his will in 1895 to leave 94% of his fortune to the establishment of the Nobel Prizes. Nobel's dynamite changed our world in positive ways, and it is not his fault that his invention found its way into weaponry. But the world remembers Alfred Nobel not for the way he earned his money, but by what he did with it.

There are many ways to create a legacy. You can invent (like Nobel), write a book or a song, or lead a people to freedom. Such methods require a skill set very few of us possess. Another way to create a legacy is to give the future something of value through money. And the ability to accumulate money is something almost every one of us possesses.

For those who hate the thought of giving up control after their death, money enables a certain measure of control to continue from the grave. Many trusts have been set up that provide ongoing funding, provided certain conditions are met. For example, a grandchild's trust income may be contingent upon completing college. Ideally, any such trust should be structured to maintain certain standards in behavior or performance, but should also be flexible enough to allow changes that enable the money to meet the goal of its donor in changing conditions.

Money's ability to move into the future intact makes it the perfect tool to create a legacy. More than a century after his death, Alfred Nobel's legacy encourages creativity and research, and it rewards people for discoveries and inventions that Nobel could have hardly imagined in the nineteenth century. This ability to touch the future can enable you to fund an education for grandchildren and great-grandchildren you may never meet, but who will know you and love you through your legacy. You can show continued support to causes near and dear to your heart by supporting or even creating a foundation that supports those causes. Your ability to affect the future is limited only by your creativity and your desire to make a difference.

Money Is Love

Let me make very clear what I mean by the above statement. Money is excellent as an *expression* of love. It is horrible as a *substitute* for love.

Because money is so flexible in its use, it can express love in ways that are impossible otherwise. A loved one may have a disease you can't even pronounce, much less treat. But if treatment exists, money can provide it. You don't have to be a college graduate to enable your grandchild to become one. You don't have to know anything about computers to provide start-up funding for your entrepreneurial geek son to create the next Google. With money, you don't have to know a lot to help; you only have to care a lot to help.

Sometimes your right brain and left brain clash as you try to understand things. As a guy, my left/logical brain has a hard time understanding why men should have to work three months to buy a ring to prove they are willing to commit to one woman. My right/emotional brain reminds me that this is a very serious expression of love, from the woman's perspective, if not the man's. Or, as Dave Ramsey more succinctly puts it, "Guys, we don't have to get it; we just have to *get it*."

Money is love has no time frame. You can express love to those who have passed by establishing a memorial fund to help a cause they supported. You can express love in the present by the simple act of buying a gift for someone for no special reason. You can express love in the future by sending money into the future to help those who will live in that future, even if you aren't one of them.

Money as an expression of love is definitely more emotional than logical, because love is that way, too. That doesn't mean that logic and discipline should be thrown out the window when it comes to intersecting money and love. You may love a son or daughter, but if they have a drug problem, giving them money that makes the problem worse is not love. Money is love means that giving or withholding money is done to help the other person, never to hurt them. Your loved one may not share your perspective, but you are more likely to have the correct perspective in such cases. Feelings of doubt or guilt should not accompany any giving of money as an expression of love.

One other thing – you can't love money. Love is humanity's greatest gift from God. Money is mentioned more times than love in the Bible, but love is clearly the most important thing, from the Ten Commandments to the Gospels. Love is intended for that which can recognize love. Money can express love – it cannot recognize it or reciprocate it.

Money Is a Mirror

My mother was orphaned as an infant. She bounced around different foster homes until her early teens, when she was taken in by Mil and Ed Prevost. Mil was a teacher and Ed was a security guard at a GM plant; they also had an eight-year-old son when my mother went to live with them. They raised her as their own until she married my father at age twenty-two. The Prevosts took in my mother when she was immersed in those difficult teenage years, which were likely made even more difficult by the traumas my mother had endured to that time.

That selfless act alone tells you a lot about my Aunt Mil and Uncle Ed. I learned something else several years ago that gives another glimpse into Mil's and Ed's souls. One year they got a notice from the IRS that they were being audited. The reason – the amounts they were claiming for charitable deductions were way out of line with the IRS guidelines for normal legitimate claims. The Prevosts would have to report to the IRS office and show proof that their deductions were legitimate.

Since Mil and Ed Prevost were as honest and meticulous as they were charitable, it was no problem for them to produce the necessary documentation. Keep in mind, to draw the scrutiny of the IRS in such a matter, your claimed deductions would have to be well above ten percent of your income. They probably gave that much to their church alone, as they were the type to take the obligation to tithe seriously. For two people who gave some of their best years to a girl who was previously a stranger, giving a substantial part of their income to charity was an easy, natural thing to do.

When I am establishing a new client relationship, one of the required documents is a copy of their latest tax return. One of the interesting items on the return is charitable deductions. I have found a clear correlation between a person's generosity and the quality of the client-advisor relationship. As a rule, a more charitable person is a less self-centered person. And a less self-centered person is more likely to listen to and follow the advice of a financial advisor.

Many people contend that how we allocate our time reflects our priorities, and our character. While I don't disagree with that contention, I contend that how we allocate our money offers an even more accurate reflection. While both time and money are valuable resources, our money balance is known, while our time balance is not. This difference makes a unit of time less valuable than a unit of money. Let me give an example. When an eighteen-year-old goes off to college, he/she will pay for that bachelor's degree with the next four years of his/her life. The parents will pay for that bachelor's degree with around $100,000. The parents will miss the money more than their child will miss the time, largely because the child sees time as an inexhaustible resource. The parents know that money is very exhaustible.

If you analyzed how you allocated your money over the last year, what would it reveal about you? A sizable portion probably went to necessities. By necessities, I mean food, clothing, shelter, transportation and medical. Within those categories, not every dollar spent is a necessity. The mortgage money on a $200,000 house is likely all necessity. The mortgage money on a $500,000 house is unlikely all necessity. If you like to shop at Neiman-Marcus and the Mercedes dealership, very little of those expenses qualify as necessities.

How much did you spend on luxuries? How much did you set aside for future obligations, including obligations to yourself? How much went to help family members? How much went to help those less fortunate than you? How much did you spend that was borrowed from the future? You may not have much control over the size of your income, but you do have control over how you allocate it.

Money is a mirror; it isn't a photograph. Others know your image from photos, not from a reflection. But photos can be altered; reflections cannot. You see your reflection in the mirror, and it shows you as you are. The way you use money reflects your heart and soul in the same way.

PS – As I write these words, Aunt Mil is 101 years old and still as sharp as a tack. God bless her.

And in rebuttal, what a MONEY MORON recommends you do:

- **Make money your cause.** A life centered on the pursuit of money is a noble cause indeed. If you're real good at it, you'll even get important stuff named after you when you're dead, like Vanderbilt University, Carnegie Hall, and Midas Muffler.
- **Use money as a weapon.** If someone is reluctant to give you what you want, and you can use money to convince them otherwise, go for it. If it was wrong, it would be illegal. And if the other guy had the money, he'd do the same to you. Remember the golden rule – do unto others before they do unto you.
- **Get your priorities straight.** You can't spend character. Or dignity, or love or any of that other stuff. Dignity, love, etc. is fine to have, but not if it comes at a price, and especially if the price is money.
- **Evaluate relationships with money.** How else can you decide who is worth wasting your time on? Put a dollar figure on everyone you know, so you can rank them, and shove the unprofitable people out of your life.
- **Make money your "Vice-God".** Just like we need a backup for the president, you should have a backup for the Almighty, just in case He doesn't work out. And I can't think of a more qualified candidate.
- **Give money instead of yourself.** There's only so much of you to go around. And truth is, most of these people wanting a piece of you would settle for a few bucks instead. If you can pay with a bad check, so much the better.
- **Hope for money.** Think of all the things you hope for. I'll bet most of them could be bought with money. So why not just hope for money? This way if you change your mind about what you hoped for, you don't have to try to exchange it.
- **Reject "Money is a Mirror".** You're far too beautiful, wonderful and complex to be reflected in something like money. Besides, I love money and hate mirrors (you would too with a face like this). If money is a mirror, I'm going to have a lot of conflicts to resolve.

YOU'RE HUMAN...

BUT THAT'S NO EXCUSE

FOR SALE: One Tulip Bulb, rare Viceroy Species; color unknown; Price: 2,500 Dutch Florins or U.S. $1,000,000. Email: janvanschnook@tulips-r-us.ne

When you picture Holland, you probably picture two things - windmills and tulips. The Dutch have been in love with tulips ever since they were introduced from modern-day Turkey in the mid-16th century. But at a million-bucks-a-bulb, those picturesque tulip fields that stretch to the horizon could never have happened.

When Tulip Mania reached its peak in The Netherlands in 1636-37, the ad you see above was plausible (though obviously not the email address). There are documented cases of a single bulb selling for 2,500 Florins, and some valued at over 5,000 Florins. One speculator offered 12 acres of prime real estate for a single rare bulb. At that time, a skilled laborer earned about 150 Florins per year. If that laborer today were to earn $60,000 per year, the price for that one Viceroy bulb is equivalent to $1,000,000 using the same conversion method.

Only a small percentage of the Dutch population got swept up in Tulip mania and paid prices in that range. From the peak in February 1637 to the end of May that same year, tulip prices declined some 90%. By 1665 bulbs were selling at no more than their modest reproduction costs. A mania's life-span is inversely proportionate to its perversity.

It's hard to imagine that such a mania could take hold today, with a better educated population and unfettered access to information. Yet we only need to turn the clock back to the start of this new millennium to see that history keeps repeating itself. Stocks historically trade at around 15 times earnings, and earnings are historically around 5% of gross revenues. During the dot com bubble, many companies had their stocks trading at *100 times annual gross revenues.*

These dot com companies were also spending money so much faster than gross revenues were increasing that the chance of ever turning profitable (which is the only reason for a company to exist or have value) was next to impossible. When reality struck, millions lost billions. The NASDAQ stock market, where almost all of the dot com stocks were traded and where over 3,000 other stocks trade, fell 78% from peak to trough between March 2000 and October 2002.

The object of desire may change. The method of gathering information may change. The method of buying and selling may change. The rationalization may change. But people don't change. Human history is the history of people making the same old mistakes in new ways. An individual can change in ways people collectively cannot. People don't change en masse; such change is the accumulation of individual change. The modest goal of this book is to change a few individual's behaviors.

The Herd Has Many Heads, But No Brains

See if this makes sense to you. An item that you badly want and need has a price that tends to fluctuate. Almost everyone else wants and needs this item, too. Demand for this item tends to peak when its price is also at its peak. When the price drops to well below its average, you can hardly give the item away. The supply of this item is rather constant, it is easy to obtain, and its usefulness doesn't fluctuate by season or by user. If we were talking about an item like a flat-screen TV or a pizza, this behavior would make no sense at all.

Humans practice this nonsensical-bordering-on-moronic behavior when it comes to investments, though. And owning investments is a lot more important than owning a flat-screen TV. Can you imagine someone in the market for a 46" Sony LCD TV saying they prefer to buy it when the price doubles, but they won't touch it when it's 40% off? That's exactly what people have historically done when it comes to investments, and have done so in just the last decade, despite our alleged financial sophistication. When the market was at its peak in the late 90's, you paid around $35 to get $1 of earnings from a stock. In the bear market of 2008, you could buy a dollar of earnings for about $9 or less; about one-fourth the price at the market peak. Was there a stampede to buy at such a time? Hardly.

America has more wealth, more desire for wealth and more opportunity to create wealth than any nation in history. So why do we have so many people who have little or no wealth despite years of hard work? One of the biggest reasons is that most people follow the behavior of people who have no wealth. If you mimic the behavior of broke people, there is an excellent chance you will be broke, too. And buying something for $35 that normally sells for $15, and then selling it when the price drops to $9 is a sure-fire way to go broke.

An ignorant person is someone who is uneducated in an area. An ignorant person is almost always capable of becoming educated if the opportunity presents itself. An ignorant person usually has a desire to lose their ignorance. You are, at worst, somewhat ignorant on money matters (we all are, including me), but you are working to change that. You are capable of learning, and even more important, you want to learn.

A stupid person is another story. A stupid person has an inability or a resistance to learn something new. Few people are handicapped by the inability to learn something new, especially anything that's covered in this book. That means that most stupid people are that way by choice. They have chosen to remain ignorant, and when you choose to remain ignorant on something you need to know, you graduate to stupid.

The dictionary defines a moron as a remarkably stupid person. And there are a startling number of Money Morons out there. (Habitually buying high and selling low is one of many symptoms). They dwell among you, and their stupidity will lead you to financial ruin if you allow them to lead you. It is important to understand that doing what the majority does only guarantees mediocrity, since mediocrity is by definition no better than average, and the majority creates the average. You aspire to be more than mediocre, and you are making the effort to be more.

There is no safety in numbers, only more of the same mediocrity. Conventional wisdom holds that there is collective wisdom in the decision of a large group. That presumes that wisdom accumulates and spreads its benefits to the entire group. The reality is a few of the more fervent members in a group (aka - the lunatic fringe) can move large numbers of people in the wrong direction. It is the loudest, not the wisest that tend to hold sway over the masses. The herd doesn't move in a direction because they determined that direction was the best after thoughtful deliberation. They typically move in that direction because a small group within the herd is shouting at the top of their lungs that this is the way to go, usually without offering any objective reason why this is the way to go.

A person becomes part of a herd in large part because they lack confidence in their own cognitive abilities. It is very difficult to swim against the current of popular opinion. You subject yourself to ridicule and ostracism by the masses whose judgment you dare call into question. You also have to firmly believe that your judgment on a matter is superior to the conventional wisdom. Most people are not willing to go on record as saying they are right and thousands or millions of others are wrong. As a result, people buy overpriced stocks and sell undervalued stocks because that is the trend of the moment. John Templeton, philanthropist, philosopher, founder of the Templeton Mutual Funds and multi-billionaire, said the best time to invest was at the point of "maximum pessimism." He became incredibly wealthy precisely because he refused to follow the herd.

Every veteran of high school is familiar with peer pressure. Because we are psychologically vulnerable during our teen years, we are more inclined to do things against our best interests and better judgment in order to fit in. The aversion to being different that we develop in adolescence is hard to shake when we reach adulthood. But adulthood is very different from childhood. There is much more freedom to be who you are, and fewer punishments and more rewards for doing what you think is best.

If you're an American, pulling away from the herd is actually pretty easy. We admire individuality. If you are successful by being different, people will flock to learn your secrets and then mimic you. It's much more difficult to leave the herd in a country like Japan, with their homogeneous culture. There is a saying in Japan that the nail that sticks up gets hammered down. Many Middle Eastern nations are still based on tribal rule. To go against the herd there will subject you to more than ridicule. Don't be afraid to think for yourself, and act on what you know, not on what you assume others know. Remember, when it comes to money, the herd is usually wrong, and they have the balance sheets to prove it.

It's Not Worth It

The only person who can never see you is you. Everyone else in the world with eyesight has the ability to meet you and view your entire physicality. You are the only one who cannot do that, as you are trapped within that same physicality. This means your perception of you will differ from everyone else's perception. Whose perception is more accurate?

When it comes to our physical attractiveness, women tend to underestimate theirs; men tend to overestimate theirs. One thing that men, women and children all do is overestimate the value of the things they own. This is known as the *endowment effect*. Once something is ours, we endow it with a greater value than the public at large will. Let's start with our own children. Is there a parent out there who didn't think their newborn baby was the cutest in history? Based on the parent's reaction, one would think their baby's first words were "Four score and seven years ago…" Based on the parent's reaction to the first successful potty attempt, one would think their kid had split the atom. Our kids are just one example of our inability to be objective when the object of attention is ours. (FYI – It's good that parents are this way to help the child develop properly, and I did all this stuff with my own kid.)

Realtors I know say one of the biggest obstacles in getting a house sold is getting a seller to recognize what the real market value of the house is. Because our house is also our home, it is very difficult to be objective about its value. This is especially true if you have made improvements that involved both your labor and your money. A part of you is in that structure, and while that has emotional value to you, it has no market value.

One reason we tend to overestimate the value of what we own is that we perceive a loss if we sell it, and there is the need to be compensated for our loss, as well as for the object itself (more on loss aversion in a bit). The objects that we most tend to overvalue are the ones that we don't need to sell and that have some usefulness to us. To get us to part with such items requires someone to make us an offer we can't refuse. If an item has outlived its usefulness to us, it may end up as part of our garage sale. At that point, what we value more than the object is our desire to be rid of the thing. One reason you find great deals at garage sales is the items for sale are no longer affected by the endowment effect.

The other time that people realistically value their objects is when circumstances leave them little choice but to sell. For example, someone may own a 1957 Chevrolet that is in good, but not great condition. Such a car probably inspires a strong emotional attachment from its owner. The owner, in order to be enticed into selling the car, might demand a price that one would pay for a car in great condition, while his is only in good condition. That difference might amount to $20,000. Now let's suppose the owner has just lost his job, and there is nothing on the horizon. Circumstances will force him into a more realistic pricing of his car in order to generate a sale. It's still a transaction between a willing buyer and a willing seller, but the seller has different priorities now that prompt a shift in his valuation of the car.

Speaking of cars and the endowment effect, why do you think car dealers encourage you to take a car home before you even buy it? Taking the car home, parking it in your driveway, watching the neighbors ooh and ahh over it creates a powerful endowment effect. It's hard to return a car after you've taken possession. In fact, ownership isn't necessary to create an endowment effect; mere possession is sufficient.

The endowment effect can occur even without physical possession. That '57 Chevy may get auctioned off at one of the televised car auctions that have become so popular. It's interesting to watch the bidding process, because the more bids a person makes, the harder it becomes to stop. There is an attachment to the object before they even acquire it, and the further the bidding goes, the deeper the attachment becomes. You have probably had a similar experience with online auctions. Once you make a bid, you feel like you have a stake in the item you are bidding for. The more bids you make, the more likely you are to bid more than you planned. You feel like you have too much invested at that point to come away empty-handed. Of course, to be the high bidder at an auction may also mean you are the biggest sucker, too. After all, despite the fact that other people thought the item you won was desirable, none of them thought it was worth what you paid for it.

The endowment effect can apply to intangibles too, such as opinions. Once we state a position on a topic, we have a stake in it, and to change our position exacts a psychological price. Winston Churchill once said that if you aren't liberal when you're young, you have no heart; and if you aren't conservative when you're old, you have no head. What Churchill didn't factor in his statement is the difficulty in letting go of long-held positions. When it comes to opinions about money, inflexibility can be a disaster. You are likely to read some things in this book that will conflict with your perceptions and opinions. In order to fully benefit from this read, it will be necessary to be open to accepting a different perspective about some aspects of money.

What Have You Got To Lose?

If you've ever watched a football game, see if this scenario sounds familiar. Your team is leading by ten points late in the game. They have built this lead with a consistent offense and an aggressive defense. Their blitzing of the quarterback has kept his passing game off-pace all day. But now, with five minutes left in the game, your team shifts to the "prevent" defense. They will stop blitzing and focus on preventing a long run after a short completion. The other team scores a quick touchdown, holds your team to a three-and-out with aggressive defense, and then moves down the field with a series of short passes that your defense willingly concedes. The opponent scores the winning touchdown as time expires. Once again, your team has snatched defeat from the jaws of victory.

What prompts a coach to change what has worked all afternoon, and replace it with a strategy that seems to prevent nothing except victory? It's simple, really – they hate losing much more than they love winning. In their defense, a loss hurts a football coach's career more than a win helps it. Football coaches are hardly alone in hating losing more than loving winning. We all demonstrate it, though not in front of 80,000 rabid fans and a national television audience.

Have you ever chosen a flat-rate option over a pay-as-you-go plan on something like phone service, even though you would probably do better with pay-as-you-go? If so, was it the feeling of loss you would feel if you got a bill that was higher than the flat-rate plan that prompted you to "prevent" such an occurrence by choosing the flat-rate plan? Have you ever bought a new car? Did you buy it in part because you did not want the potential repair bills that might occur if you bought a used car instead? Did you buy the more expensive new car even though it was unlikely the repair bills on a used car would ever approach the price differential between the new and used cars?

These are just a couple of examples of how *loss aversion* affects our decision-making in the real world. Here is what we have learned over the last thirty years of study in this area. When it comes to gains, people are pretty cautious. We tend to want the more sure thing. If given the choice of a sure $100 gain, or a chance to gain $200 or zero based on a coin flip, the great majority will choose the sure $100. They view the coin toss not as a chance to win $200, but as a chance to lose the $100 sure thing they already had.

If we flip the situation around, people become bigger risk takers. If given the choice between a sure $100 loss, or a chance to lose $200 or zero based on a coin flip, the great majority will choose the coin flip. They view the coin toss not as a risk of losing $200, but as a chance to avoid losing the $100, which is the only other option.

Loss aversion can hit us several different ways when it comes to investing. We may adopt the "prevent defense" philosophy of the football coach, and become so conservative in our investment strategy that we make it impossible to win (winning here means an investment return that exceeds inflation). We may misinterpret the temporary decline of the broad stock market to be permanent loss on a bunch of bad investments, and bail out just before the inevitable rebound. We may have bought a stock at $30, watched it rise to $50, then return to $30 where it's still overpriced. Rather than selling now at break-even, we feel like we're losing $20 a share because it was once at $50. We see a loss where there isn't one because we look backward and not forward.

The first gains are the sweetest, and the first losses are the most bitter. We enjoy a gain from zero to $100 more than we enjoy the gain from $100 to $200. This is one reason why people prefer the sure $100 to the $200 coin flip; the extra $100 isn't worth the extra risk. Going the other way, the loss of the first $100 hurts more psychologically than the loss of an additional $100. This is why, when faced with the sure loss of $100 or the chance to lose $200 or zero, most prefer to avoid the sure loss; they know it's gonna hurt.

Overall, people feel the pain of loss more strongly than they feel the pleasure of gain. Some studies estimate that losses have twice the psychological impact of comparable gains. Our aversion to losses can be good in many situations, and it has helped us survive as a species. But, when it comes to money, which is wholly man-made, loss aversion can hurt us. It can cause us to bail out on a good thing just because it is going through a bad spell. It can cause us to hang on to a bad thing because we bought it when it was good and we want it to go back there. It can cause us to act when we shouldn't and to freeze when we should act. It can cause us to play defense when we should be on offense, and vice versa. Lastly, it can turn victory into defeat.

Tied to an Anchor

My wife is one of the world's great shoppers. I don't mean great in the sense that she can spend money like a drunken sailor. Nothing could be further from the truth. Beth is very frugal (that's a wonderful virtue in a spouse, by the way), and she can spot bargains the way spy satellites can read license plates.

There is only one aspect to her shopping that I still attempt to adjust. When she arrives home to show me the kill-of-the-day, she usually says something very much like, "It sold for $75, but I got it for $8." (That's a typical original sticker/selling price ratio for her, by the way.) I have to remind her that the item *didn't* sell for $75 (or $49 or $29 or $15), which is why she eventually got it for $8.

In this example, that original price on the item was the *anchor* from which she judged the value of the item, and how good a bargain she got. That $8 item was a steal regardless of the original sticker price, but that high sticker price made the eventual selling price seem like an even bigger bargain. Beth got a great bargain in absolute terms; she got an even bigger bargain in relative terms of the anchor price of $75.

That's what an anchor price does – it shifts our perception of the value of an item and the greatness of the deal from absolute to relative terms. For example, you own 100 shares of a stock that is currently trading at $50 per share. The company has been struggling, and the consensus is that the stock is more likely to go to $40 before it goes to $60. Would you sell at this point? Before you answer, I should tell you that you paid $70 for the stock six months ago. Does that change your decision?

What if I told you that you paid $35 for the stock six months ago? Would you make a different decision now? Most people would do different things, depending on whether they paid $35 or $70 for the stock. That shouldn't matter, though. The only thing that matters is what the investment will do in the future, not what you paid in the past. But our purchase price of the stock becomes the anchor that drives our decisions, and that can make for some bad decisions.

Anchors come not only in the form of what we paid for something, or the original sticker price, but also from similar products. Chevrolet introduced a limited edition Corvette in 2009 that has a supercharged engine that produces 640 horsepower. The car's sticker price is over $100,000. A regular Corvette with a "mere" 430 horsepower engine sells for less than $50,000. If you use the limited edition Corvette as an anchor, the regular Corvette seems like a bargain, and that's just fine with Chevrolet. If you use the regular Corvette as an anchor for the limited edition Corvette, that $100,000+ price tag seems like a rip-off. But Chevrolet says the real anchor for the limited edition Corvette is the group of exotic supercars from Ferrari, Lamborghini and Porsche, which are comparable to the Corvette, but sell for much more. By using different anchors, what may seem like a rip-off can become a bargain, and vice versa.

If you've ever bought something on Ebay, you are familiar with anchoring. When you look at an item, there is a starting bid listed. The seller sets that starting bid, which is the minimum bid that will be accepted. The starting bid is an anchor. Items on Ebay often also have a "Buy It Now" price that enables you to skip the competitive bidding process by paying that price. The Buy It Now price is also an anchor. A high starting bid price will tend to push up the final selling price, though too high a starting price will eliminate potential bidders completely. A high Buy It Now price will make any winning bid below that price look like a bargain in comparison. The goal in setting these anchors is to get all the serious bidders into the process from the beginning and to make the winning bidder feel like he got a deal, regardless of what he ultimately bids.

Do old people sometimes seem cheap to you? If they are, it isn't their fault. When I was born in 1953, my parents' house cost $7,000, my father made about $4,000, and a new Chevrolet cost about $1,600. Those were their anchors. And when you understand anchors, it is easier to understand why someone in their seventies or eighties gags at the thought of a $30,000 car. It's hard to pay a dollar for a candy bar when you used to pay a nickel, even if your income has risen proportionately, too. If you're in your twenties now, someday you will be telling your grandchildren how you only paid $20,000 for your first new car, so the $200,000 cost of new cars now is ridiculous. Anchors come from points in time as well as from prices.

A Buck Is a Buck

See if this situation sounds familiar. You are driving along a highway in a sparsely populated area. Suddenly the Low Fuel indicator lights up on the dashboard. You don't know how far it is to the next gas station, but you know they are few and far between in these parts. You slow down and turn off the air conditioning to improve fuel economy and hope you make it to the next gas station. Your luck holds out; you find a gas station; you fill up, then drive like a bat out of hell to make up for lost time.

When your fuel was low and you weren't sure if you would have enough, you were very careful with it. When you filled up, you were no longer worried about running out and you stopped being careful. We are that way with most things, including money...especially money.

When we have an abundance of something, we value each additional unit less and less, which is known as the *law of marginal utility*. If you have $10,000 in the bank, an extra $100 doesn't really change anything for you. If you have $62.43 in the bank, the extra $100 may keep you from insolvency. Abundance, even the perception of abundance, leads to carelessness.

Millionaires are, by and large, careful with money, which is how they became millionaires. They remain millionaires because they continue to be careful with money, even after they accumulate a lot of it. Part of it is conditioning, habit. An even bigger part of it is these millionaires don't change their perception of a dollar's value just because they have an abundance of them. Millionaires exist largely because they refuse to obey the law of marginal utility. To them, a buck is a buck, whether it is the first one they made or the six millionth. They treat them all with equal respect.

Most people are not millionaires because most people mindlessly obey the law of marginal utility. A mechanic gets a raise of $300 a month and buys a new Harley because the raise will cover the monthly payment. A secretary gets an insurance settlement check for pain and suffering from a car accident and heads to Hawaii. Such behavior does not lead to millionaire status.

How we treat a buck is not only a factor of how many bucks we have, but also of where the buck came from. We respect most the money we earn through our own labors, and the harder we work for it, the more we respect it. In our youth, many of us worked dirty back-breaking jobs for the minimum wage. We knew the sacrifice that was made for that money, and we were careful not to waste it. As we got older and were paid more, we were still careful with that money because we worked for it, but probably not as careful as when we worked harder and made less.

Money that comes from another source is not accorded the same respect. An inheritance is usually gone by the third generation because the people who are blowing that money did not know the person who made the original sacrifice to accumulate it. The most disrespected money is that which comes from gambling. This money came from other (mostly) anonymous gamblers, and the winner isn't going to respect that money any more than the losers did by gambling it away in the first place. Casinos are well aware of how winnings from gambling are valued by the winners. If someone wins $1,000 at the roulette wheel, the casino gives him free drinks to keep him there. They know that the gambler considers that $1,000 to be different from his own money; it is "house money." Before long, the gambler will have lost it all back to the house. While the gambler took possession of his winnings, he never took ownership, and so he didn't treat it like his own money.

When I studied accounting, I learned the word *fungible*. I like the word because it sounds funny, and one can imagine it means almost anything, including dirty stuff. Like most things accounting-related, it has a mundane meaning. *Fungible* means that one unit of something can be exchanged or substituted for another unit. For example, if you deposit $1,000 in cash at the bank, and later make a withdrawal of $1,000, you don't get the same bills back. Any bills that equal $1,000 are sufficient to meet the bank's obligation to you.

We need to remember that money is fungible in our lives, too. A $100 bill you find on the floor of a restaurant is exactly the same as $100 you earn digging ditches. The $100 that goes to buy lottery tickets has exactly the same value as $100 dropped into a Salvation Army kettle. Remembering the dollars we worked hardest for, and when we had very few of them, will help us treat all dollars with the proper respect.

Where Money Doesn't Belong

I always had a problem with the movie *Pretty Woman*. I could never get past the implausibility of Julia Roberts and Richard Gere becoming more than call girl and client. I also wondered if the movie weren't sending out the message that this was somehow a viable method to meet the man of your dreams. I was finally able to figure out why the movie never clicked with me.

In this world, we have *social norms* and we have *market norms*. Social norms involve the interactions between humans. They are about helping each other and getting along. They are the glue that holds a society together. They are biological.

Market norms involve a bottom line. They are transaction-based. They can be precisely measured. They are mechanical.

We are all familiar with the old saying; it's a pleasure doing business with you. Julia Roberts' Pretty Woman would amend that to; it's a business doing pleasure with you. In either case, there is a potential clash of social norms and market norms, and any attempt to mix the two can lead to real problems.

The first thing to realize is that when social norms collide with market norms, social norms lose. This collision almost always occurs when market norms invade the world of social norms. For example, how many budding romantic relationships have come to a screeching halt because at some point the guy brought up how much he had spent on dates, and that he wasn't getting anything in return? That one comment shifted the relationship from social norms to market norms. In such a developing relationship, it also shifted the roles from girlfriend-boyfriend to hooker-john, at least from the woman's perspective. Guys, do you now understand why she went ballistic?

In business relationships, market norms should rule. Certainly, every business should treat their customers and their employees with respect, but the business will have neither customers nor employees unless it maintains an acceptable bottom line. In the long term, all employees must be judged on their ability to add value to the business. All customers must be judged on whether they add to or subtract from the bottom line. If you are an employee, the relationship with your employer should be based first on a fair exchange of labor for money.

In social relationships, social norms should rule. When you are invited to a friend's house for dinner, you bring a nice bottle of wine as a gift; you don't offer to "pay the tab" at the end of the evening. When your neighbor asks to borrow your chain saw, you lend it with the expectation he will return the favor in the future; you don't charge him rent.

Social norms should always prevail when a higher calling is involved. People are more inclined to donate blood when cookies and juice are offered as a thank you than when cash is offered as compensation. If people want to do something for altruistic reasons, you will offend them and prompt them to withdraw support if you bring money into the equation.

One of the best examples of social norms and market norms is in another movie, *The Godfather*. The opening scene has Bonasera the undertaker asking Don Corleone to kill the men who violated his daughter. The Don replies, "What have I done to make you treat me so disrespectfully? You don't ask this favor out of friendship. Instead you come to my house on the day of my daughter's wedding and ask me to do murder for money." If you introduce market norms where social norms prevail, market norms will win. But know that social norms may never return and that they never forget, either.

Choice Is Good, To a Point

Women in Manhattan are known for complaining about the lack of eligible men, as anyone who has ever watched *Sex and the City* can attest. Why is there a shortage? Was male infant mortality in Manhattan abnormally high twenty to forty years ago? Were all the men of Manhattan drafted or kidnapped? Are they all gay?

Single women do outnumber single men in Manhattan, but the ratio is about 5 to 4. One reason women outnumber men there is that women flock to Manhattan in part to land one of these high-income males. But the ratio would suggest that 80% of Manhattan women should be able to find the man of their dreams, or at least an acceptable man. But that's using logic, which has no place here.

Men in Manhattan know they have the upper hand because of the discrepancy in populations. As a result, they feel no pressure to commit to any one woman. They know there are so many single women in Manhattan, they don't need commitment to obtain companionship. The only women who succeed in their quest are the ones who are so irresistible that there is actual competition for them, which motivates a man to make a commitment. Such women might be one in ten. If we assume that half the men in Manhattan are currently looking for the right woman for a long-term relationship, the odds of a woman getting that long-term relationship are about two in five. The odds of all four women on *Sex and the City* ending up the way they did are about 2 to 3%.

As the Manhattan singles scene illustrates, too many choices can disrupt the natural order. Too many choices can make it hard to make any selection because we will always be afraid that we are passing up an opportunity for an even better selection. I think the men of Manhattan probably want a long-term relationship with the right person as much as the women do, but the men are actually burdened by the large number of choices in mates. It makes them unwilling or unable to commit to one woman because they know they will always be wondering if there weren't a "better" one just around the corner. There is a high *opportunity cost* for the single men of Manhattan.

If you have a 401k plan at work, every year you probably receive information about the plan and the investment options available. Because employers don't want the responsibility for your financial success in investing for retirement, they don't give advice; they give you choices instead. By offering a smorgasbord of mutual funds in a 401k plan, the employer feels they have met their obligation by having at least some funds in there that will enable you to reach your retirement goals. But it's your job to figure out which funds to select and how much to put into each one. If there are three to five mutual funds in each investment class, deciding may not be too hard. But what if there are ten or twenty funds in each class, and what if there are ten or fifteen investment classes listed? You may have a hundred or more decisions to make. When faced with such a task, most people will a) ask their co-workers in the adjoining cubicles what they're doing; b) put 1% into 100 different funds; c) freak out and do nothing; or d) default to the status quo.

When we are faced with a dizzying array of choices, the most common reaction is to stick with what is already in place. This *status quo bias* is why incumbents are re-elected over 80% of the time, and why the most popular of Baskin-Robbins' 31 flavors continues to be vanilla and chocolate. It's a lot of work to make a choice, and it's too much work for something like ice cream. There is also that loss aversion thing, too. If we try something different and it flops, the remorse is greater than the joy we would feel had the change succeeded. We absolutely hate it when we make a change and it doesn't work out. But there is no way something can become better without changing it.

The people who agonize most over making choices are known as *maximizers*. A maximizer expects the best all the time, from themselves and others. There are several problems with being a maximizer. Because we are presented with a dizzying array of choices in our daily lives, the time and effort required to make the best decision every time would require 56 hours a day. The pressure to make the best decision every time creates a great deal of unnecessary stress. And the chances are great that almost every decision will be accompanied by feelings of buyer's remorse.

By contrast, *satisficers* do not expect perfection from themselves or from others. Satisficers have standards, but they do not expend additional energy on something after those standards have been met. Satisficers are much more aware of the point of diminishing returns and know when their time, energy and resources can be better used elsewhere. Maximizers may do better objectively on a specific decision than a satisficer. But the satisficer will feel better subjectively about that decision than the maximizer.

In the end, the satisficer almost always ends up better off than the maximizer, both subjectively and objectively. Subjectively, the satisficer doesn't suffer from buyer's remorse. Objectively, the satisficer allocates time, energy and resources more efficiently than the maximizer, and consequently accomplishes more overall.

When it comes to making choices in life, and especially financial decisions, there are two things to remember. First, move the baseline to zero, which simply means try to ignore the status quo. Line the status quo up with all the other options and let it stand or fall on its own merits.

Remember, progress is impossible without change. Second, be a satisficer, not a maximizer. You may think that being a satisficer will mean lowering your standards, which will result in lower rewards. On the contrary, you will be able to accomplish more, and you will get more enjoyment out of each accomplishment along the way.

And The Winner Is...

If you've ever watched *Dirty Jobs* on the Discovery Channel, you have had the opportunity to become familiar with the requirements and rewards of such fascinating occupations as roadkill collector, maggot farmer, sausage maker and underwater logger. The show focuses on jobs that need to be done, but that don't have an oversupply of applicants. These are the kinds of jobs that, if your ten-year-old child professed a desire to do in adulthood, you would immediately seek therapy for the kid.

Ever wonder why you have to pay a plumber $75 an hour to fix your toilet, while your son with a Ph.D. in English Literature is working as a proof reader for $13 an hour? Both have well-developed skill sets, although they were acquired in very different ways. The plumber's skills are demanded by many more people; not many people need an analysis of *Hamlet*, but everyone's toilet goes on the fritz at some time. Plumber could never be classified as a glamour profession, so it needs to pay well enough to induce people to learn the trade and practice it.

As in most things in life, your career choice involves trade-offs between security and opportunity, between reward and risk. There will always be a demand for plumbers, and they will always pay reasonably well. Plumbers will also have less-than-desirable working conditions, and will never become millionaires from their work alone. Plumbers gain security at the price of opportunity.

These factors affect the security, opportunity, risk and reward of any job:

- The skill set necessary to perform the job. The easier it is to obtain the necessary skills, the more potential people there are to do a job, so the less the job will pay. Cardiologists make more than plumbers, who make more than janitors.
- The desirability of the job. Little boys dream of growing up to play in the NFL. They don't dream of growing up to work at the official laundry of the NFL. Little girls dream of being a famous actress. They don't dream of being a porn actress, famous or not. Working in undesirable jobs is a default, not a choice.

- The demand for the job. Since we will always need plumbers, there is security in such a career. New technologies can reduce or eliminate the demand for a job. Blacksmiths were replaced by auto workers. Auto workers are being replaced by robots.

These factors determine how much competition there will be in a specific job and what the compensation will be. If you favor a job with security, you should look for a job that requires a skill set that is broad but not necessarily deep, that has limited desirability to discourage competition, and that has demand that won't whither from new technologies or outsourcing.

If you want a job with high opportunity and high reward, prepare to do battle. Those jobs are fought like *tournaments*, and it's largely winner-take-all. You start at the bottom, which means long hours, lousy pay, and abuse from higher-ups. These conditions cull the ambivalent from the herd. Those who continue in the tournament are fiercely competitive and aren't too worried about bending the rules to succeed.

This kind of mindset has become a staple of reality shows such as *The Apprentice* and *Survivor*. In the tournament, there is nothing attractive about your current position. The only position worth having is the top one. This is the reason why CEO pay has become so obscene. The pay is not a reward for the CEO doing a great job. The pay is an inducement to get hundreds of underlings to work like hell for relatively little money, in the hopes of climbing to the top and getting the big reward.

Because upward movement in these job tournaments is based on relative, rather than absolute performance, it doesn't matter what you do, only what you do relative to the competition. As a result, you can gain by raising yourself up, or by bringing the competition down, which can create a dreadful workplace environment where back-stabbing and sabotage of co-workers are commonplace. Morale and productivity suffer, and the company itself starts to rot from within.

If you are working in such an environment, you need to ask yourself why. Do you want the top job? Are you willing to do what appears to be necessary to get it (which usually means doing more of the best and the worst than everyone else)? Do you stand a realistic chance of winning this tournament? And finally, if you win, do you think it will have been worth it?

If you don't like the way the game is being played, stop playing it. Why compete in a tournament when the price is higher than the prize? Or as comedian Lily Tomlin once said, "The trouble with the rat race is, even if you win, you're still a rat."

Misjudging the Odds

Which of these two choices would you prefer to take a chance on? Scenario One: You have to correctly guess six cards drawn at random from a deck of fifty-two. It is not necessary to guess them in order. Scenario Two: Of all the fans who attend an NFL game this year, your seat at the one game you attend is selected as the winner.

Did you select one that you thought had better odds? See if this information helps you. To calculate the odds of selecting the six cards, the formula is (6/52) x (5/51) x (4/50) x (3/49) x (2/48) x (1/47). For the NFL selection, multiply 16 games per week times 16 weeks times 79,719 attendees per game.

The odds of you selecting all six cards are 20,408,163 to 1. The odds of your being the one person selected at all those games are....20,408,163 to 1. Did you think the odds were the same for these two events? Did you think the odds were as long for either event as they actually were?

When it comes to judging the odds of things, we aren't very good, which is in part because we don't think in terms of percentages; we think in terms of experience, and not just ours. If I watch my local news, I may hear stories about a robbery, a murder and a drunken driving fatality. One might conclude this is a dangerous place and it's time to move. But this is Atlanta, with a population of five million. The odds of someone being killed here are high. The odds that it will be me are extremely low. My wife's home town of Sandersville, Georgia has a population of 5,000. Most people would consider Atlanta to be a more dangerous place than Sandersville, and might move from here to there for that reason. But if they think about it, metro Atlanta's population is 1,000 times that of Sandersville. Therefore, in order for Atlanta to be as dangerous as Sandersville, Atlanta would have to have over a thousand murders, robberies, etc. for every one in Sandersville.

When you combine loss aversion with a miscalculation of odds, you can make some serious money mistakes. You may have a low $100 collision deductible on your car as a precaution. The cost difference between a $100 deductible and a $1,000 deductible might be $200 per year. If you went 4 ½ years without filing a collision claim, you would have saved enough to pay the higher deductible. Most people go much longer than that. Many people buy health and/or life insurance that provide specific coverage against cancer. If you need these coverages, you need them against ALL risks. Because cancer is so frightening, we overestimate its probability. A heart attack or stroke is much more likely to incapacitate or kill you, but we don't act on statistics, we act on feelings. We protect ourselves from the things that frighten us the most, but not necessarily against the things that pose the biggest threats.

Misunderstanding the real odds can cause us to make bad decisions regarding investments. History shows time and time again that stocks have a strong rebound after a bear market. Yet people always think that "this time is different", so they sell in the belief that there will be no rebound this time. The one thing that has a high probability with investments is that there will be a *regression to the mean.* If the stock market has performed poorly over the last five years, it is more likely to perform better than average over the next five years. The reverse is also true. Extrapolating the recent past into the indefinite future is betting on a long shot. If you want to bet on the future movement of something, the best bet is that it will move in the direction of its long-term average. History confirms such movements, whether for the stock market, annual precipitation or a baseball player's batting average.

Frequency and severity are the two aspects to risk that we are prone to misjudge. A hurricane scores pretty high on both the frequency and severity meters, yet people continue to move to beach areas from Texas to Virginia despite the risks. Medical advances combined with increased exposure to chemicals in our environment have caused a decrease in cancer's severity (as measured by an increasing survival rate) while at the same time increasing its frequency of diagnosis. In order to accurately assess opportunities and risks, we need to know how to gather and interpret accurate data on what might happen and its effects. We also need to recognize that our perspective is but one, and is very likely to be wrong.

We can be deceived by averages, too. The New York Yankees had the highest payroll in baseball in 2008 with a total of $207,108,000, which is an average salary of $10,900,000 per player. It certainly would lead one to believe that all the Yankees must be incredibly wealthy. The median salary, where half make more and half make less, is a more modest $2,150,000. The mode, the most frequent salary, is a paltry $390,000. Averages can be skewed by a high ceiling and a few in the population at or near the ceiling. Averages can also conceal volatility in the numbers. Remember, if you stand in your kitchen with one hand in the freezer and one hand on the stove, *on average* your temperature is just right.

Great Expectations

In my line of work, it is very common for clients and others to ask me what I think the stock market will do next. After a moment of apparent deep reflection, I typically reply, "It will fluctuate." Their response varies.

As a financial advisor, one of my most important duties is to manage expectations. My answer about the stock market is accurate, and the only answer I can give honestly and with confidence. If I reply that I think the market will go up that will raise someone's expectations about the future. If I say it will go down, their expectations will go down, too. Giving either of these answers also creates the expectation that I can somehow predict the short-term future of the market. I will have created an expectation about my precognitive skills that I can never meet. If I happen to guess right with any frequency I will also create an expectation for myself, otherwise known as overconfidence. Making false predictions and promises will cause me to lose confidence in myself; more important, it will cause others to lose confidence in me. And if I don't have a client's confidence, I have nothing.

Marketers know how to manage expectations about products, which is the essence of branding. Billions and billions of dollars are spent every year by corporations to get their brand name in front of as many people as possible. The most effective branding efforts usually have a great slogan, too: "Just Do It" (Nike); "What the World Is Coming To" (Honda); "Because I'm Worth It" (L'Oreal); "Good to the Last Drop" (Maxwell House); "Ask the Man Who Owns One" (Packard) are some classic examples. Once the company has established a positive image of the brand, a positive expectation of the product is created.

Our expectations cause a shift in our actual perceptions at least as much as our actual perceptions cause an adjustment in our expectations. Here's what I mean. You are told about a new movie that critics and friends are all raving about. Everyone gives it five stars. You go see it and it is very good. You would also rate it four to five stars. On the other hand, if your friends and the critics had consistently given the movie three stars, you would have likely rated the movie three to four stars. Your expectations influenced your actual perception.

Don't believe me? How do you think placebos work? We are confidently told by experts that a drug will have a positive effect, which becomes our expectation and our actual perception moves in the direction that confirms that expectation. We don't like to be proven wrong, even to ourselves, so we make our body believe what the mind has told it. Placebos have a long history of effectiveness because people believe what they've been conditioned to believe; in this case, that a sugar pill will ease pain and suffering.

Actual perceptions move in the direction of expectations when the gap between the promise and reality is not too wide, and when reality is subjective. Your enjoyment of a movie is subjective, not objective. The movie everyone raved about might not have been quite as good as they said, but it was close enough that you were willing to give the benefit of the doubt on the difference. If the movie had been a major turkey, you might have reacted in the other direction. If you were expecting a five star movie, and it was actually a two-three star movie, you might give it one star because your disappointment was so great.

When a product or service can be judged objectively, creating high expectations can backfire, which is one reason why football coaches always seem to be downplaying their team's chances of a championship. (In the South, this is known as poor-mouthin'.) The coaches will tell the players that they are capable of winning the championship and that nothing less is expected or acceptable. But the public will hear a humble commentary about all the obstacles that need to be overcome, and that with a few breaks and God's grace, they have a chance. When the results are in black and white, you don't want your words to come back to haunt you. The backlash will leave some bad scars.

When evaluating any product or service you are offered, try to find an objective way of measuring whether reality meets expectations. Let the objective method be the yardstick you use to determine if the product or service merits your continued business. With more subjective purchases, it's less important what others think, subjectively or objectively. If you liked the movie, then buying the ticket was a good decision, regardless of what anyone else thinks. Just don't get in the habit of brainwashing yourself that a movie was good just because you paid to see it. You'll end up watching a lot of lousy movies that way.

When providing a service to others, I believe the best policy is to under-promise and over-deliver, though not by a huge amount on either side. If you under-promise too much, you may not even get the opportunity for the business. If you over-deliver too much, you may raise expectations so high for the future that you will have a hard time meeting them. If you over-promise, then you are almost certain to under-deliver, which will likely cost you a customer and create someone who will make a vocation out of telling everyone how you mistreated them.

Ever feel taken for granted? If so, don't feel bad. Those who are taking you for granted don't mean to do it, and it's actually a compliment that you are consistent enough that they slip into such a frame of mind. Taking something or someone for granted is known as adaptation, and adaptation is why we are not yet extinct. We adjust attitudes and behaviors to existing conditions. Up until the recent past, humans mostly adapted to negative conditions. In recent decades, it's more of an adaptation to abundance.

When I was a kid, we had three TV channels, all in black and white. Now I have 500 channels, and there seems to be less worth watching than there was in 1962. Back in the day, if our car had a working radio and a heater, what a luxury! Now it takes a top end sound system and heated leather seats to make the grade. The average house has doubled in size since the 1960's. We've adapted to the upgrades, and we're no more satisfied today than we were forty or fifty years ago.

We are all customers, and we all have customers. Even if you work in an office, your employer is a customer for your labor. It's important to be aware of the process of adaptation. If you buy an expensive new car, you will adapt to the performance and features of that car and will not be able to easily return to an econobox. When it's time to replace that car, you will have to get an even fancier (and more expensive) car to get the same thrill as you got with your last purchase. If you have customers, an improvement in service or product will soon become the standard, and you will have to do still more to impress people. You can't afford to stagnate, though. The competition is also trying harder, and if you don't improve in order to keep expectations low, you will lose customers to the competition. The goal is to make constant improvements in products or services without giving too much too soon. You might create expectations that will be impossible to sustain.

The most costly expectation we can have is the expectation of our own genius. This overconfidence manifests itself in a hundred different ways, from overestimating our investment prowess to thinking we're an above average driver, singer, lover, etc. Overconfidence is the endowment effect not on our stuff, but on ourselves. It's easy to think we have a great storehouse of experience and knowledge which makes us incredibly wise. But we have the worst perspective of anyone when it comes to our own abilities. If you are truly confident in your abilities, ideas and opinions, be willing to let others evaluate them. If others in the know concur with your evaluation of yourself, then you may have something. But don't let your ego let you make financial mistakes when smart people are telling you you're crazy.

Who's In Charge Here?

We are not all "created equal", despite what the Declaration of Independence says. If we were all created equal, we would all have the same intelligence, the same beauty, the same athleticism, the same lifespan. You might conclude that if we were all equal we would all have the intelligence of Albert Einstein, the beauty of Jessica Simpson, the athleticism of Walter Payton and the lifespan of George Burns. Since equality moves everyone to the average, we would likely all have the intelligence of Jessica Simpson, the beauty of Albert Einstein, the athleticism of George Burns and the lifespan of Walter Payton. Inequality is good in that it enables those with talent to flourish, benefiting all of us in the process.

There is one aspect of our lives that is equal for all of us – the size of today. For everyone in the world, regardless of their talents, nationality, gender, or station in life, every day for every human is twenty-four hours long. Everything else in this world is unevenly distributed. The amount of time you have today is an absolute, and how you use today is the purest measure of how you use what you have, in both absolute and relative terms.

You may be one of those people who feel that their twenty-four hours is not theirs, because so many others have made demands for that time. We all have demands made for our time. But never forget that your time is yours, and just because someone demands your time doesn't mean you have to give it to them. Everyone demanding your time has the exact same daily allowance of time as you. You should stand first in line for your time and give it priorities. If you respect your time, others will have to respect it, too.

The most common excuse given for not exercising is a lack of time. I say excuse and not reason because everyone has twenty-four hours, and exercising is more of a need-to-do than a want-to-do. If we say we don't have time to exercise, we're relieved of the guilt of having chosen not to do something we need to do, but don't particularly want to do. If your doctor told you that if you didn't start exercising 45 minutes every day, you'd be dead in six months, then you'd carve out a 45-minute chunk of time out of each day and move it right to the top of your to-do list, wouldn't you? Exercise is but one example of using a lack of time as an excuse for not prioritizing our time.

Benjamin Franklin said that Time is Money. He is right in many ways, but I think one way that is often overlooked is that time and money are both finite resources that often get treated like they're infinite. We don't know when our time or our money will eventually run out, and we want to think neither ever will. But they both will eventually, and what you waste today of either resource is gone forever. When it comes to time or money, winners pay for tomorrow with today. Losers pay for today with tomorrow. Winners initiate. Losers procrastinate.

When it comes to gaining control of your time or your money, there is one tried-and-true method to recognizing where those resources have been going and redirecting them to where they should go. This method can almost guarantee that the time you want to be spent in an area will be spent there. It can almost guarantee that you will save more, reduce debt, and reduce wasteful spending. In short, this method can change your life, because it will revolutionize the way you use time and money. Here it is...

Write it down.

When you set a goal or make a promise and write it down, you make an *active commitment.* You judge yourself based on your actions, not your inactions, and writing something down is an action. In the late 1950's, Yale University conducted a study. In the 1980's Harvard University conducted a similar study. In both studies, graduates of the university were asked if they had set specific written goals for themselves upon graduation. In both cases, only about 3% of the students had done so. The amazing finding was, the 3% that had established specific written goals had incomes averaging *ten times* what the other 97% were earning. And since they were all graduates of Yale and Harvard, it's unlikely any of them were working the drive-thru window. Such is the power of the simple act of writing down what you want to do.

Goals need two things: a date and an amount. If you want to lose weight, you would write down the target weight and the target date. It is also helpful to set sub-goals to measure progress along the way. For example, your goal may be to lose 30 pounds in one year. If you also set sub-goals, such as target dates for losing 10, 15, 20, 25 pounds, you will increase your chances of reaching the big goal. The sub-goals break down the large goal into more manageable pieces and give positive reinforcement along the way.

I want to use a word now that may shock and offend some of you. I'm giving you warning so that you will not slam the book shut and turn a blind eye and deaf ear to everything subsequent I say. The word is *budget.*

The reason so many people cringe at the thought of a budget is because they misunderstand what a budget is and what it is used for. A budget is often seen as a device to shackle the individual to a program of austerity and denial that sucks all the joy out of life. The budget is viewed as both an indictment for reckless spending and as a punishment for same. Someone who has to go on a budget feels the resentment and humiliation of a chastised child. *Budget* is a dirty word because there are no positive connotations associated with it.

I speak now to exalt the much maligned budget. A budget is not a loss of control over spending; it is the regaining of control over spending. A budget is your telling your money where to go, not asking where it went. A budget is not punishment in the present; it is liberation from severe punishment in the future. A budget is not a sign of financial incompetence; it is proof of proper financial stewardship. If a budget causes a reduction of short-term pleasures, it more than offsets it by greatly increasing long-term financial security, opportunity and happiness.

If you do not have a written budget and if you are not meeting financial goals like debt reduction and saving for retirement, you now have the solution to your problem. A budget does not yank you from one lifestyle to another, like a misdirected dog on a leash might get yanked. Your budget is created by you. You decide how you want your income allocated. You also create a record of where your money is currently going. A budget will show you the difference between where your money is going and where you want it to go. The shift you make from the status quo to the new priorities will be evolutionary, not revolutionary. Each month you will shift a little more money from where it was misspent to the categories that *you* have determined are important. Each change will be initiated by you because you want it. The only time someone has an externally imposed budget is when they fail to create their own budget, and an outside overseer, like a bankruptcy judge, has to assume the role.

One of the most effective psychological tools in breaking down a prisoner is creating the feeling in the prisoner's mind that he has no control. Most people experience similar psychological stresses involving that feeling of no control in their lives. You can't accomplish what you want to accomplish. You can't get a handle on your finances. Your time is not your own. If you write down what you want, whether it's a goal to manage time or manage money, you begin to take control. You are saying "This is mine!" and that you, and only you, are going to decide how it is to be used. There is no more liberating feeling.

And in rebuttal, what a MONEY MORON recommends you do:

- **Say moo.** If you've ever watched *Animal Planet*, you know that when an animal leaves the herd, that's when the wolves pick him off. Us Money Morons may not have much, but at least we got each other.
- **You be the judge of what your stuff is worth.** I've never had somebody offer me more than I was asking for something, but they always seem to offer less, which isn't what I want. You know your stuff, so you should decide what it's worth. If the rest of the world doesn't like it, they don't have to buy it.
- **Fear loss.** It's a survival mechanism. Mumble-jumble about coin flips just confuses everything. This loss aversion has been fine-tuned by thousands of years of evolution. Who are you to question the wisdom of Mother Nature?
- **Anchors aweigh, matey!** If I didn't have somebody else telling me the price, how would I know what something is worth? If it weren't for the sticker price, I wouldn't know what to pay. Just like you should know the value of your stuff, the manufacturers should know the value of their stuff.
- **Don't fungigate your money.** If you treat every dollar like it was the hardest one you ever worked for, you'll never have any fun with it. You'll never buy a bass boat, go to Vegas, nothin'. What's the fun of money if you can't blow some of it?
- **Let market norms always rule.** Social norms are too fuzzy, but market norms are crystal clear. Your date won't be offended if you think of the relationship as a transaction. It shows you know something about money, and women find that very sexy!
- **Don't let choices paralyze you.** I say get as many options as you can. There are two ways you can handle a lot of choices. One is eenie-meenie-minee-moe. The other is what I say when I go to Baskin-Robbins: One of each, please!
- **Compete in tournaments.** First of all, you don't want anyone to think you're a wuss, or worse that you have too much integrity to do the corporate version of mud-wrestling. The prize must be worth it, otherwise why would all these people be killing each other over it?

- **Roll the dice.** They say the odds of winning the lottery is about ten million to one. First of all, a number that big doesn't even compute with me and (b) if I look at the odds, I might change my mind and not play. I figure somebody's gotta win, and it might as well be me.
- **Expect the best.** If our expectations affect how much we actually enjoy something, it would make sense to brainwash ourselves into thinking that everything is wonderful all the time. Even if we're getting shafted left and right by people, our stupor will prevent us from ever knowing or caring.
- **Don't write it down.** I survived this long by being flexible. If I write something down, like a goal or a budget, I'll be forced to follow through or look like an idiot. And my image is everything to me.

DEATH BY DEBT

You owe $170,492, so does your spouse, so do each of your children and each of your grandchildren. Don't believe you really owe this much? Allow me to itemize the bill for you:

CATEGORY OF DEBT	TOTAL DEBT	PER PERSON*
Federal Government Debt	$11.4 trillion	$37,377
State/Local Government Debt	$2.8 trillion	$9,180
Corporate Debt	$10.7 trillion	$35,081
Home Mortgage Debt	$13.2 trillion	$43,278
Credit Card Debt	$2.5 trillion	$8,197
Other Household Debt (auto loans, lines of credit, etc,)	$11.4 trillion	$37,377
TOTALS	**$52.0 trillion**	**$170,492**

*total debt divided by U.S. population of 305,000,000

Please note that the above figures do not include unfunded Social Security/Medicare/Medicaid contingent liabilities, which total another $57 trillion. We won't include those numbers because they will (theoretically) be paid with future tax revenues. Back to your tab of $170,492 - will that be cash or check? (Credit cards are not accepted.)

Our per capita GDP is $45,800, which means that if every dollar earned by every man, woman, child and corporation was used to pay off our cumulative debt, that debt could be paid off in just 45 months. Of course, paying down debt has not been our pattern. Our ratio of debt as a percentage of the economy is about 470%; fifty years ago it was about 190%. Even after adjusting for inflation, our per capita debt is 5.6 times higher than it was fifty years ago. We've been digging ourselves into a deeper and deeper hole for a long time now. We have also forgotten the first rule when you find yourself in a hole – Stop digging!

Easy Money

Up until recently, credit was obscenely easy to obtain. Much of the money that made credit easy and cheap came from abroad (We currently owe Japan and China over a half-trillion dollars each). In 2003, while shopping for a mortgage, my banker told me, "Mark, with your good credit, we would be willing to loan you enough to put you into bankruptcy." Of course, one reason I have good credit is that I would never give in to the temptation to borrow excessively, just because I was capable of doing so.

Unfortunately, there are a lot of people out there who figure that if someone is willing to lend them money, it must be OK to borrow it. After all, why would someone risk lending money if there are doubts as to the borrower's ability to repay? The borrowers deferred their own judgment about their ability to repay to the lender's judgment. But there was a fundamental flaw in this line of thinking.

In the past, if someone were going to lend you money, they were going to lend you *their* money. If you went to the bank and asked for a loan for a house or a car, the bank was lending you money their own customers had made available through deposits. The lender in these situations had direct accountability if the loan ended up in default. Because of the accountability factor, the lender exercised due diligence in the underwriting of the loan – in other words, they made damn sure you could pay it back. Proper verification was made of credit and income history, and you were required to make a reasonable down payment of your own money. By requiring an equity stake by the borrower from the beginning, the risk of default and repossession was greatly reduced.

In recent years, we moved away from this model. Loans were now made by people who sold them immediately to another party. That party would package loans together and resell them to another party. That party would slice the loan packages up into smaller pieces (known as tranches) and sell them to investors. The people who processed the original loan were paid a fee for the processing and sale of the loan, but after that, they were done. The final investors were the ones at risk in the event of a loan's default, and for the most part they had no clear idea how much risk they were actually taking on. Too often, the final investors were dazzled by the expected returns, and lulled into a false sense of security that these loans were collateralized, which means they could repossess the property the loan was used to purchase.

It doesn't take a Ph.D. in Economics to know that if people borrowing money have none of their own at risk, and if the loan originators don't have any of their own money at risk, disaster can't be far off. People act in self-interest, and too often act in short-term self-interest. When the pain of honoring a contract is greater than the pain of breaking that contract, we know that most people will act in their short-term self-interest and walk away from their contractual obligations.

There has been no shortage of finger-pointing as to the causes of the great financial crisis of 2008, but there were really two root causes. One cause was people who borrowed more for a mortgage than they could afford to repay; people who could only avoid default in a best-case scenario of rising home values and steady or falling interest rates. For many of these borrowers, it all seemed perfectly safe because of the trends of the recent past, and because of the willingness of others to bankroll their borrowing.

The first cause leads us to the second cause. Wall Street firms bundled these mortgages into securities investments, held them in their own accounts (after no one else wanted to buy them any more), and borrowed against them at rates typically 30 to 40 times the investment's value. Even though fewer than 10% of mortgages defaulted, that kind of leverage by the Wall Street firms spelled disaster. Individuals borrowing more than they should have was carelessness on a modest scale, and the great majority still met their obligations. Wall Street's packaging of loans into securities and then borrowing like crazy against them was recklessness on a massive scale.

The ramifications of a mortgage default by an individual were magnified 30 to 40 times by what Wall Street firms did with that mortgage, but notice what the problem was for both Wall Street and Elm Street. They lost the ability to manage their debt. Every financial crisis has its own unique circumstances, but most of the time it goes back to debt that cannot be repaid when something bad happens, and something bad almost always happens.

The era of easy money is over, which is a good thing in the long run. The lending practices of the last few years were the financial equivalent of an all-you-can-eat buffet. There was no way some people weren't going to overindulge when there were few externally imposed limitations. Any self-imposed limitations were overpowered by the illusion that you weren't really paying for all you were getting, so get all you can. Even if no one stops you at the buffet line and even if you don't stop yourself, there will come a time later that you end up praying at the porcelain altar as penance.

Even if credit standards stay tight for many years to come, it only means that the all-you-can-eat buffet has shut down. The problem is Americans have been dining there for a long time, and they are morbidly obese with debt. While it's a good thing that they won't be able to add more debt as easily, the debt they are already carrying around is seriously endangering their financial, physical, and mental health.

The tonnage of debt Americans are carrying endangers their financial health, in that the bigger your liabilities, the lower your net worth, and net worth is what you live on in retirement. Debt threatens physical health because it creates stress which weakens the immune system and makes us vulnerable to diseases like cancer and heart disease. Debt threatens mental health because it causes marital deterioration and the loss of the support system we need to survive. Debt also makes it harder to keep a proper perspective because debt can overwhelm our thoughts, making it difficult to maintain balance in our lives.

How Much Is Too Much?

Just as every person has an individual tolerance for risk, every person has an individual tolerance for debt. There are upper limits for everyone simply because the ability to service debt is not unlimited, even for the very wealthy. If you are struggling to make debt payments and provide the requirements of life, you are past the rational upper limit for debt.

Even if someone is financially capable of servicing additional debt, he/she may not be psychologically capable. A fiscal conservative will not want to take on any more debt than necessary. They may be quite capable of making the monthly payments, but borrowing unnecessarily goes against their nature and makes them uncomfortable. If the thought of borrowing money for a purchase makes you uncomfortable, it is important to listen to that inner voice. The benefit obtained from the purchase you make with borrowed money is likely to be more than offset by the anxiety the additional financial burden brings upon you.

One of the more common determinants of whether a person has too much debt is the Debt-to-Income (DTI) Ratio, which compares a person's debt payments to his or her income. DTI Ratio is a key number lenders use to calculate a potential borrower's ability to repay any additional debt. The consensus among financial experts is that a household's debt-to-income ratio should not exceed 36%.

The debt-to-income ratio is calculated by taking the total of all monthly debt payments (mortgage, home equity loan, car payments, credit cards, student loans, etc.) and dividing that total by monthly gross income. For example, a household has total gross income of $84,000, or $7,000 per month. The monthly debt payments are as follows:

▪ Mortgage PITI (principal, interest ,taxes, insurance)	$1,645
▪ Home Equity Line of Credit	$333
▪ Car Loan 1 (purchase)	$388
▪ Car Loan 2 (lease)	$249
▪ Credit Cards	$360
TOTAL MONTHLY DEBT SERVICE	$2975

In this example, the debt-to-income ratio is 42.5% ($2,975 / $7,000). This ratio is higher than the recommended 36%, which means this household could have trouble meeting these monthly payments plus the other typical household expenses. The high debt-to-income ratio also means that any additional debt may be difficult to obtain or may require higher rates of interest to offset the higher risk of default. Total home debt service is $1,978 or 28% of income, which is the recommended maximum percentage.

Whether you can comfortably handle a debt-to-income ratio of 36% also depends on other financial obligations you may have. If you are currently paying for college for one or more children, it is an expense which could make it difficult to handle a DTI ratio of 36%. If your income fluctuates because you earn part of it by commissions, there may be months that income will be inadequate to meet your obligations. The DTI ratio of 36% is what lenders are looking for as an upper limit. Your personal upper limit may be far less if you have additional demands on your income or an income that is inconsistent.

Being a two-income household can be a mixed-blessing when deciding whether to take on additional debt. With two incomes, it is unlikely that both income-earners will lose their jobs at the same time. However, it is twice as likely that one income-earner will lose his or her job, compared to a single-income household. There is also the risk of disability or death for either income-earner. Lastly, if there is a chance that the wife will become pregnant and need to stop work, at least temporarily, the household income will drop, and the ability to service debt will be impaired. All these factors should be considered before taking on any debt, especially debt that will require several years to pay off.

Overpaying on Several Levels

Do you have money in a savings account, CD, or money market fund? What interest rate are you currently earning on that money? Do you have a car loan, student loan, credit card balance, or home equity loan? What interest rate are you currently paying on those debts? Is there a disparity in those two numbers? Is that disparity in your favor? I thought not.

Financial institutions deal with one product – money. Money is a commodity; a dollar from one institution is exactly the same as a dollar from every other institution. The only thing that makes one financial institution better than another for the customer is the interest they pay and the interest they charge. Everything else is fluff.

In order to stay in business, the spread between what a financial institution pays on deposits and what it charges on loans has to be wide enough to cover their costs and generate a profit sufficient to keep shareholders invested. That's the reason why you pay a higher rate of interest when you are a borrower than you receive when you are a lender. Also remember, you are a lender when you have money on deposit in any financial institution. It isn't the institution's money they are lending; it's their depositor's money they're lending.

If you are both a lender and a borrower, does it make sense to pay a higher rate of interest than you receive? Of course not, but people make this mistake all the time. They may have a $5,000 CD at the bank paying 5% interest, yet they have an average balance of $2,500 on their credit cards, with an interest rate of 13%. In this example, the person earns $250 interest on the CD, but pays $325 in interest on the credit card, for a net loss of $75. If the credit cards were paid off and there was only $2,500 in a CD, the earned interest would be $125. That's a $200 improvement over the current situation on net assets of $2,500 or a net gain of 8%.

I'm always amazed at people who spend a lot of time shopping interest rates offered on CD's and money markets and who seem to be keenly aware of who is offering an extra quarter-percent on deposits. However, when I ask these same people about their outstanding debt and the interest rates they are paying, they are much less informed. Their tendency is to focus on what they can get, and not what they are giving up. This disconnect may be due in part because debt tends to emphasize our mismanagement of money, something we would prefer to repress. Hence, people who focus only on interest received and not on interest paid are like the people who carefully investigate which gas stations are cheapest, but never bother to check the air pressure in their tires, a simple step that would save them much more than any price differential between gas stations.

The disparity between interest paid and interest received isn't the only way we overpay by using debt. When we borrow to buy something, we are much more likely to pay a higher purchase price than we would if we paid cash. Numerous studies have shown that consumers will pay an average of 12-18% more for an item when they buy it on credit than when they buy the same item for cash.

Economics 101 teaches that future dollars are worth less than present dollars, which is known as the time value of money. There is a tendency to apply that theory when buying something on credit. Since we will be paying with future dollars, we mentally discount those dollars by paying more for an item than we would if we paid cash now. However, when we buy an item on credit, we typically pay 15% too much for the item (relative to a cash purchase) then compound that mistake by financing the purchase at a 15% interest rate. If we take a year to pay off the purchase, we pay from 20-30% more for the item than if we had saved the money and purchased it for cash. The additional utility of getting the item sooner almost never justifies paying 20-30% more for it. There is no objective justification for the purchase, so we rationalize it by telling ourselves we've earned it. Not yet, actually.

In addition to paying too much for an item when we buy on credit, there is the simple act of buying the item in the first place. Over half of jewelry purchases are financed, even though less than 30% of sales are bridal jewelry, which is the only segment of jewelry sales that could justify buying on credit. To prove I'm not picking on women here, some 75% of new motorcycle purchases are financed, and the buyers are overwhelmingly male. Male or female, there is a much greater tendency to buy something we don't need and to buy more of it when we buy with credit rather than with cash.

When you swipe your credit card or sign your name on a credit purchase, there is no immediate sense of loss. You still have your card; you still have your pen. It is that lack of any sense of loss that makes a credit purchase easy in the first place, and it makes it easy to pay more than we might otherwise. For example, you walk into Best Buy looking for a 26" TV. You budgeted $600 to spend, which will get you a nice set in that size. Your eye drifts to the 42" sets that run about $1,400. You see they are offering 0% financing for 12 months (never mind that the finance charge is buried in the price of the set or that you are unlikely to pay off the balance in 12 months to avoid the severe interest charges). Before you know it, you are taking delivery of that 42" set.

What happened? For starters, you let yourself get distracted. You knew why you came in there. You knew how much you could spend. You can't blame the salesperson. It's their job to extract the maximum amount from you, and they know that job is made easier through attractive financing offers. Also, you didn't hand over bills, and you didn't write a check. Either of those acts would have sent off danger signals in your brain. Assuming you had $1,400 in cash on you, the physical act of handing over fifteen $100 bills (don't forget the sales tax) would have likely caused you to stop before consummation. Slightly less traumatic than paying cash would have been writing a check for the full purchase price (assuming you had that much in your checking account). The process of subtracting some $1,500 from your checking account balance would have given you pause to reflect, as you wondered how you were going to cover the mortgage, the car payment and the other bills that get paid out of this suddenly diminished checking account balance.

One of the biggest problems with buying on credit is that it doesn't hurt in the present, which makes it easy to do. The biggest problem with buying on credit is that it *really* hurts in the future, when the pleasure of a new toy has diminished, but the bill keeps showing up every month. There is a rush we get when buying something we want. It's like the warm glow from a glass of good scotch. But too much credit buying, like too much scotch exacts a price in future pain that cannot be avoided. Promising future abstinence won't ease the hangover. And when the hangover subsides and we want to feel that rush again, we're back at the mall, credit cards a-blazin'.

Stressed and Depressed

Two out of five American adults have unpaid medical bills, accumulated medical debt, or both. These unpaid bills and medical debt can make it harder to get needed health care; two-thirds of people with such burdens go without needed care because of the cost. That number is triple the rate of those without such financial burdens.

One of the reasons these people have medical bills is health problems caused by stress caused by debt problems. It's a downward spiral for many. The debt begins to pile up. The cause may be an unexpected medical bill or just careless spending. The cause is secondary to its effects. The debt and the inability to pay it create stress, which manifests itself in any number of physical ailments. The physical ailments require medical attention, but getting the medical attention might require going further into debt; so often treatment is not obtained, and the physical ailments continue or worsen. If people get the medical treatment for stress-related ailments, but get into a worse financial hole in the process, they have treated the symptoms while at the same time worsening the cause of those symptoms.

An AP-AOL survey in 2008 compared people who reported high-debt stress with those who didn't feel such stress. In comparing the two groups, the high-debt stress group:

- Had 3 ½ times more ulcer/digestive problems
- Had 3 times the migraine/headache frequency
- Suffered severe anxiety at a rate 7 times higher than the other group
- Suffered severe depression at a rate 6 times higher than the other group
- Had twice as many heart attacks
- Suffered sleep disorders at a rate 13 times higher than the other group

Stress about mounting debt and what you're going to do about it is bad enough. What is really stressful is wondering what will be done to you if you can't get a handle on your debt problem. Among the more common steps others may take when your debt gets out of control are:

- Creditor Harassment – Despite many laws on the books prohibiting such harassment, creditors continue to violate them, making legal threats, calling at all hours, insulting you, and making life generally miserable.

- Evictions – the prospect of being booted out of your home and having to find another place to stay, which will be difficult because of the eviction.
- Foreclosure – perhaps even more devastating than eviction because of the likely loss of any equity (financial and sweat) that you had in your home.
- Wage Garnishments – The embarrassment of having your employer ordered to pay your wages to a creditor is bad enough, but now you don't have the money you need to pay things like rent and insurance.
- Involuntary Bankruptcy – This bankruptcy is initiated by the creditors, not by you, the debtor. It forces you to face all your creditors at once, instead of dealing only with those who press the hardest.

The list above is a sample of what others do to you when you lose control over debt. That list is nothing compared to what debtors do to themselves when the stress of debt becomes overwhelming:

- Divorce – Money problems are the single leading cause of divorce. Losing a spouse means losing one's most important support system, which is not good for mental or physical well-being.
- Emotional Breakdown – When anxiety and depression rates climb six or seven times higher than normal, there will be casualties that require intense treatment. Many never fully recover from such a trauma.
- Abandonment – It might be the father who leaves his family and never returns, or it might be the mother who leaves her children at the shelter because she can't take care of them. For the abandoned, it's devastating.
- Suicide – When someone feels there is no way to climb out of the financial hole they are in and the future they envision has nothing positive in it, suicide may become a viable option in that frame of mind.
- Murder – Money is the main motive for murder in the U.S. Sometimes greed prompts it. Other times it is desperation over debt. Most news stories about a killing over debt problems don't report on a murder; they report on a murder-suicide.

Because money is such an important element in our lives, when we lose control over our money, we lose control over our lives. The most common feeling expressed by people who report debt problems is a loss of control over their situation. This loss doesn't just involve the loss of financial control, which is certainly the case. People overrun by debt lose control over their bodies and minds, as evidenced by the huge increase in physical and mental problems they have relative to the general population. The loss of emotional control may be the most devastating of all. We already know how the emotions of fear and greed can affect our finances. The emotional stress of owing money you can't imagine being able to repay creates an emotional time bomb that is sometimes detonated in the most revolting of crimes, such as the murder of one's own spouse and children.

Reduction, Not Consolidation

When the debts begin to pile up and just meeting the minimum monthly payments becomes a strain, the first step many people take is a debt consolidation loan. Debt consolidation is what its name implies; you take several debts and consolidate them into a single loan that should hopefully offer a lower overall interest rate than you were paying on the consolidated loans.

Since people who use debt consolidation services are typically in deep financial trouble and are looking at alternatives to bankruptcy, the purpose of debt consolidation for them is to buy time, literally. A lower interest rate may result from debt consolidation, but what the customer is looking for more than anything is a lower overall monthly payment. The reason they are seeking debt consolidation in the first place is they can't handle the current size of the monthly debt service. There are three ways to reduce the size of the monthly debt service:

- Reduce the size of the overall debt, which debt consolidation doesn't do.
- Reduce the interest rate, which debt consolidation might do a little.
- Increase the repayment period, which debt consolidation almost always does.

The only way to get a meaningful reduction in the monthly payments is to stretch out the period of repayments. Lower interest rates can reduce the monthly payments some, but there are limits there. If people are consolidating loans that average a 12% interest rate, they will probably still have an interest rate of 9%+ on a debt consolidation loan.

For example, a person has $20,000 in miscellaneous debt, with a four-year average repayment period and a 12% interest rate. The monthly payments total $527. A debt consolidation loan that reduces the interest rate to 9% and has a four-year repayment schedule reduces the monthly payment to only $498. Add in the fees to set up the debt consolidation loan, and there's no progress made here. If the repayment period is stretched to seven years, and the interest rate moves up to 10% (longer period = higher risk = higher interest rate), the monthly payment is now $332. The interest rate was reduced 2%. The monthly payments were reduced 37%. The repayment period was increased 75%. A debt consolidation loan reduces the severity of the financial suffering by increasing its duration. The overall repayment also increases in this example. Under the old plan, total repayments were $25,296 ($527 x 48). Under the new plan, total repayments are $27,888 ($332 x 84). For the record, paying more to repay a loan is not progress.

The prospects of lower monthly payments, reducing or eliminating the harassing phone calls from creditors, avoiding bankruptcy, and a general easing of emotional stress are all good reasons to consider debt consolidation. However, as is the case with any financial transaction, it is important to do your homework, shop around, and read the fine print. Be extremely wary of any plan that promises to reduce your debt a lot in a short period of time. The only ways to do that are to pay off the debt or file for bankruptcy, and the reason people seek debt consolidation is they can't do the first, and prefer not to do the second.

People often look to a home equity loan as a way to consolidate debt. It is tempting to consider a home equity loan for two reasons – the interest rate is lower than on most unsecured loans, and the interest is tax deductible, because the house is collateral on the loan. However, the fact that the house is collateral on the loan is why you should *not* consider a home equity loan for debt consolidation purposes. If you don't pay your Visa bill, Visa can't repossess anything because credit card debt is an unsecured loan, but with a home equity loan, you risk losing your home if you default on the loan. That risk is too great to take, especially if you are in a financial bind, which you are if you are considering a debt consolidation loan. The stress of an unpaid Visa bill is nothing compared to the stress of a foreclosure.

Debt consolidation tends to give the illusion of progress. Because the monthly payments are lower, it is easy to feel like the worst is behind you. However, the total outstanding debt has not diminished at all, and the total cost to repay the outstanding debt has increased because of the greater amount of interest paid over the longer repayment period. This illusion of progress leads to exactly the wrong behavior going forward.

The easing of short-term financial pressure that debt consolidation may provide makes it even easier to continue the behaviors that created the problem in the first place. Any solution to curing a person's debt problems has to begin with behavior modification. The behavior that needs modification – spending money you have not yet earned. Debt consolidation actually makes it easier to take on new debt. Because debt consolidation requires only one monthly payment of a lower amount, it isn't long before new additional debt is being added. Rarely do people who do debt consolidation cancel their credit cards. The outstanding balance on the cards may go into the consolidation loan, but the credit cards are still in force, and they soon have balances on them that meet or exceed the old balances. New offers of credit continue to arrive in the mail, too. If someone has been spending $5,000 more per year than their income, debt consolidation won't change that behavior, unless it is accompanied by a total shutdown of all sources of additional borrowing.

In the earlier example where a person had $20,000 in debt, if that person pays $527 per month, there are two things working in his/her favor. The rather high monthly payment discourages taking on new debt because there is no room in the budget. Also, the balance should be paid off in about four years. If the person in this example avoids taking on new debt for this four-year period, he/she can be debt-free and then have an extra $527 a month to save, invest, or pay cash for purchases.

With a debt consolidation loan having a seven-year payoff period, the $332 monthly payment makes it a lot easier to justify taking on new debt. Even if the person initially avoids taking on new debt because of the lower payments, he/she has to maintain that discipline for seven years, not four, in order to become debt-free. Psychologically, the temptation to acquire new debt is greater, and the period one needs to resist it is far longer. For someone who has already demonstrated a poor record at resisting temptation, such discipline is a tall order.

The only program that makes sense when debt has gotten too high is to reduce that debt. Just as the debt probably grew over a period of time, it will take time to reduce it. Just as a lack of discipline was a likely cause of the debt problem, a surplus of discipline is the only cure.

The first step in reducing debt is to cancel *all* lines of credit, which means cutting up every credit card and cancelling any lines of credit at banks, credit unions, etc. If you have a debt problem, you can't have access to any more debt – that's it. It's like an alcoholic having booze in the house – no good can come from it. Eliminating new potential debt is the first and most crucial step in ending a debt addiction. People unwilling to take this step do not deserve to be free from their indentured servitude.

The fear debtors have in cancelling all sources of credit is that they will get into a position that requires the use of credit, but the credit won't be there for them. They see their lines of credit as a safety net. It's a net alright, but the kind of net that ensnares, not the kind that saves. The best way to avoid being hurt on the high-wire isn't by having a safety net; it's by getting down off the high-wire. Credit isn't the solution, it's the problem, and eliminating any potential new credit is recognition of that fact. Eliminating new credit is the first step down off the high-wire.

When looking at how to pay down debt, the logical method would be to pay down the debt with the highest interest rate first, while still making the minimum payments on the other debts. However, if people in deep debt were logical, they wouldn't be in deep debt. What this situation requires is a method that will pay the total debt down steadily and in a manner that gets tangible and encouraging results, to sustain momentum until the last debt is cleared from the books.

The most successful method of knocking out debt is known as the Debt Snowball, made popular by Dave Ramsey. The Debt Snowball works in the following manner. You list your debts, smallest to largest by outstanding balance. You also list the minimum payments. The smallest debt you pay off immediately, not by borrowing, but by selling something. You are removing a liability by removing an asset. A garage sale is an excellent place to raise quick cash. If a part-time job for a month or two will create cash to kill a debt, that method is perfectly acceptable, too. The main thing is to get the smallest debt off the books, without adding any additional debt.

The payments that were going toward that smallest debt are added to the payment you are making on the next smallest debt. That debt gets paid off more quickly, and the money that was paying off that debt moves to the next debt on the list. As each debt is paid off, the amount every month going to pay off the next debt on the list is increased. This process speeds up the time it takes to pay off each debt and lowers the number of outstanding debts as well. Below is a table showing an example of how the Debt Snowball works:

DEBT SOURCE	INTEREST RATE	TOTAL BALANCE	MINIMUM PAYMENT	MONTHS REMAINING	NEW PAYMENT	MONTHS PAID
Target Card	16.0%	$580	$40	17	paid w/garage sale	
Sears Card	14.5%	$1,220	$85	18	$125	1-11
Discover Card	13.0%	$3,360	$120	34	$245	12-20
Visa Card	18.0%	$8,650	$245	42	$490	21-30
Home Equity	7.0%	$28,600	$360	105	$850	31-54
Student Loan	7.5%	$34,700	$366	144	$1,681	55-71
Car Loan	8.5%	$18,900	$465	48	paid off in 48 mos.	
TOTALS	av. 8.8%	$96,010	$1,681			

Notice that the new payment for each debt is the minimum payment plus the sum of the payments of the debts that have been paid off. Note that the minimum payments continue to be made for all the debts while they are waiting their turn to get an increase. In this example, the household debt is completely paid off in less than six years. Because the car loan is paid off in 48 months (before the snowball gets to it), the $465/month that was going to the car loan gets added to the student loan in month 55. For months 49-54, the $465 a month that was going to the now-paid-off car loan can go toward an emergency fund. So, in less than six years, this household eliminates almost $100,000 in debt; they have a modest emergency fund of $2,800, and they are not only debt-free, but they can now put $1,681 a month toward building their own wealth.

Who Is Fair Isaac, and Why Is He Running Your Life?

There is a TV commercial I see regularly that shows a young mechanic talking to his older co-worker. The young man has just gotten a beautiful red sports car. He tells his jealous colleague that he was able to get a "great rate" on the car because he "watches his credit like a hawk." The implication in these words is that external forces are the biggest threat to this young man's good credit standing. Identity theft is rampant, and mistakes are frequently made in recording payments, so it is important to monitor your credit to make sure you aren't a victim. But when I watch that commercial, I can't help but think that whatever an outsider might do to that young man's credit isn't as potentially dangerous as buying a shiny new sports car on a young mechanic's salary. For most Americans, the biggest threat to their credit rating comes from the person whose name is at the top of the credit report.

If you've ever borrowed money, you have some familiarity with a credit report. The credit report lists your borrowing, and more important your repayment history. Lenders use this tool to determine if they will lend you money and what interest rate they will charge you. However, looking at page after page of data on a credit report is time-consuming and different people may have different interpretations of the same data. This human element adds subjectivity, and lenders need to be able to defend a decision using objective measurements.

In 1956, two Stanford scientists named William Fair and Earl Isaac started a company that would use mathematics and computers to analyze credit risk. By far their most enduring creation is the FICO (short for Fair Isaac Corp.) score, which you probably refer to as your Credit Score. Over 100 billion FICO scores have been sold over the last half-century, which is about eleven scores for every man, woman and child who has lived on the planet during the last fifty years. The three major U.S. credit reporting agencies – Equifax, Experian, and Trans Union have been using FICO scores for nearly twenty years. (Each of these three agencies uses a slightly different computation formula, which is why your score may vary from one to the other.)

FICO scores are used by 90% of the largest U.S. banks and by 80% of mortgage brokers to determine the risk of default. In light of climbing mortgage default rates, the FICO scoring system was revamped in 2008 to give more credit points to consumers who maintain multiple lines of credit, such as home equity loans and credit cards and to penalize those who heavily use their lines of credit. These changes seem to mean that in order to improve your FICO score, you need to have more credit available to you, but that you also shouldn't use it.

FICO scores range from 300 to 850. The median FICO score in the U.S. is 723, and the average score is 678. Your FICO score is calculated based on your ratings in five general categories:

- Payment History - 35%: shows punctuality of payments in the past, but only shows payments more than 30 days past due.
- Amounts Owed - 30%: expressed as a ratio of current revolving debt to total available revolving credit.
- Length of Credit History - 15%: the longer the track record of paying on time, the better.
- New Credit - 10%: looks at new credit issued, but also at number of recent credit checks by potential lenders.
- Types of Credit Used - 10%: installment, revolving, consumer finance are main categories. Consumer finance is subprime lending. The more revolving and consumer finance credit, the lower the score.

How much of an effect does your FICO score have on your ability to borrow? Even with a low score, there is usually someone who will lend you money, provided the interest rate is sufficient for the risk. Borrowers with a low FICO score may need to collateralize a loan and/or may require a co-signer(s). Here is how interest rates on various loan types rise with a fall in FICO scores:

FICO SCORE	30-YEAR FIXED RATE MORTGAGE	15-YEAR HOME EQUITY LOAN	36-MONTH AUTO LOAN
760-850	--------	--------	--------
700-759	+.22%	+.30%	+1.43%
660-699	+.51%	+.80%	+2.53%
620-659	+1.32%	+1.58%	+4.95%
580-619	+3.49%	+3.08%	+8.37%
500-579	+4.34%	+4.33%	+9.36%

(Only 2% score below 500)

Credit scores are being used in fields that go beyond traditional lending. Insurance companies are now incorporating credit scores in underwriting insurance risks. Part of the reason for looking at credit scores by an insurer is to gauge the ability to pay the premium. Perhaps even more important is the moral hazard issue. Moral hazard refers to the risk that dishonesty might increase the risk of loss. If someone is having financial problems, it increases the chance that the insurance company may be used as a way of solving the problem through some sort of fraudulent claim. Potential employers are also looking at credit scores to get an idea of a person's ability to handle responsibility and whether personal financial problems may create greater risk for theft or fraud by the employee against the employer.

Fair Isaac Corporation offers the following tips to improve your FICO score:

- Pay your bills on time.
- If you've missed payments, get current and stay current.
- Know that paying off a collection account or closing an account does not remove it from your credit report.
- Contact creditors or see a legitimate credit counselor if there's a problem.
- Keep balances low on credit cards and other revolving credit.
- Pay off debt rather than moving it around.
- Avoid credit repair agencies that promise to remove negative, but accurate, information from your credit report.
- If you have a short credit history, don't open several new accounts too rapidly.
- Shop for a loan in a short period of time; it helps distinguish between a search for a single loan and a search for multiple credit lines.
- Don't open new accounts you don't need.

You are entitled to one free copy of your credit report from each of the three major credit reporting agencies once a year. You need to go to their joint website, www.annualcreditreport.com, and complete the online information. You can order all three reports at one time if you want to compare information on them. If you want to check your credit report periodically throughout the year, you can also stagger when you request a report from each of the agencies, which will enable you to get an update on your credit every four months. You can dispute any errors by contacting the three major reporting agencies directly:

Equifax – 800 685-1111 – www.equifax.com
Experian (formerly TRW) – 888 397-3742 – www.experian.com
TransUnion – 800 888-4213 – www.transunion.com

The use of FICO scores is so widespread that it is almost impossible to insulate yourself from its effects. Flaws in the credit scoring system, and even the credit scoring system itself, can create major financial headaches for people. It is estimated that more than 75% of credit reports have errors on them, and a third of those errors are serious enough to cause a denial of credit. Often the errors are not discovered until the individual applies for credit and is denied or is required to pay a higher interest rate. Error frequency is why it is important to be proactive and check your credit reports annually to avoid errors piling up. If you are planning to obtain credit in the near future, you should check your credit about three months before you begin the application process. If there are errors on your credit report, you will have time to get them corrected before you apply for credit.

When you apply for credit, factors other than your credit score are considered. The main items are income and employment history. Even with a high FICO score, it's hard to borrow money without an income, since an income is almost certainly where the loan payments will come from. One factor that is rarely taken into account is the borrower's net worth, which may be the best overall indicator of financial responsibility.

From the perspective of building wealth, the efforts needed to maintain a high FICO score are counter-productive. First of all, consider that we are talking about a *credit* score, based on information contained in a *credit* report. Having little or no debt is detrimental to your credit score; a thin credit history is detrimental to your credit score; refusing to use credit cards is detrimental to your credit score. In short, the behaviors that are most helpful in creating wealth and financial security are the same behaviors that tend to hurt your ability to borrow money. Bob Hope used to joke that the only way to get a loan from the bank was to prove you didn't need it. Now, if you have conducted your financial affairs to minimize your use and need for credit, you are unlikely to be offered any.

There is something fundamentally wrong when people are encouraged to have debt in order that they will have the ability to acquire more debt. It makes debt look like a financial help rather than a hindrance. Americans have been led down this path, not surprisingly, by the lending institutions. They have been telling us that our ability to buy their product in the future is contingent on our buying their product now. The FICO score is the cattle prod they use to make us take on debt we don't need, and which hurts our ability to become financially independent and immune to the lure of debt.

I'm reminded of a situation of a friend of mine. This man had a daughter who had married, and she and her husband were looking to buy their first home. The couple's credit was OK, but it was hardly perfect. As is often the case with a young couple, there wasn't a long credit history, and he had a late payment or two. They also had modest incomes and already had other debts like a student loan, a small car loan and some credit cards. They were credit-worthy, but they weren't qualified for the best mortgage rates. In their case, a 2% bump in the interest rate increased their mortgage payment 20%. When the father looked into what kind of interest rate he could get, he was informed his rate would be the same as the kids' rate because he had almost no credit history and a low FICO score. He had no credit history because he disliked borrowing money. He hadn't needed to borrow money in quite some time, since his business had grown and since he now had an annual income of nearly $1 million, and a net worth of over $10 million. He decided to loan the kids the money, at a very favorable rate. Wealth, not debt, enables you to do such things.

The Price of Friendship

What would you do if a friend or relative asked you to cosign a loan? Before you answer, make sure you understand what cosigning involves. Under federal law, creditors are required to give you a notice that explains your obligations. The cosigner's notice states:

> ***You are being asked to guarantee this debt. Think carefully before you do. If the borrower does not pay the debt you will have to pay. Be sure you can afford to pay if you have to and that you want to accept this responsibility.***
>
> ***You may have to pay up to the full amount of the debt if the borrower does not pay. You may also have to pay late fees or collection costs, which increase this amount.***
>
> ***The creditor can collect this debt from you without first trying to collect from the borrower. The creditor can use the same collection methods against you that can be used against the borrower, such as suing you, garnishing your wages, etc. If this debt is ever in default, that fact may become a part of your credit record.***
>
> ***This notice is not the contract that makes you liable for the debt.***

The previous notice may be the least ambiguous wording I have ever seen come out of Washington. It couldn't be made any clearer what a co-signer is getting into.

Before you begin thinking that no friend or relative that you would co-sign for on a loan would ever stick you with the repayment, know that there is a 75% chance that they will. Some three out of four co-signed loans end up being paid by the co-signer, or at least the co-signer is called in to repay when the primary borrower defaults. And if the co-signer doesn't repay the loan or get his friend/relative to repay the loan, the co-signer's credit rating takes the hit.

Humans have a tendency to take the path of least resistance. Despite what you may believe, loan collectors are human and will also take the path of least resistance. Here is what they see from their perspective. The person who needed a co-signer apparently does not have a good history of repaying debts in full and on time, which is why they needed a co-signer. The person who co-signed the loan apparently does pay their bills in full and on time, which is why they were approved to be the co-signer. The person who took out the loan is now living up (down) to their reputation and has fallen behind in the repayments. A cursory effort might be made to get the borrower to get back on track, but the odds of getting timely payment are much better if the co-signer is pressured; after all, this is a person who has a history of living up to financial obligations. It is not the role of the loan collector to keep the relationship between the borrower and the co-signer from being torn asunder, which is almost always what happens.

Aside from sexual infidelity, the most damaging act to a relationship is probably financial infidelity. When someone promises to repay a loan, and then they don't, they commit financial infidelity. The borrower may think they are only cheating on the lender, but they are cheating on the co-signer, too. The lender doesn't take the infidelity personally; the co-signer always does.

Very often, the person who is asked to co-sign a loan does so out of fear that if they say no, it will damage the relationship with the person making the request. There is no doubt that being asked to co-sign a loan puts a person in a very awkward position. If the person making the request is a son or daughter who needs a co-signer because they are young and don't have a sufficient credit history, that request is worth granting. However, this assumes that this son or daughter is making the request only because they have no credit, not because they have bad credit. Also, this son or daughter should have a history of demonstrated responsibility (and an income) that makes it a high probability that they will repay the loan without your help.

For everybody else who asks you to co-sign, here's what you need to evaluate. If you say no and give your valid reasons, what will this person's reaction be? If it is an irrational reaction (which is what we fear), what kind of reaction is it? If they threaten to sever the relationship over this issue, that threat tells you there was not much of a relationship there and that this person would be very likely to stick you with repaying the loan. If they threaten any physical action, that confirms you made the right decision. This person won't repay the loan because they will probably be in jail at some point soon.

You may be concerned about damaging the relationship by saying no, and you fear you may be blamed for the damage. Remember, you are saying no to the request, not to the relationship. If the other person lets your declination affect the relationship, it may be that this relationship was never mutually beneficial, but instead parasitic, which you don't need.

Lastly, realize that 75% of co-signed loans get defaulted, and if you look at the figures for borrowers who need a co-signer because of bad credit (as opposed to no credit), the default number is closer to 90%. There is about a 90% chance this person is going to stick you with the bill, which is going to damage the relationship *and* your finances. In such a circumstance, you are infinitely better saying no. Say no, and they'll be mad at you. Say yes, you'll be mad at them, and poorer. No contest, in my book.

Here's one last tip that may help you decide whether to co-sign a loan. If you yourself have the money on hand that the person is looking to borrow, would you be willing to make the loan yourself out of your own funds, with the proper legal paperwork to bind the borrower to repay the loan? If your answer is yes, you might as well make the loan yourself. Your risk is virtually the same, and at least you will receive the interest. Would you also be willing to take the loan out yourself and have the person who is asking you to co-sign pay you back directly? If the answer to both of these is a resounding no because it sounds too risky, the answer to co-signing the loan should be an equally resounding no because the risk is almost identical.

Before you cosign, the Federal Trade Commission offers the following advice:

- Be sure you can afford to pay the loan. If you're asked to pay and can't, you could be sued or your credit rating could be damaged.
- Even if you're not asked to repay the debt, your liability for the loan may keep you from getting other credit because creditors will consider the cosigned loan as one of your obligations.
- Before you pledge property to secure the loan, such as your car or furniture, make sure you understand the consequences. If the borrower defaults, you could lose these items.
- Ask the lender to calculate the amount of money you might owe. The lender isn't required to do this calculation, but may if asked. You also may be able to negotiate the specific terms of your obligation. For example, you may want to limit your liability to the principal on the loan and not include late charges, court costs, or attorneys' fees. In this case, ask the lender to include a statement in the contract similar to: "The cosigner will be responsible only for the principal balance on this loan at the time of default."
- Ask the lender to agree, in writing, to notify you if the borrower misses a payment. That will give you time to deal with the problem or make back payments without having to repay the entire amount immediately.

- Make sure you get copies of all important papers, such as the loan contract, the Truth-in-Lending Disclosure Statement, and warranties — if you're cosigning for a purchase. You may need these documents if there's a dispute between the borrower and the seller. The lender is not required to give you these papers; you may have to get copies from the borrower.
- Check your state law for additional cosigner rights.

Opportunities Lost

A Chinese saying goes: "Luck is when preparedness meets opportunity." One of the unseen and unmeasured costs of debt is that it leaves one unable and/or unprepared to take advantages of opportunities. Some examples:

- Making monthly payments on a depreciating asset, like a boat, leaves you unable to use that money to regularly invest in an appreciating asset, like stocks.
- You find someone who is selling a classic car you've always wanted at a fraction of its true value because of financial problems. You can't get financing because your debt/income ratio is too high to get approved.
- You are disqualified as a co-signer on your daughter's first home because you already have too many obligations, one of them a loan you co-signed for your cousin, who has since defaulted.
- You have the opportunity to quit your job and start your own business, but your income will take a hit in the first year or two. You can't handle the income drop because your monthly debt service is too high.
- You are unable to help your son with his college expenses as much as you would like, because 45% of your income is used to service debt. As a result, he has to borrow extensively for college, continuing the cycle.

These examples are hypothetical. You probably have your own real-life examples, which are probably more poignant than these.

I have my own variation on the Chinese saying: Light Load + Liquidity = Luck. If you keep your debt load as light as possible (ideally, nothing more than a 15-year fixed rate mortgage) and if you have money set aside in a liquid asset like a money market account, you will be amazed how many opportunities will cross your path. More important, you will have the ability to take advantage of those opportunities.

Here in Georgia we have a creeping vine called kudzu. It was brought over from Japan to control erosion, but since it has no natural enemies here, it goes wherever it pleases and can grow a foot a day. Unless aggressively controlled, it wraps itself over everything, including fully grown trees, which eventually die from lack of sunlight and the weight of the kudzu.

Debt is like kudzu; unless it is aggressively controlled, it will quickly spread to the point where it is out of control. You are like the tree; the debt will cover you up to the point where it suffocates you, and you eventually collapse and die from the weight of the burden.

And in rebuttal, what a MONEY MORON recommends you do:

- **Forget that $170,492 per person debt stuff.** Did you co-sign anything for that federal, state or corporate debt? I didn't think so. Just let 'em try and collect it from you without a signed agreement!
- **Urge Congress to default on debt to foreigners.** These people buy our treasury bills and then bad-mouth us, so I say forget 'em. We owe Japan a half-trillion dollars. If we don't pay them, what are they gonna do, attack Pearl Harbor *again*?!
- **Assume if they're OK lending it, you're OK borrowing it.** Are you a financial expert? Well, the people lending the money are, and if they say it's safe for you to borrow that much, who are you to question their judgment?
- **Remember that present pleasure is worth future pain.** You've been told that a future dollar is worth less than a present dollar. It stands to reason that future pain hurts less than present pain. The pain of paying a big debt later is therefore less than the pain of denying yourself an indulgence today.
- **Don't let debt stress you out.** What's the worst that can happen if you don't pay? They take their stuff back. If they go after your income, just quit your job. There are no more debtors' prisons, and your health isn't at risk unless you borrowed from Tony Soprano.
- **Keep even with your better half.** If your wife is charging up a storm, go buy a bass boat. Or vice versa. Just don't let your partner get too far ahead of you in the spending game. Fair is fair.
- **Get it now.** Something in the present is worth more than something in the future, so it makes sense that you should pay more to have it now than to wait and get it for less later. It's more fun, too.
- **Agitate the bill collectors.** My favorite trick is to use one of those air horns when they call me at dinner time. It's more fun than poking a pit bull with a sharp stick! If that's not your style, derogatory comments about their mother works pretty good, too.
- **Work off the books.** They can't garnish your wages if you don't have any (nudge, nudge, wink, wink).
- **Walk away.** Not from the temptation; from the obligation. Bankruptcy laws exist to be used. Don't be shy about trying them out.

Don't be shy about walking away from spouses, children, co-signers etc., either. If it comes down to you or them, you know whose side you're on.

- **Consolidate, don't eliminate debt.** Wrap it into one neat little package with one monthly payment that's lower than what you pay now. So what if you're on the hook for ten years instead of five? That's also about 500 Lotto jackpots in the meantime, and you're bound to hit at least one.
- **Worship the FICO god.** Do not, under any circumstances risk not getting credit in the future by not using credit now. If you need to borrow money from a lot of different places now to raise your credit score, by all means do so. A high FICO score is worth a low net worth.
- **Consider co-signing.** Are you so selfish that you can only think about how co-signing affects you? They wouldn't ask you if it wasn't important. You should be honored you were asked. It's a sign that your friendship is considered strong enough to withstand you being left holding the bag.

CHAMPIONS START WITH DEFENSE

Baseball has been used as a metaphor for life thousands of times. One more analogy can't possibly hurt.

Pitchers are unique among baseball players. They exist totally for defense. When a pitcher is allowed to bat, he is almost always at the bottom of the batting order. The American League has the designated hitter, specifically to spare the pitcher the embarrassment of batting.

The pitcher is one of only nine positions on a team, yet pitchers typically make up about half the players on a team's roster, which is, in part, because no pitcher is expected to play more than 20% of the time. Actually, most play far less than that 20% figure.

The eight teams that made the major league baseball playoffs in 2008 had a combined payroll of $838.2 million. Of that total, $372.5 million, or 44.4% was paid to pitchers.

If you are even a casual baseball fan, you know that there is nothing more frustrating than to watch your team's starting pitcher do a great job, watch your team scratch and claw their way to a late-inning lead, and then watch a relief pitcher give up a tape-measure home run that costs the team the game. That slight defensive gaffe erases all the previous hard work.

Too many people focus their financial efforts strictly on offense. Specifically, they focus almost exclusively on earning an income and on growing their investment portfolio. They rarely give much thought to protecting what they have accumulated or to protecting their ability to accumulate more in the future.

These people are akin to the baseball team with a great offensive lineup, but no pitching. Such a team will routinely score 10 runs a game. They will also routinely give up 12 runs a game. Such a team may lead the league in offensive statistics, but they will almost never make the playoffs.

In your personal financial situation, what good is it to have a great return on your investment portfolio, only to lose it in a lawsuit because you lacked adequate liability insurance? What good is it to work years to get to a great job only to lose it to an uninsured disability? What good is it to create a lot of home equity, only to lose it after the fire, when you find out you were underinsured? What good is it to exercise daily and eat right, only to fall victim to some disease because you don't have health insurance that enables you to get the treatment you need? What good is it to work hard, make money, provide a comfortable lifestyle for your family, only to see them lose it all when you die prematurely, with only enough life insurance to pay for the funeral?

The savings of a lifetime can be wiped out in the twinkling of an eye. It happens all the time, although it shouldn't. The purpose of this chapter is to make sure it doesn't happen to you.

You heard the word *insurance* mentioned several times in a previous paragraph. Yes, that's what we're talking about here. Yes, talking about insurance can be boring (though it doesn't have to be). Yes, talking about insurance forces you to focus on a lot of worst-case scenarios. Yes, spending money on insurance premiums seems like a waste unless you have a loss and file a claim. And yes, if you choose to ignore this chapter because of the above statements, you might as well ignore the rest of this book, too. Without a willingness to put your defense together first, all the rest is for naught.

I worked several years for an insurance company (as an underwriter, not in sales). I got to review thousands of claims during that time. Some of those insurance claims made me appreciate the randomness of events, and their consequences. For example, one man survived his plane sliding off the runway at LaGuardia into the bay, only to get home to North Carolina in time to see his home destroyed by a hurricane. In another case, a young driver was driving to the beach with her parents, and she assumed the intersection was a 4-way stop. It wasn't, and the collision that resulted left her mother paralyzed for life. Then there was the young father who went to the all-night convenience store for some medicine for his sick infant daughter. He was shot and killed in the robbery. Insurance would not have prevented any of these tragedies. Insurance does play a big part in making the unbearable bearable, as it did in these three cases.

One of great stressors of human beings is uncertainty. More specifically, it isn't the uncertainty of events, but rather the uncertainty of consequences that is the real source of stress. When you have a defense against the consequences of a bad scenario, the stress of the uncertainty goes away. You are able to say to yourself, "Regardless of what may happen in the future, my family and I will be all right." The ability to truthfully make such a statement will free you up to generate a financial offense that will stand up to anything the future may hold. Your financial foundation is built on rock, not sand.

In the movie *Unforgiven*, Clint Eastwood plays Will Munny, a bounty hunter. After his young partner kills for the first time and is remorseful, Will Munny tells him, "It's a hell of a thing, killing a man. You take away everything he has, and everything he's ever going to have." The last part of Munny's statement is what affects me. If you are reading this book, you are probably serious about making your financial future better than your financial past. You may not fathom what you are putting at risk if you ignore the advice of this chapter, but you risk everything you have, and everything you're ever going to have. Imagine what "everything" might include.

Better Off Dead?

Hopefully, you have never seriously contemplated if you would be better off dead. There is one group however that has certainly contemplated that question more than the general population. I'm talking about people who have become disabled.

Becoming disabled, even temporarily, takes a heavy toll on a person. First, there is the physical trauma that created the disability. Something happened to the body that causes it to not function properly. Whether from injury or disease, the body endures the great stress from the impact of whatever caused the disability and the stress of the body's efforts to heal.

Second, there is the psychological toll of a disability. The onset of a disability may require us, for the first time, to contemplate our own mortality. We may realize finally that we are quite fragile and vulnerable. We may lose our greatest sense of purpose when we can no longer work. The psycho-logical stress of diminished capacity can often be harder to bear than the physical disability itself.

Lastly, there is the financial toll that a disability exerts on the disabled person, and also on that person's family. The problem with a disability from a financial perspective is that income goes away, but expenses do not. In fact, expenses typically increase when someone becomes disabled. From a strictly financial perspective, many people who suffer a long-term disability would be better off dead.

Do not misunderstand what I am saying. Physically, mentally and spiritually, a disabled person is not better off dead. Here's what I need you to understand – when you die, your income ceases, but so do your expenses. And most people have some life insurance to help their loved ones deal with the financial strain. When you become disabled, your income ceases, but your expenses do not. They are likely to rise, in fact. And more Americans are underinsured for disability insurance than are underinsured for life insurance. The way to be sure that you will never be someone who is financially better off dead is to understand the risks of disability and understand how to protect yourself from those risks.

Yes, it can happen to you. One reason people don't contemplate disability insurance is because they don't seriously contemplate a disability. This misperception is especially true for people who work in "safe" jobs, where the risk of an on-the-job injury is small. Most disabilities are the result of something that occurs away from the job. Most disabilities are actually the result of illness, not injury.

ODDS OF A DISABILITY OF 90+DAYS BETWEEN NOW & AGE 65

Age of Person	Risk of Disability of Any One Person	Risk of Disability to Any One Person Out of Two
30	46.7%	71.6%
35	45.1%	69.9%
40	43.0%	67.5%
45	40.1%	64.1%

(The statistics for two people are important if both husband and wife work.)

AVERAGE DURATION OF A DISABILITY OF 90+ DAYS AT VARIOUS AGES

Age at Beginning of Disability	Duration
25	2 years, 2 months
30	2 years, 8 months
35	3 years, 1 months
40	3 years, 6 months
45	3 years, 11 months
50	4 years, 2 months
55	4 years, 5 months

Source: 1985 Commissioners' Disability Individual Table A

PROBABILITY OF DISABILITY VS. DEATH PRIOR TO AGE 65

Age	Ratio
30	2.31 to 1
35	2.21 to 1
40	1.95 to 1
45	1.69 to 1
50	1.53 to 1
55	1.33 to 1

Source: 1985 Commissioners' Disability Individual Table A and 1980 CSO Mortality Table

There are several points I want you to get from the previous tables:

- There's at least a one-in-three chance you will be disabled for more than three months in your working life.
- If you are married, there is a two-in-three chance that one of you will be disabled for more than three months in your working life.
- The odds of being disabled decrease with age, but only because there are fewer years to go until retirement.
- The odds of a long-term (over 90 days) disability within the next five years increase with age.
- Disabilities tend to be short or very long. If your disability lasts 90 days, it will probably last more than two years if you're young and last more than four years if you're middle-aged.

Worker's Compensation is not a substitute for disability insurance. Worker's compensation is designed to cover medical expenses and, in many cases, lost income, but these benefits are only payable to workers who are injured in the course of employment. That group is a very small percentage of people who become disabled. The overall goal of worker's compensation policies is to have 95% of injured employees back at work within four days. Many people on long-term disability are out for four *years*. Also, in order to receive worker's compensation benefits, you relinquish the right to sue your employer.

Social Security Disability is not a substitute for disability insurance. To be eligible for SSDI, you must first have paid into the system for forty quarters or ten years. If Social Security case workers decide you are capable of any work, you are not eligible for benefits. If you are deemed eligible for benefits, they won't start until the sixth month of disability. The amount you receive is based on your lifetime average earnings, which are likely to be considerably less than your current earnings. Social Security Disability benefits are also reduced by any worker's compensation benefits you receive.

Unemployment insurance is not a substitute for disability insurance. Unemployment insurance benefits vary by state, but in most states the maximum benefit period is 26 weeks. To become eligible, you must become unemployed through no fault of your own. Benefits are based on your earnings, but each state sets a cap on maximum benefits a person can receive. Lastly, you must continue to actively seek work and report weekly to the state unemployment office to remain eligible for benefits.

Disability insurance policies are typically broken down into short-term policies (26 weeks or less) and long-term policies (over 26 weeks). We will focus on long-term policies, because a long-term disability is more damaging; a short-term disability can be handled from your emergency fund.

The amount of income benefit available under a disability insurance policy is related to the disabled worker's income. Most policies limit the income benefit to no more than 60 to 80 percent of the person's earned income. Since few disabilities are permanent and since full replacement of lost income would be a disincentive to return to work, these percentage limits serve a purpose.

Most disability insurance policies have a waiting period before benefits start, known as the *elimination period.* The longer the elimination period, the lower the insurance premium will be. When you choose your elimination period, you should realize you will be self-insured for that period. If you know you can cover six months of lost income out of savings, then selecting a 180 day elimination period is appropriate. A longer elimination period might be the key to making disability insurance affordable for you. It is better to have a disability insurance policy with a longer elimination period than you would like than to have no disability insurance policy at all.

The other part of a disability insurance policy that is flexible is the *benefit period*, which is the maximum length of time benefits are payable. Most policies do not pay a benefit past age 65 since it is assumed you would have retired by that age. When you look at the average duration of disabilities on the previous table, it is prudent to select a benefit period of no less than five years. Typical benefit periods are for 2, 5, 10, or 20 years or to age 65.

Some points to keep in mind when evaluating disability coverage:

- Think long term. A policy that covers you to age 65 is best, even if you take lower benefits and a longer elimination period to afford it.
- Make sure your policy is non-cancellable (except for non-payment of premium) and has level premiums to age 65.
- Look for a waiver-of-premium provision, which means premiums are waived during a period of total disability.
- Look carefully at the policy's definition of *disability.* Some policies pay benefits if you can't engage in your occupation. Others pay if you can't engage in any occupation. *Partial disability* means you can't perform one or more important duties of your occupation. *Residual disability* means your income is reduced (but not eliminated) as a result of your disability. The broader the definition of disability, the better for you.
- Not everyone is eligible for disability insurance. If you have a heart condition or certain other pre-existing conditions, if you are starting a

new business or work in a hazardous occupation, coverage may be prohibitively expensive, if available at all.

- See if your employer offers disability insurance, which is the first best place to get it. Alumni groups, professional and similar associations may also be able to provide group coverage.

A Most Selfless Act

Next to a permanent total disability, the worst financial disaster that could befall a family is the premature death of the breadwinner. A few generations ago, when the husband was typically the only one earning an income, his premature death was truly a disaster. Today we have more households where both spouses work. However, when both spouses work, the premature death of either spouse can create a real financial hardship for the surviving family members. We also have more single-parent households than ever before. The premature death of that single parent would be emotionally devastating to the children; it doesn't need to be compounded by financial devastation, too.

Life insurance is unique among insurance products, but not because of the policy itself. With almost any other type of insurance, the person who pays the premium receives the benefit of the coverage the policy provides. When you purchase and pay for disability, auto or health insurance, you are protecting yourself from financial hardship resulting from a loss. Others may also benefit from the coverage, but when buying these types of coverage, you are acting in self-interest (though you are not being selfish).

Here is where buying life insurance is different. The person who pays the premium is typically the same person whose life is being insured. This situation means that the person paying the premium is the only person who cannot possibly benefit financially from the payment of the policy benefit. The person paying the premium must in fact lose his/her life in order for the policy to generate a financial benefit.

The financial sacrifice isn't the only act the insured person/premium payer makes. This person also has to acknowledge his/her own mortality and the real possibility that they will die before their time. One's mortality isn't an easy fact to accept, nor is it easy to crystallize the possibility of one's premature demise into a legal contract.

Of all the things we can do to improve ourselves financially, I believe that making sure we have adequate life insurance is the most important. So many of the things we do with money we do for selfish reasons. Sacrificing pleasures to pay a life insurance premium and making sure those you love the most will be financially OK if you depart too soon are the most selfless acts you could ever perform with money. It is unlikely you could ever demonstrate love through your checkbook any better than by writing the premium check for a life insurance policy that benefits you only in ways that could never be measured by mere money. Such selflessness will become a large part of your legacy.

The term *life insurance* is really a misnomer; a marketing strategy if you will. It should properly be called *risk-of-premature-death insurance*, but it's already hard enough to convince people to buy the product. Such a name change for the sake of accuracy would not be helpful. I just want you to know what you're buying when you buy life insurance. It isn't a Live-Forever, or even a Live-Longer policy (imagine how easy it would be to sell something like that!). Buying life insurance may be one of the few times that being a pessimist can be helpful.

Imagine a college campus, perhaps the one you may have attended. Let's say there are 10,000 students on campus, with an average age of 20. Here's what we can predict with surprising accuracy:

- A total of 100 students won't live to age 30.
- A total of 200 students won't live to age 40.
- A total of 500 students won't live to age 50.
- A total of 1200 students won't live to age 60.

It's sad to envision the students at this campus and realize the 100 of them won't be around for their 10th reunion or that 500 of them won't be around for their 30th reunion. This uncertainty and its financial consequences to others is why life insurance was created.

The need for life insurance is based on the need to replace lost income for persons who depend on the insured for income. If no one depends on you for income, nor is likely to in the future, then you would not have a need for life insurance. Some people who have no dependents, but who would like to leave an estate to loved ones, will often obtain a life insurance policy or maintain one they already have. In such cases though, the life insurance policy is a nice-to-have, and not a need-to-have.

Age and health are the two major factors that determine the insurance premium and even insurability. Someone who is young and healthy can get life insurance at very reasonable rates. If a young person anticipates marriage and children in the future, it is wise to get necessary life insurance now. Not only are the premiums higher if you are older when you get the policy, but health issues could develop between now and the time you actually need the insurance, which could make life insurance prohibitively expensive, and perhaps even unattainable.

How much life insurance is needed is a function of several variables, and the method of calculation can affect the number that is generated. The main thing to keep in mind when calculating how much life insurance you need is you want the beneficiaries to maintain the lifestyle they would have had, had you continued to live a normal lifespan.

One starting point to calculating how much life insurance is needed is to calculate the present value of the deceased person's future net income after taxes. This calculation basically involves estimating the person's net income over his/her remaining working years, then using a reasonable discount rate (a reverse interest rate, if you will) to determine how much money would be needed today to generate a stream of income identical to what the deceased person would have made if he/she had lived to normal retirement age.

Listed below are some examples of calculations of needed life insurance. Everyone's situation is unique, so it is a good idea to run calculations specifically for you. Some numbers, like inflation rate and investment return, require an educated guess (not wishful thinking). You can run these same calculations using your own numbers at my web site, www.marathon-forthelongrun.com/calculators.cfm.

INPUT

What is your current income before taxes?	**$50,000**
What percentage of this income will your family need?	**90%**
For how many years will your family need this income?	**35**
What do you expect the rate of inflation to be over this time period?	**4%**
What investment return do you expect over this time period?	**8%**
Enter the total of one-time payments your family will have. (i.e.-funeral costs, college expenses, mortgage expenses, other debts the insurance will pay)	**$25,000**

RESULTS

Based on these inputs, you need this much life insurance:	**$915,726**

INPUT

What is your current income before taxes?	**$75,000**
What percentage of this income will your family need?	**75%**
For how many years will your family need this income?	**25**
What do you expect the rate of inflation to be over this time period?	**3%**
What investment return do you expect over this time period?	**8%**
Enter the total of one-time payments your family will have. (i.e.-funeral costs, college expenses, mortgage expenses, other debts the insurance will pay)	**$50,000**

RESULTS

Based on these inputs, you need this much life insurance:	**$893,539**

INPUT

What is your current income before taxes?	**$150,000**
What percentage of this income will your family need?	**70%**
For how many years will your family need this income?	**15**
What do you expect the rate of inflation to be over this time period?	**4%**
What investment return do you expect over this time period?	**7%**
Enter the total of one-time payments your family will have. (i.e.-funeral costs, college expenses, mortgage expenses, other debts the insurance will pay)	**$250,000**

RESULTS

Based on these inputs, you need this much life insurance:	**$1,550,471**

Life insurance policies can be divided into two basic types: term insurance and whole life insurance. We will discuss term insurance first since it is the type of life insurance most people would need.

Term life insurance provides protection for a fixed period of time, or stated term. It is the most cost-effective type of life insurance because you are buying coverage against a contingency, rather than a certainty. Basically, you buy term life insurance *in case you die* during the stated term.

Term insurance is appropriate for someone who is raising a family and will have financial obligations to others for several years to come. Over that period of time, this person's financial obligations to others should decrease and his/her own assets should increase. Eventually, this person will no longer need life insurance because any remaining financial obligations can be covered out of personal assets. As an example, a thirty-year old father of two small children may need term life insurance for the next 20 years to be sure there is enough money to raise and educate his children. When he is fifty-years old and his children are adults, his own personal assets should be sufficient to meet any remaining obligations.

With term insurance, if you don't die during the stated term (and it is assumed you prefer not to), then you get nothing back. You paid for pure protection and ended up not needing it (lucky you!).

Since the risk of a person's death increases with each passing year, the premiums for term insurance should be expected to increase with each passing year, which is the case for policies known as annual renewable term. Most people don't purchase such policies. If people know they have a twenty-year financial obligation, such as parents with small children, they will usually get a twenty-year level term policy. As the name implies, the policy is in effect for twenty years, and the annual premium stays the same for those twenty years. Most level-term policies range from five to thirty years.

It is important not to underestimate how long you will need to have term insurance. If you take out a fifteen year level term policy and you find you still need insurance after those fifteen years are up, the premiums will be much higher for a new policy. Also, you may have developed a health problem in that fifteen year period that makes insurance very expensive, or even unattainable. It is better to pay a little more in the early years and lock in both the premium and the coverage than to risk having no insurance in the future, when it is still needed.

If you are offered life insurance through work, just remember that your coverage probably ceases when your employment does. Such coverage can be inexpensive, but it shouldn't be your only life insurance. If you Google 'term life insurance quotes', you can compare rates from different carriers. The internet is a good place to begin finding individual coverage, which can't be cancelled because of an external factor like a job change. If you need life insurance, you need life insurance that you can control.

Whole life insurance is insurance you buy that will last your whole life, as will the premiums. Whole life insurance is needed when you will have outstanding financial obligations *whenever you die.* Two common examples are someone who has a disabled child that will need care for the rest of that child's life or someone with a high net worth who faces a large estate tax bill upon their death.

Whole life insurance is considerably more expensive than term insurance because as long as the premiums are paid, the death benefit will also be paid. Also, the premiums on a whole life insurance policy remain level from day one. The premium remains level, but the risk of death increases every year. In order to make level premiums work, the policy gets over-funded in the early years. That over-funding offsets the under-funding in the later years. The over-funding creates cash values, which are an asset to the policyholder. The cash values can be used to pay premiums; they can be borrowed, or they can be refunded to the policyholder if they choose to terminate the policy.

Premium payments that are considered over-funding need to be invested. For decades, the insurance companies chose the investments and assumed the investment risk. By law, the investments the insurance companies chose could not be risky, which meant mostly bonds. In 1976 *variable life insurance* was introduced as a new type of whole life policy. Variable life insurance shifts the investment risk to the policyholder. The range of investment options is broader than with traditional whole life policies, with stock mutual funds being the preferred investment. There is the possibility of better investment returns, but also the possibility of loss. There is no guarantee of investment return or of minimum cash value.

Variable universal life insurance is one of the more recent product developments, and it is the most common type of whole life insurance today. In addition to giving the policyholder flexibility in choosing investments, the policyholder has the ability (within limits) to adjust both the premiums and the death benefit. Such flexibility is a function of both the cash reserve and the investment performance of the policy.

Whole life insurance policies have historically paid lucrative sales commissions and as a result, have been sold when a lower cost, lower commission term policy would have been more appropriate. If you have a need for permanent life insurance, then some type of whole life insurance is your answer, but when an insurance agent is touting the advantages of a whole life policy, be sure that you really need life insurance that will never go away. Equally important, make sure you are willing to pay an insurance premium for the rest of your life. Lastly, be very wary of pie-in-the-sky investment projections. Any agent who assumes you will average double-digit investment returns for the rest of your life is not to be trusted.

To Your Health

You can tell how important something is to the American people by how much that issue is politicized. By that standard, there has hardly been a more important or more politicized issue over the last fifteen years than health care. Health care and health insurance are such important issues because everyone needs to attend to his/her health, and everyone, with the exception of the extremely wealthy, needs health insurance to assure getting proper medical care in a crisis.

Medical care expenses can be broken down into three categories:

1. *Ordinary medical expenses* are those that are considered routine. Regular medical and dental exams, treatment of minor illnesses, and routine medications would fall into this category. Ordinary medical expenses are those that occur year in and year out, with little variance. There is no need for insurance to cover these expenses. Covering these expenses through insurance tends to only add a layer of expense. The main reason most group health insurance plans include coverage for ordinary medical expenses is to encourage members to be proactive in

their health care through regular exams and the like. HMO stands for Health *Maintenance* Organization.

2. *Extraordinary medical expenses* go beyond the routine, but are not uncommon. Examples might include an appendectomy, a broken wrist, or hepatitis. While many families could manage to pay for an extraordinary event, very few would choose to do so. The certainty of a higher health insurance premium is preferable to the uncertainty of a medical bill that could come to several thousand dollars.
3. *Catastrophic medical expenses* are those that result from a catastrophic illness or injury. A serious car accident, an organ transplant, or the onset of advanced Alzheimer's disease would all fall into this category. Even the super-rich would prefer to pay for insurance against these expenses, than to absorb the expense on their own. For most people, an uninsured catastrophic medical event would leave them with only two options: surrender their financial health to recover their physical health, or surrender their physical health because of the inability to afford the needed medical care.

Approximately 15% of the U.S. population is without health insurance. One in five working class adults is uninsured. One in ten children is uninsured. The lower percentage of uninsured children compared to uninsured adults may indicate that being responsible for the health care of others is a motivator to getting health insurance. In any event, some 45 million Americans are uninsured. These uninsured tend to be on the lower economic rungs and also live where injuries, illnesses and accidents are more prevalent. They are at greater risk for a catastrophic medical expense, with the least ability to pay for it. (I assume that if you're reading a book like this you have health insurance if it's attainable. If I assumed incorrectly, put the book down and don't come back until you get properly covered.)

Of the 85% of Americans who have health insurance, 90% of them have group health insurance, most typically through their employer, which makes about 230 million Americans covered through group health insurance. A major advantage of group insurance is easier eligibility for coverage, as it is the group as a whole, not the individuals in the group, that are underwritten. Another advantage is lower premiums, due to the economies of scale a group offers.

The disadvantages can include less flexibility in choosing your coverages or in choosing your physicians. An even bigger disadvantage to group health insurance is the potential loss of coverage should you leave the group. While you have the ability to continue the coverage for a period of time after leaving a job, there is a time limit, and the cost of coverage increases dramatically. For better or worse, group health insurance has become the predominant retention tool in American businesses today.

The per capita cost of health care continues to rise at twice the overall inflation rate. There are several reasons for this increase:

- Since 85% of Americans are covered by health insurance, they are not as careful consumers. When the insurance company is paying the bill, we are much less likely to question overcharges or comparison shop. Out-of-pocket expenses amount to less than 20% of total payments.
- Health insurance, in addition to making us less careful consumers on price, also makes us more voracious consumers of health care. We are more inclined to use services that have little or no cost to us. It's like an all-you-can eat buffet – you almost always eat more than if it were a la carte.
- Advances in technology create new treatments. New technologies are usually expensive, as early users have to offset much of the development costs of the technology. Newer technologies also tend to be more complicated, increasing their costs.
- We are getting older, baby boomers especially. The disproportionately large baby boomer generation is entering their 60's, and the amount of health care services they will consume in the next two decades will shoot up dramatically. Americans spend one-half of their total lifetime medical expenses in the last five years of their lives. A lot of baby boomers are closing in on that number.
- While health insurance companies can contract to pay lower prices than an uninsured person will pay, the administration layers in the insurance companies and in the health care providers (which are necessary to deal with the insurance companies) create additional costs.
- Medical malpractice suits and the fear of them have led to the practice of defensive medicine. Unnecessary tests and procedures are the most obvious result of increased litigation. Higher medical malpractice insurance premiums also lead to higher medical costs.

To help counter the rising costs of health care, and to give the consumer more control over their health care choices, *Health Savings Accounts* (HSAs) were created in 2003. A Health Savings Account is an alternative to traditional health insurance; it is a savings product that offers a different way for consumers to pay for their health care. HSAs enable you to pay for current health expenses and save for future qualified medical and retiree health expenses on a tax-free basis.

You must be covered by a High Deductible Health Plan (HDHP) to be able to take advantage of HSAs. An HDHP generally costs less than what traditional health care coverage costs, so the money that you save on insurance can therefore be put into the Health Savings Account.

You own and you control the money in your HSA. Decisions on how to spend the money are made by you without relying on a third party or a health insurer. You will also decide what types of investments to make with the money in the account in order to make it grow.

You must have an HDHP if you want to open an HSA. Sometimes referred to as a catastrophic health insurance plan, an HDHP is an inexpensive health insurance plan that generally doesn't pay for the first several thousand dollars of health care expenses (your deductible) but will generally cover you after that. The minimum deductible in 2008 for an HDHP is $1,100 for an individual; $2,200 for a family. Also, your HSA is available to help you pay for the expenses your plan does not cover.

Many health insurance policies give you options between HMOs, PPOs, HDHPs and Indemnity programs. When choosing which option is best for you and your family, premiums will certainly play a part in that decision. Don't forget to look carefully at the benefits offered by the different options, including deductibles, co-pays and the percent the plan pays. Some key areas to look at include:

- Maximum lifetime benefit payable
- Pre-existing condition limitations
- Lifetime benefit limit for a particular treatment, such as substance abuse
- Annual deductible and co-pay requirements, for individual and family
- Annual out-of-pocket limits
- Primary care physician coverage and benefit payable
- Maternity care coverage, for women of child-bearing age
- Physician services in a hospital, including emergency care
- Outpatient surgery coverage and benefit payable
- Emergency care at a hospital
- Ambulance services
- Allergy shots and serum coverage and benefit payable
- Prescription drug coverage and benefit payable
- Diagnostic tests, laboratory work, X-rays
- Mental health coverage and benefit payable
- Semiannual dental exam coverage and benefit payable
- Oral surgery coverage and benefit payable
- Home healthcare services coverage and benefit payable
- Chiropractic care coverage and benefit payable
- Hospice care coverage and benefit payable
- Medical equipment rental/purchase coverage and benefit payable

Long Term Care

Much has been made about the pending transfer of wealth from the "greatest generation" to their "baby boomer" children. The articles I read typically talk about how this transfer creates a great opportunity for us financial advisors to increase our business. I have not yet read an article that mentions that this huge transfer will be muffled by the health care expenses these elder citizens will face near the end. A lot of the wealth accumulated by the greatest generation will go not to their chosen heirs, but to those providing care to them in their last years.

Consider this one fact – of all the health care expenses we will incur over our entire lives, one-half of them will be incurred in the last five years of our lives. Part of that imbalance can be blamed on inflation, but most of it is the result of needing more intense and more expensive care as we typically decline in health as a prelude to passing on.

Medical advances have made possible new treatments to extend life spans in ways we couldn't imagine thirty or forty years ago. Since we have the ability to extend the length of life (though not necessarily its quality), we are naturally using that technology. The result is increasing life expectancies and more years at the end of our lives, where we receive extensive and expensive care.

Here is a typical example of what I'm talking about. A couple enters their eighties with their home, their social security and a half-a-million dollars in savings. The husband develops Alzheimer's disease. For the first year, he is able to remain at home, but the in-home health care expense is $50,000 for that year. He then has to go to a nursing home, where he lives for two more years before dying. The bill for those two years comes to $215,000. The widow's health also declines during those three years (having a spouse with Alzheimer's is very stressful), and she also goes to a nursing home, where she passes away after eight months and $75,000 in expenses. The children who were expecting to inherit about $500,000 will end up inheriting about $160,000. So much for the greatest transfer of wealth in history.

The figures I'm quoting in the preceding paragraph are not inflated. Some parts of the country cost more, some less. But, living in a decent nursing home in this time runs about $100,000 per year. Medicare does not cover long-term care. Medicaid provides for long-term care, but almost exclusively to the aged, blind and disabled group of eligible beneficiaries. Income and asset requirements are so strict to qualify for Medicaid long-term care, you would be considered destitute by most people in order to qualify. You also can't give assets away in anticipation of becoming eligible for Medicaid. Lastly, the amount Medicaid pays the care providers is considerably less than private insurance pays. You may logically assume that the quality of care is less as well.

If you are a baby boomer, you may already have experienced the high cost of long-term care through your parents. When you reach their age, the costs will be even higher. In twenty-five years, if these costs continue to increase at the 7% annual rate they have been, that $100,000 per year nursing home will be over $500,000. If you are thirty years old and long term care costs continue to increase 7% per year, a one year stay in a nursing home when you're eighty could run $3,000,000.

It is the prospect of such enormous expenses that makes long-term care insurance something to be seriously considered. Currently, about 60% of the population over age 65 will need some type of long-term care over their lifetime. As medical advances increase the ability to keep us alive, that percentage can be expected to rise even higher in the future. It won't just be the elderly who can be kept alive through constant care. People who suffer from accidents and debilitating diseases, but who are in the prime of their lives will be adding to these numbers. Suffice it to say, it's at least an even-money bet that the average citizen in America today will have a need for long-term care at some point in his/her life. Whether they will be able to afford it is a very different bet.

There are a lot of different opinions on when is the best age to apply for long-term care insurance. The advantages to applying when you are young (say, in your forties) are lower annual premiums and less chance a health problem will raise your premiums or disqualify you. The disadvantages are that you will pay that premium for more years, and you may be paying those premiums when there are a lot of other financial pressures on you.

I think that once you turn fifty, it's time to start looking at long-term care insurance. I don't necessarily mean you have to buy a policy when you turn fifty. However, fifty is an appropriate age to begin looking at different carriers, their coverages and their premiums. Once again, it is easy to get quotes online. You can make online comparisons and see how premiums change by waiting two, five, or ten years. Making such premium comparisons has a potential pitfall, though. It assumes your health status doesn't change; only your age does. If you make a decision to wait five years, you may develop a medical condition that makes long-term care insurance far more expensive, or even unattainable.

When you are looking into long-term care policies, there are several characteristics and variables to look at. Changing different values for different benefits can greatly affect the premium. Here are some key items to examine:

- *Guaranteed Renewable.* Most policies are guaranteed renewable, though premiums may increase for an entire group of insureds.

- *Types of Care Provided.* Coverage is typically provided for:
  -skilled nursing care, which is daily nursing and rehabilitative care by skilled medical personnel based on doctor's orders.
  -intermediate care, which is occasional nursing and rehabilitative care by skilled medical personnel based on doctor's orders.
  -custodial care, which is primarily to handle activities of daily living (ADLs) such as walking, bathing, dressing, eating, taking medicine or using the toilet. It can be provided without professional skills or training.
  -home health care, which is received at home and includes part-time skilled nursing care, speech therapy, physical therapy, occupational therapy and help from homemakers.
  -adult day care, which is received at centers designed for the elderly who live at home but who are alone during the day. The level of care is similar to home health care, and transportation is typically provided.
- *Alzheimer's Disease Coverage.* If Alzheimer's disease is a pre-existing condition, there may be some exclusions or limitations. If there is a family history of Alzheimer's, premiums may be higher. There may be exclusions for other mental disease or cognitive impairment.
- *No Prior Hospitalization.* Prior hospitalization is generally not required before entering a nursing home.
- *Elimination Periods.* Common elimination periods are 30, 60, 100, or 180 days. The longer the elimination period, the lower the premium. When adjusting characteristics, it is better to lengthen the elimination period than to lower benefit amounts or shorten the duration of coverage.
- *Aggregate Benefits.* Purchasers can select a daily benefit amount and a lifetime maximum amount. The higher the benefit amount, the higher the premium.
- *Inflation Protection.* Purchasers can select an annual percentage increase for their aggregate benefits. Since this protection can more than double the amount payable between the purchase date and when the policy is used, adding inflation coverage increases the premium substantially.
- *Eligibility for Benefits.* Most policies base eligibility on the insured's ability to perform certain activities of daily living (ADLs). Check the policy to see the list of ADLs and how many the insured must be unable to perform before they are eligible for benefits.
- *Spousal Coverage.* Coverage for spouses can usually be written at a 10-20% discount when the same company writes both policies.

Protecting Your Castle

For most of us, our single most valuable possession is our home, and we naturally need to protect ourselves from loss related to that asset. Homeowners insurance is a package policy that combines all the needed types of coverage into one policy.

Since most people have a mortgage on their home, the mortgage company will mandate homeowners insurance coverage. It is perfectly acceptable and better for you if you select the insurance policy, rather than the mortgage company selecting it. If the mortgage company obtains the coverage, they will focus on protecting themselves only, and their only exposure is the loan value on the dwelling. The mortgage company will also not shop around for the best rates, since the premiums are always paid by you. The mortgage company will always need to be listed as a loss payee on the policy, and they may want the premiums to be escrowed into the mortgage payment. That's all fine, but you should be the one selecting the policy because you pay the premiums, and there are a lot of coverages that affect only you, as you will soon see.

Even if you have no mortgage on your home, you still need homeowners insurance. The premium for a policy, compared to the risks it covers is a bargain. There are two rules when it comes to buying any insurance. Don't pay a lot for a little coverage; don't risk a lot to save a little. Not having homeowners insurance would definitely violate that second rule.

The first thing to look at is who is insured under a homeowners policy. Usually the person or persons listed as owner(s) and resident(s) of the property are also listed as named insured(s). Family members residing in the house are also covered, which includes children away at college temporarily. Other persons under age 21 in the care of the named insureds, such as a foster child or exchange student, are also covered.

Coverages on a homeowners policy are broken down into two broad categories: property coverages and liability coverages. Each of these coverages are further broken down into subcategories.

Under property coverages, the first category is for the dwelling itself. Other property coverages are usually based on a percentage amount of the dwelling coverage. The dwelling is defined as the dwelling on the residence premises listed on the policy (usually your street address) and any structure directly attached to the dwelling, like an attached garage. The land itself is not insured on a homeowners policy.

The amount of coverage is based on the calculated cost to rebuild the structure as it was before the loss. The policy states that this is what the insurance company is agreeing to do – to put you and your dwelling back into the position you were in before the loss.

Most people will find that the replacement cost of their dwelling exceeds the market value of their home, which is especially confusing when you consider that market value also includes the land. However, the insurance company isn't promising to pay you the market value of your home. They are promising to rebuild your home, just as it was, which is always a more expensive proposition than buying a similar home at market value. As a way of comparison, it would be more expensive to repair a car after major damage than to replace it. Because you can replace a damaged car with an identical one, insurers will replace rather than repair when it's cheaper to do so. But every home is unique, and that's why the promise by the insurer is to repair, not just replace. If the policyholder elects not to rebuild after a major loss, the insurance company will usually negotiate a buyout at or near market value.

Other structures on the residence premises are covered under the homeowners policy. The typical limit is 10% of the amount of the dwelling coverage. If your dwelling is covered for $200,000, other structures are covered for an additional $20,000. Other structures could include a storage building, a fence or a swimming pool. There are three major exclusions under this coverage. Once again, land is excluded. Also, any structure used for a business or any structure that is rented out are excluded from coverage.

Personal property owned or used by an insured person is covered anywhere in the world. The amount of coverage for personal property usually starts at 50% of the dwelling coverage. Again, this coverage is an additional amount of insurance and doesn't reduce other coverages. With this amount of coverage, the insurer will pay you the market value of an item you have a loss. The problem with this type of reimbursement is that market value is almost always less than replacement cost. For example, if a five-year old television is stolen, its market value is less than the cost to replace it with a comparable new one, and you would have to make up the difference on your own.

More commonly, the policy is written with coverage for personal property at 70-75% of the dwelling amount, and personal property is insured at its replacement cost, rather than just market value. There is an additional premium for this additional coverage, typically around 10% more. This extra coverage is worth having, both for the additional protection as well as for eliminating the hassle of determining the value of items after a loss.

Certain types of property have limits of coverage under a homeowners policy. For reasons involving potential fraud and loss-adjustment problems, items such as cash, valuable papers, firearms, silverware, jewelry, furs and business property have dollar limits of coverage. Many items that have such coverage limits can be covered on the homeowners policy by scheduling those items. Scheduling involves requesting specific coverage, providing appraisals and paying an additional premium. It is always a good idea to check your policy carefully for such limitations and to arrange additional coverage if you need it. If you had a theft of $10,000 of jewelry, you would not want to find out after the loss that you were only covered for $1,000.

The last of the property coverages handles loss of use, when the residence premises cannot be used because of a loss covered under the policy. This amount of additional coverage is usually 20% of the amount of the dwelling coverage. For example, if your home were to be damaged in a fire, the loss of use coverage would pay for renting another place to live while the damage is repaired. If a civil authority requires you to leave your premises because of an occurrence on other property (i.e. – the fire marshal orders you to evacuate because of a neighbor's gas leak), loss of use coverage can be used then as well.

Coverage for the dwelling and other structures on the property is stated as all-risk, with stated exclusions, which means that there is coverage for a loss unless the loss is caused by something specifically excluded by the policy. Some of the more common exclusions include freezing, flooding, earth movement, neglect, war, wear and tear, ordinance or law and, of course, intentional loss.

Personal property is covered for specific losses that are listed in the policy. The most common losses are covered, like theft, fire, vandalism and plumbing-related damage. When looking at what kinds of losses are or are not covered, it is important to remember that the insurance is in place to protect you from losses that are beyond your control and that have a low degree of predictability.

One of the most common losses is theft, which is why insurers offer a substantial discount if you have a monitored security system installed. The discount is often enough to offset most of the annual cost of such a system. These systems also monitor for smoke, fire and carbon monoxide. I recommend them for every homeowner, especially when the cost to you is essentially subsidized through reduced insurance premiums.

The second broad area of coverages involves liability protection. This personal liability insurance is part of the homeowners policy, and it protects an insured person against a claim or lawsuit because of property damage or bodily injury caused by the negligence of the insured person. This coverage is in effect anywhere in the world you happen to be. Some examples of covered losses include:

- Your backyard cookout accidentally sets the neighbor's house on fire.
- You accidentally hit your golfing partner with an errant tee shot.
- Your son carelessly runs over another student on campus with his bike.
- A guest in your home trips on the cracked sidewalk and sues you for bodily injury, pain and suffering, emotional distress, etc.
- You accidentally break an expensive vase while antique shopping.

The insurer also provides legal defense and will defend you even if a lawsuit is groundless. The insurer's obligation to defend you ends when the amount paid for damages from the occurrence equals the policy limits.

The amount of personal liability coverage is selected by the policyholder. As a practical matter, any coverage under $250,000 is inadequate in today's litigious atmosphere. Higher liability coverage adds very little to the premium and is well worth the protection it affords.

The last type of coverage under the homeowners policy is for medical payments to others. Insured persons under the policy are not eligible to receive medical payment benefits. This coverage is usually for a relatively small amount, generally $5,000 or less. The purpose of this coverage is to make sure someone injured on your premises or due to your actions can receive medical attention without having to resort to a lawsuit. For example, a child running on your property trips and breaks a collarbone. Even though you may have no legal liability, medical payments coverage could be used to pay for necessary treatment.

If you own a condominium, as opposed to a detached single-family home, a condo-owners policy provides most of the same coverages, except the dwelling part of the coverage is different. Since a condo owner technically owns the airspace rather than the structure itself, the building is usually covered under the condominium association master policy. If your dwelling is classified as a townhouse, you may need a homeowners policy, as you may be the owner of the external structure.

Even if you are a renter, you still need coverage. A renters policy provides coverage for your personal property and liability coverage. Renters may be at greater risk from theft loss or to damage to personal property caused by other tenants' negligence. Your own negligence in your rental dwelling could cause loss to others, leading to lawsuits against you. These higher risks makes a renters policy a necessary part of a good defense strategy.

No Opting Out Here

All the types of insurance discussed up to now have been insurance you could choose to have or not have (the exception being dwelling coverage if you have a mortgage). If you choose to drive a car, you have no choice but to have auto insurance. It's the law in every state.

In a typical year, there are over six million auto accidents in the U.S. In these accidents, just under three million people are injured, and some forty-thousand are killed. Property damages total a quarter of a *trillion* dollars. The potential to maim, kill and destroy when behind the wheel is why auto insurance is mandatory. The laws exist to protect others from your negligence. Auto insurance is also needed to protect you from the negligence of others.

One of the first things to understand about auto insurance is that the insurance is first on the car and then on the driver. On an auto insurance policy, specific vehicles are listed. The only other cars that could be covered on that policy would be a newly acquired vehicle (There is a time limit to add a new car to the policy before it is no longer covered.); a temporary substitute auto, like a rental car, is covered; trailers owned by the insured driver are also covered for liability.

If someone drives your car with permission, your auto insurance is the primary coverage if that person has an at-fault accident. If the person driving your car has his/her own auto insurance, that insurance will be secondary to your auto insurance, which is what I mean when I say the insurance is first on the car and then on the driver. This is the reason you should always be careful in lending your vehicle to anyone. If they have an accident that your insurance company has to pay for, you may have a lot of explaining to do to your insurance company to prevent a cancellation.

Your insurance is also there for you if you are driving someone else's car and have an accident. As I said, the insurance is first on the car, but suppose you borrow a friend's car, have an at-fault accident and find out only then that your friend had no auto insurance. Your insurance will step in to cover you up to your policy limits. In this example, let's suppose that your at-fault accident caused some serious injuries to others, that your friend did have auto insurance, but he/she had low limits of coverage, too low to compensate the victims. Your insurance would step in to cover the shortfall up to the point your insurance reaches its limits of coverage.

After declaring the cars to the insurance company, you declare the drivers of those cars. Insured drivers include family members in the household, so it is necessary to declare those teenage drivers, too. Yes, the premium for them is higher, but not as high as it will be if the insurance company finds out they were undeclared drivers. Persons using your car with your permission are covered, though this should be a rare occurrence unless you don't mind risking a cancellation. Lastly, if you are using your insured auto on behalf of another person or organization (such as running an errand for your employer) and you have an at-fault accident, that person or organization is also covered on your policy if they get sued as well as you.

As with any insurance, an auto insurance policy has exclusions. Among the more important ones, the most obvious is the exclusion for any intentional injury or damage you cause. If you remember Kathy Bates in the movie *Fried Green Tomatoes,* after she intentionally rams a Volkswagen into oblivion, she tells the shocked owners, "I'm older and I have more insurance." Point of order – her insurance company would have denied any claim because it was an (extremely) intentional act. Also, if you use your vehicle as a taxi, coverage is excluded. If you use your car in the automobile business (the definition is broad), coverage is excluded.

The states require that you have liability coverage to protect others in the event you cause an accident. Other coverages are optional; though, if you have a loan on a car, the lender will require comprehensive and collision coverages (more on those in a bit). Most states have minimum liability limits around 25/50/10. What do those numbers mean? The first number means that there is a $25,000 limit for bodily injury to any one person. The second number means there is a $50,000 limit for bodily injury to all persons injured in the accident. The last number means there is a $10,000 limit for all property damage resulting from the accident. Remember, these coverages do not cover an insured driver or an insured vehicle. These coverages are to protect others.

Note how low those numbers are. Any one person who is seriously injured is likely to incur medical bills exceeding those limits. Those are just the medical bills, too. There are additional damages, like lost wages and pain and suffering. And $10,000 for property damage won't cover one used sub-compact that's totaled. Having liability coverage at these limits is better than nothing, but not by much. Remember the rule - don't risk a lot to save a little. Choosing low limits of liability to save on the insurance premium is violating that rule.

Despite the mandatory insurance laws, one of the next seven cars you pass is unlikely to have any insurance. The percentage of uninsured drivers varies widely by state (from 4% to 32%), but nationally the average is 14%. The drivers with no insurance are also the worst drivers, with the fewest assets. Why else would they violate the law in this manner? Their insurance would be expensive because of their driving records, and they don't have the income or assets to pay for it.

As a general correlation, the worse the driver, the less insurance they have. We know that one driver in seven is uninsured. It is estimated that another 35-40% of drivers carry only the minimum required coverages. Those facts mean that about half the drivers out there have little or no liability insurance. They're the worst drivers, and they're coming after you.

If you are a careful person (and reading this book would indicate that you are), then the chances are greater that you will have an accident with an at-fault driver who is uninsured or underinsured rather than have an at-fault accident. This is where an important coverage on your own auto policy comes in. There is a coverage called *uninsured/underinsured motorist coverage*. It is not mandatory, so many people decline the coverage. Some feel they are paying for the other guy's insurance, but that's not the case. In the event that you are involved in an accident that is not your fault, and the other driver has a) no insurance, or b) inadequate insurance, your uninsured/ underinsured motorist coverage will pay you for your medical bills, property damage and pain and suffering.

Since you may be more likely to use this coverage than you are your liability coverage, it makes sense to have it on your policy. The premium is much less than the liability premium, in part, because the states regulate the premium closely to encourage people to get it. Uninsured/underinsured motorist coverage can also be applied if you are hit by a hit and run driver or if you are hit by an at-fault driver while you are walking, jogging or riding a bicycle.

Your uninsured/underinsured coverages can be as high as, but not higher than your liability limits; moreover, I recommend they both be the same. How high should they be? I recommend no less than 250/500/100. That's $250,000 per person, $500,000 per accident for personal injury and $100,000 per accident for property damage. Any serious injury is likely to exceed $100,000 in medical bills, and pain and suffering is typically calculated as some multiple of the medical bills. Totaling someone's Mercedes SL will get you to the property damage limit very quickly. Remember, you can double the coverage without doubling the premium. Don't assume the rate goes up in proportion to the coverage; it doesn't. You may be surprised to find out how little it costs to get your coverages up to these limits.

The other coverage that is there for personal injury is medical expense coverage, which is very similar to the medical expense coverage on the homeowners policy. The amount of coverage is usually small, and coverage is not based on fault. If you have good health insurance, you may not need this optional coverage on your auto policy.

There are two types of coverage for damage to your own auto. *Collision* coverage is the more expensive of the two because more is paid out under the coverage. Collision is basically when your vehicle hits or is hit by another car or when your car hits something stationary that it shouldn't have, like a telephone pole, a building, a fountain. Collision losses are paid regardless of fault, but you have a deductible you select, and that part of the loss is what you pay out-of-pocket.

If damage to your car is not considered a collision loss, it will be considered an other-than-collision loss (clever, huh?). Most insurance policies refer to this coverage as comprehensive coverage. It covers things like fire, theft, hail damage, flood and being attacked by a deer.

Speaking of deer, let me clarify the difference in comprehensive and collision coverages with an example. You are driving down a country road and a deer bounds out in front of your car. You can't stop in time, so you have only two choices – hit the deer or swerve into the ditch. My advice is to hit the deer, and for several reasons. The deer may total the car, but the ditch may total the car and you both. Also, since the deer was a moving object that got into your path, hitting it is considered a comprehensive loss. It's not classified as an accident, and since most people have a lower deductible for comprehensive coverage than for collision coverage (comprehensive coverage is a lot cheaper than collision coverage), your out-of-pocket expense would be less, too. If you go into the ditch, it is a collision loss. Your moving vehicle struck the stationary ditch. Also, going into the ditch is considered a single-car loss-of-control accident, which isn't good for you. If it happens at 2am, the claims adjuster is going to start thinking you were drinking prior to the accident. You also have no evidence there was ever a deer, since Bambi loped off when you chose the ditch. Your rates are almost certain to go up at the next renewal.

If you finance a car, lenders will require you to have comprehensive and collision coverage, to protect them. They will also limit the size of the deductible, usually to $500. Their fear is that too high a deductible may cause you to walk away from the car after a loss, rather than come up with a large deductible out-of-pocket.

Incidentally, when your auto is paid for and has a reduced value, you can then consider dropping the comprehensive and collision coverages. Don't drop the coverage unless you are willing to self-insure in the event of a total loss of the vehicle. It may make sense to drop these coverages for a $5,000 car, but not for a $10,000 car. It might make more sense to raise the deductible on such a vehicle to $1,000. A higher deductible can lower the premium substantially, yet a major loss isn't all on your shoulders.

The liability coverages and the collision coverages are the coverages that are the most expensive, in part because what is paid out under those coverages is the result of the driving habits of the insured(s). Moving violations and at-fault accidents will do more to raise those rates than anything else. Also, insurance companies may forgive a driving incident, but they won't forget. The first mistake may result in higher costs, but the second one will get you surcharged for everything. The best way to keep your auto insurance premium down is to keep your driving record clean.

Other Insurance

If you are found liable for damages to someone, there's a lot at stake. If you're rich, everything you've worked for is at risk. Even if you're not rich, everything you work for in the future might be at risk.

An umbrella policy gives you liability coverage above anything you might already have on your auto and homeowners policies. It provides defense and pays damages for lawsuits brought against you or your family. While there are some exclusions, the coverage is broad and can cover instances that are not covered by auto or homeowners insurance. This coverage is also stacked on top of auto or homeowners coverage, increasing your protection for claims covered by either policy. Premiums are very reasonable. For $10-15 a month, a family can get $1 million of coverage, typically.

If you own a boat, motorcycle, snowmobile, ATV or other motorized vehicle, you need at least liability insurance, even if not required by law. The risks of a liability suit against you are just as great with one of those vehicles as they are with a car, and homeowners and auto policies specifically exclude coverage for losses related to such vehicles. You may also want or need to insure yourself against loss of the vehicle itself. I will assume that you do not own such toys unless they are fully paid for, so any comprehensive/collision insurance is to protect you from loss.

Some people equate insurance with gambling. They think it's a bet between the insured and the insurer. Insurance is actually the opposite of gambling. When you gamble, you create a risk of loss where none existed before. When you buy insurance, you take the risk of a large and unpredictable loss and transfer it to the insurance company. You trade the sure loss of the premium payment to avoid the potential losses that would be catastrophic to you and your family. A gambler doesn't use insurance because a gambler doesn't avoid unnecessary risks; he/she creates them.

And in rebuttal, what a MONEY MORON recommends you do:

- **Believe like me that "The best defense is a good offense".** When I type that statement into Google, I get 93,400 hits. I didn't read any of them, but when you get that number of hits, it just *has* to be true.
- **Explain to me again what baseball has to do with insurance.** I know a team likes to get an "insurance run" in the late innings. And the Seattle Mariners' ballpark is named for an insurance company. Beyond that, I'm lost.
- **Don't worry about becoming disabled.** There's only a 1-in-3 chance it'll happen. By my math, that means there's a 2-in-3 chance it won't happen. I prefer to remain optimistic.
- **If you do become disabled, think in positive terms.** You don't have to work, and other people have to do things for you. It makes me almost envy the disabled.
- **Buy life insurance when it can actually save your life.** Your auto insurance will replace your car, and your homeowners insurance will replace your home. Your life insurance should replace your life. Otherwise, it's just a scam.
- **Don't get life insurance on *your* life.** Ever heard of the self-fulfilling prophecy? As soon as you buy life insurance, your days are numbered. Did you ever hear of anyone buying life insurance who didn't die eventually? I didn't think so.
- **Don't pay for life insurance on *your* life.** If life insurance on me is supposed to benefit the wife and kids, shouldn't they be the ones paying for it? I would start by reducing the kids' allowance.
- **Get health insurance so you don't have to take care of yourself.** When I see what health insurance costs, I'm not about to eat right, exercise and quit my vices to use it *less*. In my book, HMO stands for Help Me Overindulge.
- **Avoid those Health Savings Accounts (HSAs).** They may save you money, but you have to become a more careful consumer, too. Comparison shopping for health care? That's the kind of pain that makes me need to go see a proctologist.
- **Use my alternative to long-term care.** Here's the way I see it. Long-term care is expensive, so long-term care insurance must be expensive,

too. But, you can avoid needing long-term care. How, you ask? Simple – half your medical expenses occur in the last five years of your life, and a lot of that is for long-term care. Avoid the last five years of your life, and you avoid half your medical expenses. In these last years, you're probably old and in a nursing home, so they're not "good" years anyway. I still have to work out a couple of details, like knowing when the last five years begin and the best method of avoidance, but I'm working on it!

- **Assume homeowners insurance is a rip-off.** First the insurance company tells you the cost to rebuild your house is more than the value of the house *and* land. What are you, some kind of moron? Then they tell you they'll replace your old stuff with new stuff for a slightly higher premium. Sure it's in the contract, but are you so gullible as to believe they'll actually do it when the time comes?
- **If the insurance company is replacing new for old, it makes sense to pad the claim a little.** If someone steals your 19" television, tell the insurance company it was a 32" set. Get a new living room set by staging a "covered loss." You paid these guys for years. It's time they paid you for a change.
- **Just get the minimum coverage for auto insurance.** I'm not wasting money on insurance premiums to pay the other guy, even if it was my fault he got hurt. He can sue me if he wants. I don't have anything, and you can't get blood from a stone.
- **Forget that uninsured/underinsured coverage.** These deadbeats drive around with no insurance, so you have to buy insurance to protect *yourself?!* I don't think so. Just sue the hell out of them if they injure you or your family.
- **Blame Bambi.** If you have a single-car accident, always claim a deer ran out in front of your car, and you hit the tree swerving to miss it. If you run into a light post downtown, claim it was a dog or a *really* big rat.
- **Avoid the sure loss.** I'm talking about the premium payment. If I have to make the choice between the small risk of a big loss or the sure risk of a small loss, I'll take my chances. Only an idiot gambler would bet on a sure loser. I'll get the insurance I'm required to have, but that's it. Getting more insurance than required is like admitting defeat before the contest even begins. That's a loser mentality, not mine.

MONEY AT WORK

When I interviewed for a teaching position after college, the man who hired me told me that I would never become rich from my labors. He may have said that in part to lower my expectations regarding salary. Mostly, he was giving me sage advice that wealth is not created by the work we do, as much as it is by the work our money does. Only a handful of people in this world (most of whom would fall under the broad category of "celebrity") can generate enough income so that income alone can create wealth. For the rest of us, wealth is created by first working for our money, then making some of that money work for us.

College graduates this year can expect to earn about $5 million in their lifetimes. They will also need about $3 million when they retire after 45 years of work, with 20-25 years of retirement ahead of them. It is unlikely any of these people will save 60% of their income for retirement, nor do they need to. They can regularly invest about 10% of their income for their entire working life and hit the $3 million mark by retirement day. The person will earn $5 million; ten percent of that $5 million will earn another $2.5 million over the same period. This is the power of money at work.

I could have titled this chapter *Investments*, but that is a fuzzy term and is too often misused. There are two essential ingredients to creating wealth. Any wealth formula that does not include these two ingredients is at best a transfer of wealth and at worst a theft of another's wealth. These two essential ingredients are *Work* and *Delayed Gratification*. Anyone who claims that wealth can be created without these two ingredients is a fraud.

There is no magic formula to creating wealth. Work. Earn. Invest. Repeat. That's it. It's not complicated, merely hard, which is why so few people are wealthy. Most people are willing to do the work. Most people aren't willing to do the delayed gratification. Delayed gratification requires discipline and a long-term perspective, two virtues sorely lacking in the general population today.

Just as work is an essential ingredient to creating wealth, work is an essential ingredient to anything claiming to be an investment. Simply put, an investment does work. Here are some examples of what is and isn't an investment:

- Stock in a gold mining company is an investment. Gold is not. The gold mining company does work – it generates a product used by industries and consumers. Gold purchased as an "investment" is idle. Any price increase (or decrease) is based on speculation of future supply and demand. The gold itself is powerless to control its price. Even if the price of gold falls, the gold mining company can continue to create wealth by mining and refining gold for the market.

- A rental house is an investment. Vacant land is not. The rental house provides a service in the form of shelter to the tenants. The service provided generates income to the owner in the form of rent payments. Even if the market value of the property falls, the rental house can still create wealth because it is doing work by providing shelter. Vacant land is idle, like gold is idle. It is purchased with the expectation that someone will come along in the future and offer more than the current owner paid for it. While it may happen, it again is speculation. Price fluctuation is again based on supply and demand, and the vacant land has no control. Vacant land also generates a tax liability, reducing any potential gain.
- Futures contracts are either insurance or speculation, but they're not an investment. Futures contracts are an agreement between two parties to buy/sell a commodity or financial instrument at a certain future date, at a set price. For example, a wheat farmer sells a futures contract to sell his wheat at a set price on a future date. He is buying insurance against the price of wheat falling below the contract price by that future date. While the buyer of the wheat contract is essential to the deal, the buyer is speculating that the price he pays for the wheat in the contract will be less than the market value of the wheat on the settlement date. The buyer makes money if the market price is more than the contract price on the settlement date; he loses money if it's less.
- Buying stock in a casino is an investment. Buying lottery tickets is not. The casino is a business, whose goal is to make a profit. Even though their business is gambling, they control all aspects of the game, including the payout. The law of large numbers enables the casino to know that the larger the number of bets made, the more predictable the outcome. The casino creates wealth by providing entertainment to its patrons, be it in the lounge or at the gaming tables. A lottery ticket is a game of chance, a zero-sum game. If you win (highly unlikely), your winnings still come from others' losses. No wealth is created, only transferred.

Since an investment does work, there are a couple of truisms about investments. The first is, the more work it does, the more it will earn. The second is, it can only do so much work at a time. The more productive the investment, the better its return will be. An investment in alternative energy is likely to be more productive than an investment in a shoe factory. Neither investment will make you rich overnight. The shoe factory might have steady, but unspectacular, profits. The alternative energy company may not be profitable for years, but can make up for it when a viable product makes it to market. An investment makes you rich over time, not overnight.

The Only Standard

There are so many terms and measurements in the world of investments that it can be frustrating trying to figure out what they all mean, and which ones are important to you. When looking at investments, you can go crazy trying to judge an investment by analyzing alpha, beta, standard deviation, intrinsic value, P/E ratios, Sharpe ratio, and your eyes are starting to glaze over, so I'll stop there.

What every investor is most interested in at the end of the day is the performance of the investment. Many investors, especially those who need to draw an income from their investments now, focus on a measurement known as yield. Yield is the money the investment gives up to the investor; the investment *yields* that money to the investor. In the case of bonds, the yield is the interest payments that are sent to the bond holder. In the case of stocks, the yield is the dividends a stock pays to its shareholders.

Focusing on yield can create a couple of problems. First, yield is an incomplete and sometimes deceptive measure of an investment's performance. For example, many of the stocks that pay the largest dividends are in mature industries with little growth potential. Annual stock dividends average about 2% of stock values for the market as a whole. If you find a stock that is paying a 4% dividend, it may also be a stock that is flat or losing value over time. Bonds have higher yields than stocks, but those interest payments are everything as far as the bond's performance goes. Any rise or fall of the bond's value is the result of credit rating changes or interest rate changes. When the bond is held to maturity, you get the face value back – no more, no less.

The second problem with focusing on yield is that a person may structure a portfolio around yield, to generate a certain level of income. But, the structure of that portfolio may also be detrimental to that investor's long-term needs and goals. For example, if a retired investor needs to receive an income equal to 5% of his portfolio's value, he might need to have 75% of the portfolio in bonds yielding about 5.5%, and 25% in stocks paying about 3.5% in dividends. The potential problem with such a portfolio is that its long-term growth after these payouts is not likely to keep up with inflation, resulting in our investor suffering a decline in his standard of living in the future. Additionally, if interest rates fall over time, the bond investor will have a difficult time finding new bonds that pay the same kind of interest rate as before, without having to buy bonds that have a higher risk of default.

The only number that really matters when judging the performance of an investment is total return. Total return includes any interest or dividends an investment yields, plus it includes capital gains and unrealized appreciation in the investment's market value. Total return gives the truest picture of how an investment is doing and whether it is measuring up to your expectations.

By focusing on total return, you are able to structure a portfolio that can not only meet income needs now, but also in the future. You can properly diversify your portfolio to prevent getting slammed by any one sector. You prevent the income tail from wagging the investment dog.

Now, that investor who needs to draw 5% of the portfolio's value for income this year may wonder how he can do that, if his portfolio doesn't yield that amount. It's quite simple – sell enough assets each year to generate the necessary income. It doesn't matter if the income you receive was generated by interest, dividends or capital gains – it's all money. In fact, if you are drawing income from a taxable account, it could be to your advantage to have more income from capital gains than from interest or dividends because interest and dividends are regular income and are taxed at a higher rate.

When you receive a paycheck from your employer, do you question whether the money that went into that check came from operations, investments or capital gains? No, it just matters that the check is good. The same is true with income from an investment portfolio. You should be concerned only with total return. Whether your income is generated by interest, dividends or capital gains is a very secondary consideration. Money from any of these sources spends exactly the same.

The following charts compare two scenarios. The one on the left shows a portfolio that has a 6% annual return. This portfolio is set up to generate income from interest and dividends (yield). The yield is 5%, which is the annual income to the investor. The portfolio has a net growth of 1% per year (6% return – 5% yield), which also means that the income to the investor grows by 1% per year, well below the investor's inflation rate. In order to tap additional income, this investor would need to sell some of the assets, though that would reduce future portfolio size and income.

The chart on the right is a portfolio with an 8% annual return. This portfolio is composed of assets based on their total return, not their yield. Assets are sold annually to generate income. The investor still draws 5% of the portfolio's value each year for income. Because the portfolio's total return is 8% compared to 6%, the net growth of the portfolio is 3% per year, as is the annual increase in the investor's income. The difference isn't too noticeable in the early years, but by year ten, the gap is quite wide. By the thirtieth year, income and portfolio value for the total return investor are both nearly double what they are for the yield investor.

	Yield Portfolio (6% Return)		Total Return Portfolio (8% Return)	
Year	Account Value	Income	Account Value	Income
1	$1,000,000	$50,000	$1,000,000	$50,000
2	$1,010,000	$50,500	$1,030,000	$51,500
3	$1,020,100	$51,005	$1,060,900	$53,045
4	$1,030,301	$51,515	$1,092,727	$54,636
5	$1,040,604	$52,030	$1,125,509	$56,275
6	$1,051,010	$52,551	$1,159,274	$57,964
7	$1,061,520	$53,076	$1,194,052	$59,703
8	$1,072,135	$53,607	$1,229,874	$61,494
9	$1,082,857	$54,143	$1,266,770	$63,339
10	$1,093,685	$54,684	$1,304,773	$65,239
11	$1,104,622	$55,231	$1,343,916	$67,196
12	$1,115,668	$55,783	$1,384,234	$69,212
13	$1,126,825	$56,341	$1,425,761	$71,288
14	$1,138,093	$56,905	$1,468,534	$73,427
15	$1,149,474	$57,474	$1,512,590	$75,629
16	$1,160,969	$58,048	$1,557,967	$77,898
17	$1,172,579	$58,629	$1,604,706	$80,235
18	$1,184,304	$59,215	$1,652,848	$82,642
19	$1,196,147	$59,807	$1,702,433	$85,122
20	$1,208,109	$60,405	$1,753,506	$87,675
21	$1,220,190	$61,010	$1,806,111	$90,306
22	$1,232,392	$61,620	$1,860,295	$93,015
23	$1,244,716	$62,236	$1,916,103	$95,805
24	$1,257,163	$62,858	$1,973,587	$98,679
25	$1,269,735	$63,487	$2,032,794	$101,640
26	$1,282,432	$64,122	$2,093,778	$104,689
27	$1,295,256	$64,763	$2,156,591	$107,830
28	$1,308,209	$65,410	$2,221,289	$111,064
29	$1,321,291	$66,065	$2,287,928	$114,396
30	$1,334,504	$66,725	$2,356,566	$117,828

The point of this example is to be sure you understand that total return is what you are seeking and how you should judge an investment. Total return is what will generate the income you will need for decades, as well as generate the growth you will need to sustain and grow that income. The total return portfolio can also enable you to leave a more substantial legacy to those people and causes important to you.

Prognosticate This

Below is a fifty-year history of the S&P 500. While the long-term trend is clearly up, it has not been in a straight line. For proof, compare 1974 with 1972, or 2002 with 1999. Also, notice how quickly the index recovered after those drops. Bear markets average about 15 months in length; bull markets average about 40 months. However, half of the gain of a bull market typically occurs in the first six months, before most people even recognize the bear market is actually over.

STANDARD & POORS 500 YEAR END VALUES

YEAR	VALUE	CHANGE	YEAR	VALUE	CHANGE
1956	44.72	---	1982	145.30	+20.7%
1957	41.70	-6.7%	1983	163.41	+12.5%
1958	55.45	+33.0%	1984	179.63	+9.9%
1959	55.61	+.3%	1985	211.78	+17.9%
1960	61.78	+11.1%	1986	274.08	+29.4%
1961	68.84	+11.4%	1987	257.07	-6.2%
1962	66.20	-3.8%	1988	297.47	+15.7%
1963	77.04	+16.4%	1989	329.08	+10.6%
1964	87.56	+13.7%	1990	343.93	+4.5%
1965	92.88	+6.1%	1991	408.78	+18.8%
1966	86.61	-6.8%	1992	438.78	+7.3%
1967	92.24	+6.5%	1993	481.61	+9.8%
1968	103.01	+11.7%	1994	470.42	-2.3%
1969	85.02	-17.5%	1995	636.02	+35.2%
1970	95.88	+12.8%	1996	786.19	+23.6%
1971	103.94	+8.4%	1997	980.28	+24.7%
1972	116.03	+11.6%	1998	1279.64	+30.5%
1973	96.57	-16.8%	1999	1394.46	+9.0%
1974	76.98	-20.3%	2000	1366.01	-2.0%
1975	100.86	+31.0%	2001	1130.20	-17.3%
1976	102.03	+1.2%	2002	855.70	-24.3%
1977	89.25	-12.5%	2003	1131.13	+32.2%
1978	99.93	+12.0%	2004	1181.27	+4.4%
1979	114.16	+14.2%	2005	1280.08	+8.4%
1980	129.55	+13.5%	2006	1418.30	+10.8%
1981	120.40	-7.1%	2007	1468.23	+3.5%

In looking at the previous chart, two observations can be made. In the long-term, the trend is undeniably upward. In the short-term, there is no trend – returns are all over the place. Two-thirds of the time, the annual return of the S&P 500 wasn't within 5% of its average return of 8.5%.

The chart of S&P 500 returns helps illustrate the futility of trying to time the market. How many people at the end of 1974, when the S&P 500 had dropped by a third and was lower than its value ten years earlier, anticipated a 31% gain the next year? How many people in early 2000, when the S&P 500 had nearly tripled in five years, expected the ride to end with the worst bear market since the great depression?

In order for market timing to work, you need to be right at least 80% of the time, which means you have to guess right 4 times out of 5 to beat a buy-and-hold strategy. You have to be able to predict with a great deal of accuracy when the market is reaching its peaks and its troughs. Since the market tends to move very quickly when it changes directions, being a little too early or a little too late in your predictions can cause you to lose a lot of the gain and absorb a lot of the losses.

You also have to be willing and able to act on your predictions. For example, you would have to be willing and able to:

- Buy heavily when your investments have lost 34% of their value over the last two years, as they did in 1973-74 or when your investments have lost 40% of their value, as they recently did in 2001-2002 and in 2008.
- Sell heavily when your investments have tripled in a ten year period, as they did in 1982-92 or when they tripled in a five year period, as they did in 1995-2000.

Even if you had the ability to move at such times, could you make yourself pull the trigger? Could you dive into water that people were fleeing out of like the Fourth of July beachgoers in *Jaws*? Could you tear yourself away from a party that made the toga party in *Animal House* seem like an Emily Dickinson poetry recital? The empirical answer is No.

There is never a shortage of people willing to tell you which way the market is going next; they're a staple of CNBC programming. If these people actually knew short term market moves, they'd be hunkered down with Warren Buffet, Donald Trump, et al, plotting to take over the world. They wouldn't be blabbing the most valuable secret on the planet to you for free on cable TV. Even a broken clock is right twice a day, and such prognosticators are right about the market about as often as a broken clock. They also should be relied on as much as a broken clock.

If investing in stocks were a smooth ride, everyone would do it all the time. If you could have a consistent return that tripled the post-inflation return of bonds, why wouldn't you take it? People can take the returns; many can't take the process of getting those returns.

When molten steel is poured from the blast furnace into ingots, it isn't usable in that form. The steel we use in our most demanding applications requires a process of hardening and tempering. The steel is repeatedly heated and cooled and intermittently struck with great pressure. This process removes impurities, relieves stresses and increases toughness. You have probably seen a blacksmith heat an iron bar in a furnace, pound it with a hammer and dunk the bar in cold water. He is making the steel stronger, though it's not an easy time for the steel.

You are the steel. The heat is the bull market; the cold water is the bear market. The pounding is your refusal to try to time the market or to give in to euphoria or panic during the peaks and troughs. It's not an easy process, but it's the best way to create the kind of wealth that survives for generations.

When you take a *longer term perspective*, the volatility of the market is much easier to take. While there have been peaks and dips, the line has a remarkably consistent upward trend, even when the declines of 2008-2009 are included. Knowing this long-term trend line makes enduring the bulls, bears, and hammer blows easier to take.

In the long run, markets always have a regression to the mean, which is another way of saying they move closer to the long-term average. A period of above-average growth is followed by a period of decline. A period of below-average returns is followed by a strong bull market. Excesses in either direction get corrected; it just takes some time.

In recent years, short-term market movements have become increasingly exaggerated. I'm old enough to remember watching Walter Cronkite on the news, and if the Dow Jones Average moved 1% that day, that was Walter's lead story, because if the market moved that much in a day, there was an economic reason for it. The market was dominated by institutional investors, like pension funds. Those professional money managers maintained a long-term focus and were not governed by emotion.

Today we have 24/7 business channels and more financial internet sites and bloggers than one can imagine. We also have individuals, rather than professionals, managing retirement portfolios. With the demise of the traditional pension, and its replacement with the 401k, along with online trading accounts, individuals are making their own investment decisions. These individuals are being assaulted with financial "advice" from all sectors. They also have the ability to move their life savings around with the click of a mouse. Because the owner of the assets is also the manager of the assets, emotion is a major part of investment decisions. As a result of all this emotion-based decision-making, short-term market volatility is much greater than in the past. In this new era, if the Dow Jones Average moves 1% today, it is considered a quiet day on Wall Street.

Here is one final testament to the futility of trying to time the market, or allowing short-term market moves to dictate your actions. Over the last twenty-five years, the average investor in equity mutual funds has earned less than one-third the return of those mutual funds. During this period of time, the average U.S. equity mutual fund has had a return of 8.6%; the average investor in those funds has averaged a return of 2.6%. How can this be?

There is a simple explanation for this discrepancy. Most people bought their mutual fund(s) after the market had been climbing for an extended period of time. They finally decided to get on the train before it left the station, but they were also getting on board at or near the peak of that market. Then the market began a correction, and the mutual funds that had seen the biggest gains (and which attracted the most new investors) also had the biggest declines. Those investors who jumped in and bought near the peak of the market are the same ones who gave in to their fears and sold before their investment sank even lower. Just as they expected the bull market to run forever, they expected the bear market to do the same. And since they bought high, their paper losses in a market decline were worse than for the methodical investor, goading them to do something to stop the bleeding. The end result for this type of investor was that they bought high and sold low, a sure-fire recipe for failure. In the long run, buying high can be corrected with patience. But if you sell low, the damage is done.

Don't Just Do Something, Stand There

The increasing short-term volatility of the stock market is the result of people tinkering with their accounts on an almost-daily basis. People tinkering with their accounts on an almost daily basis are the result of the increasing short-term volatility of the stock market. The preceding isn't so much circular logic as it is a vicious circle.

Americans are by nature tinkerers, and they are by nature impatient. These are good qualities much of the time. Our economy was built largely by those who wanted a better mousetrap and weren't going to stand around waiting for someone else to build it. Many of our greatest industries were built by impatient tinkerers. But a desire to tinker combined with an impatient streak is likely to wreak havoc with your investment goals.

Before the internet, if someone liked to tinker with their investments, that investor would call their broker and direct the changes to be made. The broker was happy to oblige because the broker made a commission on every trade, whether it worked out or not. The broker would also recommend trades, especially to clients who tinkered, because such clients were receptive to changes. Clients too often mistakenly equate trading activity with diligence over the account by the broker, forgetting that the broker's motivation is likely to be a profit first for the broker and then for the client.

With the internet, two impediments to frequent trading are gone. There is no longer a need for a personal broker to execute a trade, and there is no longer the traditional broker's commission to pay. Tinkerers can choose from online brokers like E*Trade, Scottrade, TD Ameritrade, Schwab and others. Low trading costs are the main points of comparison among the online brokers. E*Trade advertises 100 commission-free trades for new customers. TD Ameritrade offers thirty days of free trades for new customers.

Notice that the word "trade" is a prominent part of the name of many online brokerage firms. The word "investment" is noticeably absent. Online brokerages appeal to those who trade frequently, their target market. Revenue for these firms is directly related to trade frequency in the accounts. Even if someone opens an account with an online brokerage and doesn't plan to trade with any frequency, the temptation may become too great not to increase trading frequency. The free market information and research offered by the online brokerages is there, as much to increase trading frequency (and brokerage income) as it is to help you select a winner. Many online brokerages charge an inactivity fee, leading customers to trade more frequently than they would otherwise.

Here is the basic difference I see between a trader and an investor – a trader buys the stock; an investor buys the company.

A trader tends to look at data regarding the stock. That data tends to be more short-term oriented, and the trader seeks large short-term movements in a stock's price. A trader has a clearly defined exit strategy, a tightly defined set of criteria that will trigger a sale. It may be a price point or a time limit. A trader will usually set an increasing price trigger for a sale (to lock in gains), a decreasing price trigger for a sale (to control losses) and a time limit to hold a stock if it flounders. Stock ownership has a finite life to a trader.

An investor tends to look at the company itself. The process probably starts by using the company's product or service. The investor may begin by eating at their restaurant, buying their lawnmower or staying at their hotel. That favorable impression with the product or service leads the investor to research the company first, and the stock second. If that research reinforces the initial positive impression, an investment is made in the company through the purchase of the company's stock.

An investor will have an open-ended policy on stock ownership, with the hope that it will never be necessary to sell. A decision to sell will be based on changes to the company, not on changes to the stock. If the industry a company is in undergoes a fundamental change, if the company's direction changes, if there is a major challenge to the company's market share or to its structure, those changes may prompt an investor to sell. A stock price change not related to a change in the company or its market would not be a trigger for an investor to sell.

A trader is, by nature, focused on the short-term. The strategy is based on short-term price movements that fall (significantly) outside the normal range. If the trader could not expect to generate gains that exceeded the gains of a buy-and-hold strategy, there would be no point. A trader has three costs that exceed those of an investor:

- Trading costs. Even if the trader uses an online brokerage, the costs of frequent trading can add up. In addition to per-trade charges, there are additional fees and charges that can add up quickly.
- Tax costs. The gain from a profitable sale is taxed at best as a capital gain and at worst as regular income. In any event, realizing the gain also realizes the tax liability.
- Time costs. A trader will have to expend much more time and effort than an investor in order to realize a superior return. While traders will typically factor trading and tax costs into their performance calculations, few of them keep track of how much time they spend on their trading activities, and fewer still attach a cost to that time.

Day Trader Survives Shootout but Fails to Beat Long-Term Odds.

Publication: Knight Ridder/Tribune Business News Publication Date:
25-FEB-02

By Jim Auchmutey, The Atlanta Journal-Constitution
Knight Ridder/Tribune Business News

Fred Herder killed himself one point-and-click at a time.

The retired chef got a bloody warning of what could happen on a hot Thursday afternoon in July 1999. He already had lost thousands of dollars day trading stocks when a colleague, who had blown even more, Mark Barton, huffed into the Buckhead offices of All-Tech Direct. Herder looked up from his computer monitor and glimpsed a revolver. Diving under a table, he heard shots and felt a burning sensation in his back.

Less than two weeks later, Herder hobbled back into All-Tech on crutches. When friends asked how he could resume day trading so soon after he was wounded by the toxic passions it could arouse, he was stoic. "Something like that could happen anywhere," he said. "It could happen at McDonald's."

Those passions eventually pulled Herder under. Late last year, his life's savings vaporized, he was forced to take a new job in a new city, Augusta. It didn't work out.

Barton's catastrophic reverses triggered the worst mass killing in Georgia history. Herder claimed only one victim: himself.

When Fred Herder committed suicide on Nov. 29, it had been less than 2 1/2 years since the Buckhead shootings. It seemed longer.

Herder began day trading during the Internet souffle of the late '90s, when speculating on the minute-to-minute fluctuations of stock prices looked to be a new and exciting way to strike it rich. By the time he took his life, the headlines had moved from dot-com layoffs to recession to the crash of the highest-flying Internet contraption of them all, Enron. The sad end of a failed day trader seemed like an attachment to yesterday's e-mail.

Day traders are still out there nervously punching keyboards and swigging antacid. But their ranks have thinned since the go-go days when they were emblematic of the uncharted world of online finance. With the decline of the stock market and an increase in regulatory scrutiny, day trading companies such as All-Tech have closed branches amid falling trading volume. At the peak of the phenomenon two years ago, the Securities and Exchange Commission estimated that nearly 7,000 people nationwide were trying to make a living day trading.

Day trading, the internet bubble, and this news article might all seem like very old news now. But it's important not to forget the lessons to be learned here:

- You don't need to be a day trader to go broke. Keeping your day job may postpone the day of reckoning, but even trading in your spare time can lead to financial disaster if you don't do it well.
- Buying on margin magnifies losses even more than gains. If you have $25,000 and you borrow another $75,000 on margin, and that $100,000 investment goes up 25%, you made $25,000 (less interest charges). If that $100,000 investment loses 25%, you've lost *all* your money (plus interest charges). Psychologically, losses make us feel twice as bad as comparable gains make us feel good. Total losses are devastating, financially and psychologically.
- Traders are seeking a timing advantage. The only difference between market timers and traders is that market timers are trying to guess what the broad market will do in the short term. Traders are trying to guess what individual stocks will do in the short term. Market timers aren't affected by the fate of individual stocks. Traders are affected by the fate of the market, in that their stocks will be drawn lower in a bear market.
- Trading demands a commitment of time and energy and concentration. An ad for an online brokerage shows a man in New York bragging that he just bought stock in an Asian energy company on the Hong Kong Exchange at 2am. That he has the ability to do that is impressive. That he is actually doing it seems rather sad to me.

At the end of the day, I believe the real difference between a trader and an investor is patience – I believe the investor has a lot more of it than the trader. The trader wants the returns but doesn't want to wait for them. To that end, the trader must assume more risk. Everything comes with a price, and the price of greater returns in less time is more risk.

Charlie Munger is Warren Buffet's lesser known partner in Berkshire Hathaway. The two of them are probably the greatest investors (not traders) in history. The best year for most traders is unlikely to match an average year for Berkshire Hathaway. In his own words, here is Charlie Munger's investment philosophy.

"We're partial to putting out large amounts of money where we won't have to make another decision. If you buy something because it's undervalued, then you have to think about selling it when it approaches your calculations of its intrinsic value. That's hard. But if you buy a few great companies, then you can sit on your ass. That's a good thing."

Moron-Proof Money-Making

If you're reading this book to find my secrets to "beat the street", this section is as close as you're gonna get, so pay attention. For our purpose here, we will define "the street" as the S&P 500. Our goal is to outperform the S&P 500, but without taking on any more risk than the S&P 500. In fact, to make sure we don't drift from the S&P 500, we invest *only* in the S&P 500. (This example is for demonstration purposes; in real life, you diversify.)

I know what you're thinking. If we only invest in the S&P 500 and we are trying to outperform the S&P 500, the only way to do that is by timing the market, to move in and out of the S&P 500 in such a way that we capture more of the peaks and less of the valleys. You already know how I feel about market timing, so rid yourself of this notion right now.

I propose something more radical. I propose we avoid the peaks and become aggressive toward the valleys. Now you probably think I'm advocating market timing, moron style. What I'm advocating doesn't require any type of prognostication; it is brilliant in its simplicity and will lead to superior investment returns.

Here's how this system works. Take a percentage of your income this month and invest it in the S&P 500. Do the same thing next month. And the next month. And the next month. Keep doing it as long as you are earning an income. Then stop and see how much you've got. That's it.

No, I haven't lost my mind. You don't believe that something so basic, so uncomplicated, so moronic in its simplicity could possibly yield above-average returns. It can, it does, and I'll prove it momentarily.

This sure-fire method of superior returns was not created by me, and it's possible you're already using this method without realizing it. If you are investing money into your 401k every month, and you put the same amount every month into the same investments, you are following this method. It has a formal name, too – Dollar-Cost Averaging.

Here's how it works in its simplest form. If you put $100 a month into a mutual fund, and the share price that month is $25, you'll buy four shares. If the share price the next month drops to $20, you'll buy 5 shares. You automatically buy more shares when the price is lower and fewer shares when the price is higher. In this simple example, you bought 9 shares for $200, or $22.22 per share, even though the average price during this period was $22.50.

The following chart shows a dollar-cost averaging plan with the S&P 500. The initial annual investment is $5,000 per year, and increases 4% per year. The year end value of the S&P 500 is the share price we use for purchases.

ANNUAL INVESTMENT	SHARE PRICE	SHARES BOUGHT	CUMULATIVE SHARES	CUMULATIVE INVESTMENT	ACCOUNT VALUE
$5,000	$103.01	48.54	48.54	$5,000	$5,000
$5,200	$85.02	61.16	109.70	$10,200	$9,327
$5,408	$95.88	56.40	166.10	$15,608	$15,926
$5,624	$103.94	54.11	220.22	$21,232	$22,889
$5,849	$116.03	50.41	270.63	$27,082	$31,401
$6,083	$96.57	62.99	333.62	$33,165	$32,218
$6,327	$76.98	82.18	415.81	$39,491	$32,009
$6,580	$100.86	65.24	481.04	$46,071	$48,518
$6,843	$102.03	67.07	548.11	$52,914	$55,924
$7,117	$89.25	79.74	627.85	$60,031	$56,035
$7,401	$99.93	74.06	701.91	$67,432	$70,142
$7,697	$114.16	67.43	769.34	$75,129	$87,827
$8,005	$129.55	61.79	831.13	$83,134	$107,673
$8,325	$120.40	69.15	900.28	$91,460	$108,393
$8,658	$145.30	59.59	959.86	$100,118	$139,468
$9,005	$163.41	55.11	1,014.97	$109,123	$165,856
$9,365	$179.63	52.13	1,067.10	$118,488	$191,684
$9,740	$211.78	45.99	1,113.09	$128,227	$235,731
$10,129	$274.08	36.96	1,150.05	$138,356	$315,206
$10,534	$257.07	40.98	1,191.03	$148,890	$306,178
$10,956	$297.47	36.83	1,227.86	$159,846	$365,251
$11,394	$329.08	34.62	1,262.48	$171,240	$415,457
$11,850	$343.93	34.45	1,296.93	$183,089	$446,055
$12,324	$408.78	30.15	1,327.08	$195,413	$542,484
$12,817	$438.78	29.21	1,356.29	$208,230	$595,113
$13,329	$481.61	27.68	1,383.97	$221,559	$666,532
$13,862	$470.42	29.47	1,413.43	$235,421	$664,908
$14,417	$636.02	22.67	1,436.10	$249,838	$913,390
$14,994	$786.19	19.07	1,455.17	$264,831	$1,144,043
$15,593	$980.28	15.91	1,471.08	$280,425	$1,442,071
$16,217	$1,279.64	12.67	1,483.75	$296,642	$1,898,670
$16,866	$1,394.46	12.09	1,495.85	$313,507	$2,085,900
$17,540	$1,366.01	12.84	1,508.69	$331,048	$2,060,884
$18,242	$1,130.20	16.14	1,524.83	$349,290	$1,723,362
$18,972	$855.70	22.17	1,547.00	$368,261	$1,323,768
$19,730	$1,131.13	17.44	1,564.44	$387,992	$1,769,588
$20,520	$1,181.27	17.37	1,581.81	$408,511	$1,868,549
$21,340	$1,280.08	16.67	1,598.49	$429,852	$2,046,189
$22,194	$1,418.30	15.65	1,614.13	$452,046	$2,289,325
$23,082	$1,468.23	15.72	1,629.85	$475,128	$2,393,001

This is a forty-year investment plan, representing the forty-year working life of most Americans. The share prices are the year end values of the S&P 500 for each year from 1968-2007. This period includes some the biggest bull and bear markets in our history, so it includes the best of times and the worst of times.

Here are some important observations to be made from the preceding chart:

- Annual investment increased, but as a percentage of income, it stayed the same.
- In only 6 of 40 years was the account value lower than the year before.
- In all six of those down years, more shares were bought than in the year before.
- Total shares owned grow every year; only the rate of growth varies.

Now here is the best part. Over the 40-year period we used here, the S&P 500's share price grew at an average annual rate of 6.9%. That's the return it takes to raise a share price from $103.01 to 1,468.23 in forty years. The average annual return of this portfolio was (are you ready?) 8.5%.

The *investment* returned 6.9%. The *investor* received 8.5%. Investing $5,000 a year to start, bumping it up 4% per year, doing it for 40 years and ending up with $2,393,001 requires an average annual return of a shade over 8.5%. The difference between the investment return and the investor's return is totally the result of dollar-cost averaging – automatically buying more shares when the price drops and fewer shares when the price rises. An important caveat here - dollar-cost averaging does not ensure a profit or prevent a loss. Such plans involve *continuous* investments in securities regardless of fluctuating prices. You should consider your financial ability to continue making purchases during periods of low and high price levels.

If our hypothetical investor had been able to find an investment with an even 6.9% return (i.e. – the share price going from $103.01 to $1,468.23 in a straight line), the account value at the end of the forty years would have been $1,769,097. Compare that to $2,393,001. The difference between 6.9% and 8.5% in this example is 35% more money.

You don't need to be smart to become wealthy. You don't need to time markets or even understand markets. You just need to invest regularly and consistently. You can set up a program like this at work or online, and then let it virtually run itself. Let your friends knock themselves out trying to figure out a way to "beat the street." You don't have to waste that time and effort, and you will surely beat whatever they conjure up as an investment scheme. Dollar-cost averaging is the most successful and the most democratic method of creating wealth ever devised. Power to the people.

I O U

A *bond* is simply an IOU that is issued by a corporation or government entity, and is wrapped in precise legal and financial wording. When you buy a bond, you are lending the money to the issuer of the bond.

Bonds typically have several features. The first is the *face value* of the bond, with $1,000 being the most common face value. Face value is sometimes referred to as par value. The second feature is the *maturity date* of the bond, which is the date the borrower agrees to repay the face value of the bond. The period to maturity varies according to the needs of the borrower. For short-term cash flow needs, the borrower may issue bonds that mature in six months. For long-term needs, like financing a factory, the borrower may issue bonds of twenty or thirty years.

The third key feature of the bond is the *stated interest rate*. The interest rate the borrower will state for a specific bond offering is based on a couple of factors. The first factor is the prevailing interest rates at the time. For example, if the prevailing interest rate at the time for a ten-year bond is 7%, borrowers won't get anyone to buy their bonds if they only offer 5 or 6%. They also don't want to pay more interest than they have to, so they won't offer the bond at 8 or 9% either.

The second factor affecting the interest rate is the borrower's credit rating. Just as your credit score affects your ability to borrow money at lower interest rates, the same applies to corporate and government borrowers. Credit rating agencies like Standard & Poors and Moody's provide ratings for publicly traded bonds. If a bond issuer has a credit downgrade, it will have to pay a higher interest rate to attract new money. A credit upgrade will enable it to pay a lower interest rate and still attract new capital.

Some bonds are issued with a Call provision. This provision allows the issuer of the bond to redeem the bond prior to the maturity date, often by paying a small additional premium to the bond holder. This feature is useful for a borrower who thinks its credit will improve in the future, allowing it to borrow at a lower interest rate. The issuer may also hope to be able to pay off the entire debt before the maturity date and wants to retain the option of doing so.

Most bonds are not bought directly from the issuer, but are bought and sold in the secondary bond market. The bond market creates liquidity and stable pricing for bonds, since many bond holders don't plan to keep the bond until its maturity date. If you own any bonds, they were probably bought through the bond market, rather than from the bond issuer directly.

Other factors being the same, the longer the time to maturity, the higher the interest rate the bond will pay. This relationship makes sense, since the longer the time to maturity, the greater the uncertainty that something negative might occur. Interest rates might rise, and you as the lender would lose that opportunity to get a better return. Also, the longer the time to maturity, the greater the chance the borrower might default on repaying the debt. The same standards apply to you. You can get a 15-year fixed-rate mortgage at a lower interest rate than a 30-year mortgage. More time means more risk. More risk means more reward.

If you bought a bond and held it to maturity, and the issuer of the bond didn't default during that time, then you would get exactly what you expected. Even if interest rates jumped up and down the whole time you held the bond, you still received your annual interest payments, and you received the face value of the bond at the maturity date. One problem you may face after that bond matures is finding another bond that offers the same reward for no more risk than the old bond. If interest rates have fallen, that may be hard to do. Low interest rates are good if you're a borrower, but not if you're a lender.

What happens if you choose to sell a bond before the maturity date? This is what the bond market is for. The price you get for the bond may not be the face value of the bond, though. A change in interest rates or in the issuer's credit rating can affect the market price for the bond. For example, you want to sell a corporate bond that pays 7% interest, but interest rates have risen since that bond was issued and a comparable bond now pays 9% interest. Why would anyone buy your bond for a 7% return, when they can get a comparable bond that pays 9%? In order for your bond to sell, the price has to be lowered so that the $70 annual interest payment, plus the payment of the $1,000 face value at maturity makes the total return equal 9%. In the case of rising interest rates, the bond would sell for less than $1,000. If interest rates were falling, the bond would sell for more than its $1,000 face value.

The risks involved with owning bonds can be broken down into the following categories:

- *Interest Rate Risk* - Changes in interest rates will affect the value of your bond. Rising interest rates lower the value; falling interest rates raise it.
- *Default Risk* - The issuer of the bond may become unable to pay the interest payments and/or the principal payment at maturity.

- *Reinvestment Rate Risk* – As you receive money from the bond, either from interest payments or principal repayments, you may not be able to get another bond with the same return for the same credit rating (risk).
- *Inflation Risk* – Interest rates are based on what the market thinks the inflation rate will be like in the future. If the inflation rate is higher than anticipated, your bond will lose actual purchasing power.
- *Maturity Risk* – The longer the time to maturity, the greater the risk, because the longer into the future we go, the less certain we are what will actually happen.
- *Call Risk* – If you own a callable bond, you are likely to face a forced redemption (a call) when interest rates drop. This means the higher returns you were planning on with the called bond are no longer there, and you won't find the same return in the market without taking on more risk.
- *Liquidity Risk* – There is the possibility that there isn't a ready market for your bond. Treasury bonds don't have this problem, but some municipal bonds and high-yield (junk) bonds have this problem.

Bonds as a whole have lower volatility than stocks. Bonds as a whole also have lower long-term returns than stocks. Since stocks involve a greater risk, they should provide a greater return than bonds over the long term. If you are bondholder, you get paid before the stockholders of that company get paid. Bondholders get their money first, but they never get more than what the bond agreement calls for. Stockholders aren't assured of anything, but they get everything that's left after the company's obligations are met.

Bonds are the primary investment for those who favor stability and modest growth over larger returns. Trusts, endowment funds and insurance companies have large bond holdings because a modest return is preferable to a large potential loss, as can be the case with large stock holdings. These entities are paying out a regular stream of income and need to know that flow will not be reduced or interrupted. Also, as fiduciaries they cannot risk the lawsuits that might come if they were accused of taking on too much risk to increase the returns of these portfolios.

Bond returns over the last eighty years have averaged 5-6% per year. Inflation over this same period has averaged just over 3% per year. Interest rates are a function of inflation. When inflation is higher, interest rates must also be higher to induce people to save rather than spend. Bond returns have historically been 2-3% above inflation, because that is how much incentive people need to buy a bond rather than spend the money now. Bonds are an appropriate investment for preservation of capital, but not for growth of capital, especially if you want growth of capital well in excess of the inflation rate.

Owning, Rather than Loaning

When you're a lender, as you are when you own bonds, you make a decision to limit your gain for the opportunity to move up the line in the order of getting paid back. You have chosen greater security over greater opportunity. There is nothing wrong with that choice and that is the appropriate choice regarding any money that you will be spending within the next five years. In the short term, the return *of* the money is more important than the return *on* the money.

Saving is what you do for the short term. Investing is what you do for the long term. When you invest money that won't be spent for decades to come by you or your heirs, you want to invest in a way that gives you the best long-term returns. And as long-term investments go, stocks are the way to go.

Think about the wealthiest people you know. Bill Gates isn't wealthy because he created computer software. He is wealthy because he is a (very large) stockholder in the company that manufactures and sells that software. Warren Buffett is currently the richest man in the world. Warren Buffett doesn't loan money. He figures that if a company is worth lending to, it's worth owning. The wealthiest people you know personally are probably owners of their own businesses, or stockholders in companies. Even if these people have inherited their wealth, that wealth was almost certainly created through ownership in a corporation. When you're a stockholder, you own a piece of the company. You're just like Bill Gates or Warren Buffett, albeit on a much smaller scale.

At this point, let me tell you what I'm not going to tell you in this section:

- I'm not going to make short-term market predictions. I can speak with some confidence about the stock market in the long term (more on that later). Neither I, nor anyone else can accurately predict market moves over the sort term.
- I'm not going to tell you how to "beat the street" (other than dollar-cost-averaging). The advice in this book is about helping you do better with money. Beating the street is not part of that objective. What you learn from this book will enable you to do better financially than most of your peers, but this is not a competitive sport, so stop thinking in terms of beating anyone or anything.

- I'm not going to dive into stock analysis. If I go beyond a few basic terms about stocks, I risk losing you. If you want to read about stock-picking analysis, there are tons of books out there on the subject. Read them if you want, but they aren't likely to help much. I also hope you have better things to do with your time.
- I'm not going to structure a stock portfolio for you. I don't know you, and unless I know you, I can't know what specific investments are appropriate for you to invest in. The last thing you are going to find here is some cookie-cutter recommendations that sound like an excerpt from *Money* magazine.

In the last fifty years, America has been rocked by the following:

- The Cuban missile crisis
- The assassination of President Kennedy
- Urban riots
- The Vietnam War
- The resignation of President Nixon
- 'Stagflation'
- Iranian hostage crisis
- AIDS
- Savings & Loan collapse
- The Gulf War
- The impeachment of President Clinton
- The tech bubble burst
- September 11
- The worst bear market since the crash of 1929
- The Iraq war
- The Afghanistan war
- The subprime mortgage meltdown

Imagine if, in 1958 you could have known that the above events would happen. Would you have been optimistic about the future? Probably not. Would you have been optimistic about investing in the future? Almost certainly not.

In the last fifty years, Americans have also had the following:

- An average increase in life expectancy of 8 years
- A doubling of cancer survivor rates
- A doubling of heart disease survivor rates
- A tripling of per capita GDP
- A halving of the percentage of the population living in poverty
- A quadrupling of farm productivity
- 125,000 new U.S. patents

- A decline in high school dropout rate of 75%
- A quadrupling of college degrees earned annually
- The collapse of the Soviet Union
- Legislated equality for women and minorities
- Men on the moon and robots on Mars
- China emerging as one of our largest trading partners
- The invention and widespread use of microwaves, personal computers, cell phones, cable TV, digital recording, fax machines, laser printers, the internet, artificial organs and thousands of therapeutic drugs

Go back to 1958. If you saw the second list, would you feel more optimistic? You might feel a little better, but you might also think that the bad at least offset the good, if not overwhelming it.

How did the stock market react during this period to the mixture of progress and catastrophes? Over the last fifty years the S&P 500, perhaps the single best indicator of the American stock market went from 42 to 1400. This increase does not include stock dividends, which when added brings the average annual return for this index to almost 9%.

A pessimist in 1958 would have invested in bonds, and he would have earned an average annual return of about 5.5% over the next fifty years. An optimist in 1958 would have invested in stocks, and would have had an average annual return of about 8.5%. A $10,000 investment by the pessimist would have grown to $145,420. A $10,000 investment by the optimist would have grown to $590,860. After discounting for inflation, the pessimist's gain is $89,580; the optimist's gain is $535,020, which is almost six times better.

While the optimist had a far better return, he/she also had a far bumpier ride, including two bear markets that each reduced his portfolio's value by 40%. The price for better returns is volatility that can be enough to make you want to toss your lunch.

Why do stocks roller coaster more than bonds? Bonds are affected primarily by inflation, which affects interest rates. Inflation numbers rarely shock us, so panic in bond markets is rare. Also, if bonds are held to maturity, bond holders will get exactly what they expected to get when they bought the bond, with no surprises.

Stocks prices are based on expectations of future profits. These expectations are greatly affected by current events. Catastrophic events can quickly alter our expectations for the worse. Events, good and bad, affect our expectations of profits, usually much more than they affect actual profits. In the short term, the stock market is a voting mechanism, reflecting our expectations of profits. In the long term, the stock market is a weighing mechanism, reflecting the actual profits. The history of actual profits is a fairly smooth, fairly continuous upsloping line. Our expectations of profits are constantly buffeted; by greed and fear; by good news and bad news; by taking the recent past, good or bad, and extrapolating it out into the indefinite future. It is the human element that causes the markets to vibrate like a car with four unbalanced wheels. But even as the human passengers are bounced around, the vehicle progresses steadily down the road.

While the long-term trend for stocks is clearly upward, that trend applies to stocks as a whole, not to individual stocks. The S&P 500 could never go to zero; the value of an individual stock could. Because an individual stock could become worthless, one important rule to remember is to never invest more in an individual stock than you can afford to lose permanently. Many people fall in love with a stock and let it become a disproportionately large part of their portfolio. It may be intentional; it may just be the result of that stock growing faster than the rest of the portfolio. Intentional or accidental, it's dangerous to let it happen.

One of the most common situations of a person owning too much of one stock occurs with employer's stock. Employers often offer employees the chance to buy company stock at a discount. Employers also often fund some or all of the employer's contributions to a 401k plan with company stock. Employees don't have to keep the 401k contributions in the employer's stock, but many do, out a sense of loyalty or because it's a company they know and are comfortable owning.

It isn't disloyal to rebalance your portfolio by trimming an oversized proportion of company stock. It isn't wise to purchase shares of company stock at a discount if you are limited regarding your ability to sell it. When Enron collapsed a few years ago, many of the employees who suddenly found themselves out of work were hit doubly hard because a large part of their retirement funds were in Enron stock. Bouncing back from a job loss is hard, but doable. Bouncing back from the eradication of your retirement portfolio, especially if you're over 50, is almost impossible.

I have seen my investment portfolio drop by more than 20% at least three times. These drops were due to market downturns, not because of anything toxic in the portfolio itself. All the investments remained intact and were able to do their part in bringing the portfolio back to new highs. If you have 20% of your investments in one stock and that stock becomes worthless, that situation is a crisis.

A bear market is like a sprained ankle; it's painful, but time enables a full recovery. Owning a suddenly-worthless stock that comprised 2-3% of your investment portfolio is like losing a toe - painful, permanent, but hardly incapacitating. Owning a suddenly-worthless stock that comprised 20% or more of your portfolio is like losing a leg; you'll probably survive, but you will never be capable of what you were before. It's a permanent disability. Owning a suddenly-worthless stock that comprised one-third to two-thirds of your portfolio is like losing an arm, a leg and an eye; you may survive, but life as you knew it is gone forever. Owning a suddenly-worthless stock that was your whole portfolio is like losing your head; Game Over. Putting too many eggs in one basket can cost you an arm and a leg and a lot more.

So what are some of the things to look for in a stock you want to add to your portfolio? Here are some factors to focus on:

- Price Earnings Ratio, or P/E Ratio – This ratio is the stock's price, divided by its earnings over the past year. If a stock's P/E ratio is 10, you would pay $10 to get $1 of earnings, an expected return of 10% if earnings do not change. If a stock's P/E ratio is 25, you would pay $25 to get $1 of earnings, an expected return of 4% if earnings do not change. Stock prices are based on *future* expected profits. If you buy a stock with a P/E ratio of 25 over a stock with a P/E ratio of 10, your chosen stock needs a much faster rise in earnings to justify the higher price you paid. Growth stocks tend to have higher P/E ratios because their earnings are expected to grow faster than average. Value stocks tend to have lower P/E ratios because their earnings are not expected to grow rapidly, but they are priced well for their expected growth. Growth stocks have higher potential reward, but also higher risk in the higher price paid up front. Below is the history of the S&P 500's P/E ratio. Note that abnormally high P/E ratios (1929, 1999) are followed by steep drops. When stock prices rise well ahead of earnings growth, the market inevitably corrects to a more reasonable P/E ratio. Also note that the periods of abnormally high P/E ratios were preceded by a period of abnormally low P/E ratios.

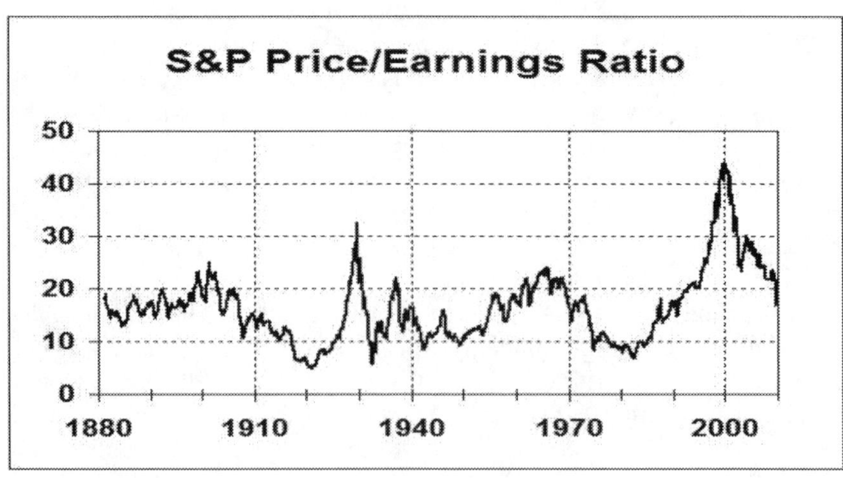

- The industry the company is in – Utility companies tend to have steady if unspectacular earnings, and typically pay above-average dividends. Technology companies are in a growth industry, where profits and losses can both be high, as can the attrition rate. You need to know if the industry is one that fits with your investment goals and risk tolerance.
- The company's position in its industry – Established industry leaders will have less chance for phenomenal growth, but they will also likely have good growth that will enable them to survive against competitors and a changing market. Newer entrants in an industry will need something different to attract customers and take market share from the giants. A company that is growing only because the industry is growing may not be as good as an investment as a company that continues to grow market share in a slower-growth industry.
- The company's management – Top management in a company should come across as stewards of the stockholders' assets, not as hotshots willing to risk those assets for their own ego gratification. The more frequently a CEO is appearing in the media, the less likely this criterion is being met. In reviewing a company's financial statements, steady growth in earnings and dividends and low levels of debt are numbers that reflect good stewardship.
- Be aware of the "buzz" on a stock – I don't mean to pay attention to the buzz on a stock coming from CNBC, *Money* magazine or the guy spouting off at a cocktail party. Just be aware that the more a stock is being talked about in such places, the more likely it is that people are buying it that have no idea what they are buying and are driving the price up to places it has no business being.
- Your Emotions – It is easy to get excited about a stock, then use selected information to justify the decision you've already made. The fact that you are considering a stock means you are already predisposed to buying it. Be aware of this fact and look very closely at any information that may indicate buying the stock is not a good decision. Most people who buy a stock that tanks had indications of the outcome before they ever bought the stock; they chose to ignore the warning signs, though.
- Your Intelligence – Our tendency is to overestimate our positive traits, and intelligence is near the top of that list. I'm not saying you aren't smart; it's just that there's a good chance you aren't as smart as you think you are. Or as an old boss once said of a co-worker of mine, "If I could buy him for what he knows, and sell him for what he thinks he knows, I could retire tomorrow." To protect your portfolio, make sure such a statement can't be applied to you and your investment IQ.

Strength in Numbers

If the prospect of selecting and monitoring a portfolio of individual stocks intimidates you (If it doesn't at least a little, then re-read the previous paragraphs about emotions and intelligence.), then using mutual funds as your primary investment vehicles may make a lot more sense for you.

A mutual fund is simply a collection of stocks, bonds or other securities that are purchased by a group of investors and managed by an investment company. When you buy a share of a mutual fund, you are buying a piece of the entire portfolio of that mutual fund.

According to the most recent Morningstar listings (Morningstar is a leading evaluator of mutual funds), there are over 26,000 mutual funds out there. Many mutual funds have several classes for different types of investors, so the actual number of different mutual funds is in the 8,000-9,000 range. These are broken down into well over fifty different categories.

For almost any investment category you can think of, there is probably a mutual fund that will enable you to invest in it.

Here are the most important features of mutual funds:

- *Diversification* – When you own even one share of a mutual fund, you own a piece of every asset owned by the mutual fund. For example, if you own even one share of a mutual fund that is an index of the S&P 500, then you own a small piece of all 500 companies that make up the S&P 500. Mutual funds enable smaller investors to get a properly diversified portfolio that might otherwise require a million dollars or more without using mutual funds.
- *Asset Allocation* – If you should have a portfolio consisting of 25% bonds and 75% stocks, you can buy individual mutual funds to get to that asset allocation, or you can buy a single mutual fund that is already set up with that allocation. Mutual funds enable you to invest in the categories you need to be in, without having to have millions of dollars, or hundred of different securities in your portfolio.
- *Liquidity* – Open-ended mutual funds (which most funds are) are required to buy back the shares from shareholders at market price upon demand. There is never a problem of having to hook up a buyer and a seller or of what price will be paid. If you sell shares of a mutual fund on Tuesday, the share price at the end of business on that Tuesday is the price you will be paid, along with everyone else who sold shares of that fund on that day.
- *Professional Management* – Along with diversification, professional management is probably the best feature of the mutual fund. By

directing others to look after the day-to-day oversight of your portfolio, you are freed from having to do it. You are also freed from making the difficult decisions to buy, hold or sell a security. Since these managers invest on behalf of thousands or millions of anonymous investors, the cost of this management to the individual is affordable, much lower than hiring a portfolio manager on your own. These professional managers have access to analysis that individuals can't afford. Lastly, professional management takes the emotion out of the decision process, which can be the biggest aid to investment returns.

Because you and thousands/millions of others are *mutually* investing in a fund, you are able to afford to buy a diversified portfolio, you are able to afford top-notch management at a reasonable cost, and you are able to maintain flexibility to add or subtract to your holdings as your needs change.

There are two basic types of risks when dealing with securities. *Systematic* (market) risk is the risk associated with overall movements of the market. No matter how many stocks you own, you are subject to the systematic risk of the stock market. You can't get the gains of investing in the stock market without accepting the systematic risk of being in the stock market.

Non-systematic risk is the risk associated with an individual security that is separate from systematic risk. This risk includes owning stock in a company whose earnings might not meet expectations, whose management might be indicted, whose product might be subject to a recall or whose credit rating might be lowered. Non-systematic risk stems from the company, not the market.

In order to diversify away non-systematic risk, a portfolio needs thirty or more different securities in it, with no security worth more than 4-5% of the entire portfolio. To set up such a portfolio might require hundreds of thousands of dollars. Approximately half the mutual funds on the market allow an initial investment of $1,000 or less. For people who are starting an investment program or who don't have hundreds of thousands to invest, mutual funds are the only way to avoid non-systematic risk. It's also important to remember that no one has ever been wiped out by systematic risk because the stock market never goes to zero. The same cannot be said of individual stocks that can often become worthless. Someone who owns one or two stocks because that's all they can afford is running the risk of being wiped out. It is precisely that type of risk to the smaller investor that mutual funds were created to eliminate.

When looking at mutual funds, there are several factors to review in deciding whether a fund is appropriate for your portfolio. While past performance is one factor to consider, let me remind you of the disclaimer that goes out with every investment: Past Performance is neither a predictor nor a guarantee of future performance. Very often, a mutual fund that has been red-hot gets featured in *Money* magazine or similar publication. The publicity leads to a flood of new investment in the fund. The managers are unable to invest these new funds with the same kind of success they previously had. Often, these red-hot funds were small and had generated huge returns because one or two stocks in a portfolio out of thirty or forty stocks in the portfolio hit it big. When the newest investors don't get the anticipated returns, they are the first to pull out. These new investors probably take a hit, but so do the original investors, who would have been better off had the mutual fund not been the beneficiary of the publicity.

Here are some of the main things to look at when evaluating a mutual fund:

- *Category* – The first thing to decide on is what fund category you are looking for. Related to category is the fund objective. For example, you may be looking for a U.S. large-company stock fund with growth as the objective, or you may be looking for an International Bond fund with income as the objective. Even if you have only one objective (say, growth), you would want to have funds in different categories to spread the risk.
- *Historical Performance* – Look for consistent above-average total returns over long periods of time. It's OK for a fund to underperform a little in bull markets if it also outperforms in bear markets. Look for consistency over 3-year, 5-year and 10-year periods. Also, be aware if one year of really good or bad returns is skewing the returns for a period. Compare a fund's performance to other funds in that category. Comparing a government bond fund to a developing markets stock fund is an apples-to-oranges thing. They are likely to have widely varying performance, in large part because they also have widely varying risk.
- *Expense Ratio* – This ratio is the cost of the management of the fund. Expense ratios average a little over 1% but the ratios vary widely. Approximately 10% of mutual funds have expense ratios exceeding 2%. Actively managed funds have higher expense ratios than index funds, which only buy and sell to reflect the index they mimic. That developing markets stock fund will have a relatively high expense ratio since there is likely to be a higher volume of trading in the fund and since global research has a high price tag. That government bond fund, on the other hand, may have an expense ratio that is less than half of the developing markets stock fund. Once again, compare expense

ratios of funds in the same category. The expense ratio is deducted from the fund before calculating its total return numbers. Fund managers can justify higher expense ratios with higher returns, but abnormally high expense ratios can indicate careless stewardship. If the returns decline, it's unlikely the expense ratio will do the same.

- *Fund Management* – When you are looking at a fund's historical performance, also check to see if the current manager(s) is/are responsible for that performance. Good performance may be the product of the previous manager; the new guy might be a question mark. If the mutual fund you are looking at is part of a large family (Fidelity, Vanguard, T. Rowe Price, etc.), a new manager probably has a proven track record with another fund in the family. Stable management with a history of good returns and reasonable expense ratios is what you want.
- *Beta* – A measure of volatility, and hence of risk. The Beta of the market as a whole is 1.00. If a mutual fund has a Beta of 1.20, it can be expected to rise 20% more than the market when the market goes up; it can also be expected to drop 20% more than the market when the market goes down. If a mutual fund has a Beta of .80, it can be expected to move up or down 20% less than the market.
- *Load or No-Load* – This is the sales charge of the fund. No-load funds do not have a sales charge and are usually bought directly from the mutual fund company by the investor. Load funds have a sales charge and are usually bought through a financial advisor. The sales charge (load) is usually 3-5%, and it can be charged up front or also charged over a period of years, which might appear misleading without proper disclosure by the advisor.
- *Turnover Ratio* – This ratio is a measure of the trading activity in the fund. A high turnover ratio may result in a higher expense ratio. A high turnover ratio may also create a greater tax liability for shareholders. If the manager sells a security for a gain, the tax liability on that gain is on the shareholders in proportion to their ownership. Because of the tax liability generated by sales within the fund, it is possible to have a tax liability for a fund that dropped in value in that year. This situation occurs when the fund is in a taxable account and the markets were down that year. You can control such events by having funds with lower turnover ratios in taxable accounts.

When comparing index funds to actively-managed funds, you will notice that expense ratios in index funds are lower, which is natural, since there is no active management and little trading in the fund. However, it's important to remember than an index fund is like a ship with a sail, but no rudder. When the S&P 500 was climbing 20% a year in the late 90's, everyone was putting money into S&P 500 index funds, which was one reason why the S&P 500 kept climbing. Since such an index fund is required to mimic the S&P 500, it has to buy stocks when they are added to the S&P 500 and sell them when they get deleted. When it was announced that Yahoo was being added to the S&P 500 in two weeks, the share price went from $104 to $147 in the interim, which was what the index funds had to pay for it. (It trades at around $15 a share today.) When the S&P 500 started to fall in 2000, those index funds had to sell stocks in proportion to the index, not based on what was best to keep or to sell. This requirement helped drive the S&P 500 still lower. When the waters are calm and the wind is blowing you in the direction you want to go, a rudder may seem unnecessary. But when the storms arrive, the rudder may be what keeps you from drowning.

Money-market mutual funds have become a popular place to "park" money. These mutual funds have a consistent share price of $1.00, and their rates of return vary directly with short-term interest rates. Money-market funds hold assets such as treasury bills, negotiable CD's and short-term commercial paper (loans to corporations). The quality of the investments is high, and default risk is thus extremely low. By regulation, money-market funds cannot invest more than 5% in any one issuer; the maximum time to maturity is thirteen months, and the weighted average maturity of the portfolio cannot exceed ninety days.

Most Americans who have investments have at least some of their investments in mutual funds. Most employee-directed retirement accounts, like 401k's, have mutual funds as the primary, if not the sole investment option.

Most Americans accumulate wealth through a systematic investment program, most commonly through their employer's retirement plan. When you are building wealth through dollar-cost averaging with a systematic investment schedule, mutual funds are the best way to go. When you buy stocks, you need to buy in blocks of 100 shares to avoid additional costs. That limitation rarely fits with a person's systematic investment schedule. Mutual funds are typically purchased in dollar amounts, not share amounts. Most employer-sponsored retirement accounts don't limit the minimum size of the systematic investment. Even for mutual funds purchased directly, two-thirds have a minimum systematic investment of $100 or less. You can also instruct the mutual fund to automatically reinvest dividends, interest and capital gains into additional shares of the fund. More than any other financial invention, mutual funds have enabled the average American to accumulate wealth with the same advantages that used to be available only to the very wealthy.

Money You Can't Outlive

Imagine you are in your early 70's. You've been retired for five years. You have social security, a small pension and about a half-million dollars in an IRA. Your home is paid for; your bills are modest. You and your spouse are in decent health, and you live a comfortable, but modest, lifestyle.

A bear market strikes, and your $500,000 IRA is now at $350,000. What adjustments are you going to make? Going back to work isn't an option (age, health, lack of marketable skills). Your modest lifestyle doesn't have much discretionary spending to be cut. Your social security and pension don't provide much income, and medical expenses continue to rise. If the market goes any lower, you calculate you'll be broke around age 80. Broke at 80 – it's a terrifying thought.

The prospect of outliving their money is one of the worst scenarios most retirees can imagine. It isn't just the financial strain; the loss of independence and dignity associated with having to ask relatives or agencies for assistance is a psychological strain, too. With the disappearance of traditional pensions, the prospect of outliving your money is more common now than at any time since the Great Depression. There is a financial product that replaces the traditional pension – the annuity.

Annuities have many features similar to life insurance. Annuities are also sold by life insurance companies. Both life insurance and annuities protect against the loss of income. Life insurance replaces income if you die too soon. Annuities replace income if you live too long.

The most important feature of an annuity, the feature that makes it unique, is the promise to pay a lifetime income to the annuitant, regardless of how long that person lives. Traditional pensions were an annuity in the sense that they made the same promise to pay as long as the retiree or spouse were living. In the case of an annuity, it basically works this way. You pay premiums to the annuity company. There is no set amount or timetable. You can make a lump-sum payment, periodic payments, whatever. That money grows in your account. When you are ready to begin your annuity, a calculation is made for a regular income based on the value of your account and your life expectancy from mortality tables. There is a calculated interest rate for the money's growth during the period payments are made to you. If the annuity company calculates you were going to live fifteen more years, and you live twenty more years, it doesn't matter. They still have to pay you the same amount at the same interval as long as you're drawing breaths.

What if you were expected to live fifteen more years and you're hit by a bus one year after getting the annuity? In that case, the annuity company won that bet. It is actually more complicated (more on that in a bit), but the basic idea is you get a guaranteed income for the rest of your life, however long that may be. The possibility of outliving your income has been eliminated. That is the most reassuring aspect of the annuity and its strongest selling point.

As you might have guessed, annuities are not as simple as what I've just laid out (What insurance contract is ever simple?). Let's start with the most basic difference, the type of annuity. A *fixed annuity* is one that pays a fixed rate of return for the period the money is in the account. The rate of return may be adjusted periodically, but it can never go below a certain amount, a guaranteed floor to protect owners during low interest rates. Fixed annuities invest primarily in bonds and other fixed instruments. Fixed annuities would be chosen when the guarantee of the rate of return is more important than the size of that return.

Variable annuities allow the owner of the annuity to invest in equities, through mutual fund offerings within the annuity. The owner can choose different levels of aggressiveness in the investments. If the annuity won't be used for income for decades to come, a more aggressive investment strategy would make sense. There is no minimum guaranteed return with a variable annuity; there is no floor. The value of the account could go below the amount invested. There is also no ceiling on the return. An aggressive investment strategy could yield returns double or triple what a fixed return might offer. As with any investment strategy, which product is appropriate for you should be based on your financial goals and your risk tolerance.

Annuities are sold by insurance companies because they offer an insurance aspect to them. If you should die during the accumulation phase (you haven't started taking an annuity income), the beneficiaries of your annuity are guaranteed to never receive less than the amount you invested in the annuity. For example, if you invested $100,000 in a variable annuity, the market went down and the $100,000 was now worth $90,000 and you died, your beneficiaries would receive the $100,000 you invested, not the $90,000 that the investments were worth at your death. In this same scenario if the investments had grown to $110,000, your beneficiaries would receive the full $110,000. The insurance aspect of the annuity says that if you die before you start taking an annuity income, your beneficiaries will receive the amount you invested or the amount that is in the account, whichever is *greater.*

Because the annuity is considered an insurance contract, it also enjoys a benefit of life insurance contracts – the growth of money invested in an annuity is tax-deferred until the money is withdrawn. Tax-deferral is one of the great advantages of qualified retirement plans like IRAs and 401ks, but there are none of the contribution limits with annuities like there are with qualified retirement planes. Because of the tax-deferral feature, holding an annuity in a qualified retirement plan is unnecessary. Since annuities have higher expenses to provide their features and since you don't need tax-deferral in a qualified plan (It's already there.), it's better to have an annuity on its own, and keep stocks, bonds and mutual funds in the retirement account.

When you take money out of an annuity, part of the money is taxable and part isn't. The part you contributed comes out tax-free, and all the growth gets taxed as regular income. The amounts are pro-rated for every distribution from the annuity. For example, if you invested $100,000 in an annuity, and it grew to $200,000, half the balance came from your contributions and half was tax-deferred growth. As a result, half of each distribution will be a tax-free return of your contribution, and half will be taxed as regular income. Annuities do have many of the same rules as IRAs regarding distributions, such as a penalty for withdrawals before age 59½ and required minimum distributions after age 70 ½.

It may seem strange, but only about 5% of the people who purchase an annuity chose to *annuitize*, which I need to define. If you have an annuity, and you decide you want a guaranteed lifetime income, you give up your claim to the money in the account in exchange for a guaranteed stream of payments for the rest of your life. The regular payments (usually monthly) are based on the amount in the annuity and your life expectancy. If your life expectancy is twenty years, but you only live two, you lose. If your life expectancy is twenty years and you live thirty, the annuity company loses.

Most people find that they prefer to take regular *withdrawals* from their annuity (Yes, you can do that.). They take a regular income similar to the annuitized income, but the lump sum in the annuity is still there for them or their beneficiaries. Someone has to live considerably longer than the norm for annuitization to be better than withdrawals. Most people dislike the thought of surrendering the principal in the annuity enough that they choose the withdrawal method instead.

You can start taking withdrawals, and if you later choose to annuitize, the amount of your annuity payments will be based on what is left in your account. A caution – annuity companies limit the upper age someone can annuitize, which makes sense. If you are 85 years old, the life expectancy tables may have you living four more years. Your family history and good health indicate you have an excellent shot at making it to the century mark, which is why you want to annuitize. This situation is known as adverse selection in insurance parlance. Insurance companies don't want to write life insurance on someone who's likely to die too soon, and they don't want to annuitize an annuity policy for someone who's likely to live too long.

As I said, many people want the security of a guaranteed lifetime income, but they struggle with "losing" all that money if they die too soon. There are different ways to set up an annuity regarding annuitization:

- *Single-Life Annuity* – This type is what we've talked about so far. The payments last for one person's life. When the annuitant stops breathing, the payments stop coming.
- *Joint-and-Last-Survivor Annuity* – This arrangement pays as long as any of the named annuitants survives. This annuity is commonly used with a married couple. The regular payments continue until both husband and wife are deceased. The amount paid monthly is less than with a single-life annuity, but is likely to be paid for a longer period of time.
- *Single-Life-With-Period-Certain Annuity* – This type is a single life annuity with a provision that if the annuitant doesn't live a minimum period of time (typically, ten years) a designated beneficiary will receive the payments until the "period certain" is up.

Annuities in recent years have come up with some interesting features. They are designed to encourage people to invest for the long-term by giving them some assurances regarding income. A guaranteed minimum withdrawal benefit allows the owner to withdraw a fixed percentage of the paid premiums until 100% of the paid premiums are withdrawn, even if the account value is below the amount of premiums paid. A guaranteed minimum income benefit is similar, but states the guaranteed benefit in dollars.

Some annuity contracts have added a guaranteed amount to annuitize. This feature may state that if you leave the money in the annuity for a stated period of time (say, ten years), they guarantee that you can annuitize the contract based on a guaranteed amount (say, a doubling of the money that's been there for ten years). While people might not plan on annuitizing, knowing that there is a guaranteed rate of return if they go that route can give the annuity owner needed piece of mind in a down market.

Annuities are long-term investments. Plan on leaving your money in them for at least a decade. Most annuities have surrender charges for the first five to seven years. The higher expenses of annuities make them inappropriate except as long-term investments. Annuities have also paid high commissions to the sales person (5-8% of the amount invested, typically). Since an annuity sale is lucrative to the seller, they are often sold when they are not appropriate. It's a shame these sales occur because annuities are excellent investment vehicles in the right circumstances.

When they get sold to people who shouldn't have them, it taints the product and drives away people for whom an annuity might be exactly what they need.

A Word about Real Estate

As I write this chapter in the early fall of 2008, Congress is debating a $700 billion bailout of the credit markets due to problems created largely by defaults in the subprime mortgage market. After a period of abnormal price inflation in real estate, prices are contracting in real estate at levels unseen since the Great Depression. Considering the unusual rise in prices previously, this adjustment is just a normal market correction. Real estate is subject to the same market forces as any other investment. We tend to forget that fact, because real estate is usually less volatile than the stock market.

Until recently, a popular show on cable TV was *Flip This House*. As the name implies, people bought a house, made modest improvements and then resold it for a quick profit. Such activity fueled the spike in real estate prices, which enticed even more to speculate in this manner. It resembled a game of musical chairs, a case study of the one-greater-fool theory, which states that you can pay anything for something, as long as there is one-greater-fool who will pay more.

While this type of real estate speculation has run its course for the time being, many people still hold real estate as an investment. The most typical type of real estate investment is the house or apartment rented to others. The owner/landlord buys a property and hopes that the rental income will at least cover the expenses of the property. If that happens, the pay down of the mortgage, as well as any market price appreciation, will be the owner's gain.

I have no objection to people investing in real estate in this manner, and such investors do provide needed housing to people who cannot or choose not to buy a home of their own. However, I have seen many people get into real estate as an investment and then become discouraged by unforeseen issues. If you are contemplating becoming a landlord, please consider these factors before buying any property:

- Why is the current owner selling? What do they know that you don't? Why do they think it's better to sell than to hold? Which of you is guessing correctly? Unless you know they *have* to sell, be suspicious.
- Know your cash flow. I don't mean best-case scenario, I mean worst-case scenario. If you can't manage your worst case-scenario on cash flow, you will lose the property – it's just that simple. Cash flow

crises result from underestimating expenses and/or overestimating income.

- Assume a worst-case scenario regarding cash flow. Assume a six-month period of vacancy between tenants. Assume major repairs and maintenance are needed every year. Assume property taxes increase almost yearly. Assume insurance premiums rise faster than inflation. You don't have to assume your mortgage will increase because you should never buy investment property unless you can get a fixed rate mortgage. A variable rate mortgage on rental property greatly increases the chance you will default on the loan due to cash flow problems.
- Know the competition. Potential tenants will be looking at several places to rent, and you need to be competitive on both price and features. Most new landlords overestimate the actual market rental rate for their property.
- Know the potential tenant market. Because of low interest rates and liberal lending policies in recent years, most of the people who wanted to own their own home were able to buy one, which means the pool of high-quality tenants has been somewhat depleted. You need to know the ability of tenants to pay the rent in full and on time and the likelihood they will not damage the property during their time there.
- Your commitment of time and aggravation will be more than you think. If you manage the property yourself, you will be the one who gets called at 3am because the toilet doesn't work. The tenants aren't going to try to fix something because that's what they are paying you to do. If you hire a professional management company, their fees will likely erode any profit you hoped to make.
- Being an owner/landlord is an active investment, not a passive one. If you compare the potential return of rental property to a mutual fund, you need to factor in your time, as well as to count every dollar that goes into the property in comparing returns. If you spend 20 hours a month managing the property and your time is worth $50 an hour, that's a monthly expense of $1,000. To not factor your time as an expense is to say your time has no value. You wouldn't tell your employer that, would you?
- Real estate is a concentrated, leveraged position. People who wouldn't dream of putting 50% of their investments in one stock don't think twice about putting 50% of their investments in one piece of property. Add in the fact that the property has a loan of 75% of its value, which is a lot of eggs in one basket.
- If you want to invest in real estate, but don't want to be a landlord, consider investing in Real Estate Investment Trusts (REITs). You can

invest in real estate through mutual funds that invest in REITs. You can gain from rental income and price appreciation; you have professional management at a very reasonable cost, and you have liquidity on demand. REITs also enable you to have a diversified real estate portfolio without having to personally buy several different properties.

"Investments" You Should Probably Avoid

Collectibles – This category includes anything from coins to cars to record albums. If you want to collect such items because you like them, that's fine. Don't consider them as investments, though. Remember what I said about an investment doing work. Most collectibles do nothing more than collect dust. If you are spending money that should be going into a 401k plan on collectibles, stop. Collectibles should be spent with discretionary income, because they are discretionary purchases, not investments. If you can set up a museum for your collectibles and charge admission, the collectibles might be considered an investment. Otherwise, they're just toys.

Options on Stocks You Don't Own – A call option gives the buyer of the option the right to buy a particular stock within a specified price within a specified time. A put option is the opposite, giving the buyer the right to sell. You pay for an option, and if you don't use it by the expiration date, it's worthless. A put option could make sense if you owned a stock and wanted to insure a minimum selling price for a limited time. On the other hand, if you were worried about the stock's price declining, you might be better off selling it now. Here is a direct quote from the textbook I used to pass the Certified Financial Planner exam, *"Buyers of calls are betting that the price of the underlying common stock will rise, making the call option more valuable. Put buyers are betting that the price of the underlying common stock will decline, making the put option more valuable. Both put and call options are written by others who are betting the opposite of their respective purchasers."* Betting is a zero-sum game, the opposite of investing.

Futures Contracts – This agreement provides for the future exchange of a particular asset between a buyer and a seller. A futures contract is typically between a hedger and a speculator. The hedger has an asset he needs to sell in the future and wants some guarantee of the price he will receive. A hedger may also have a need to make a future purchase and wants a guarantee of the price he will pay. A wheat farmer might be a hedger of wheat on the sell side; a bakery might be a hedger of wheat on the buy side. A deal is not typically made between two hedgers; one of them is typically a speculator. The speculator is making a bet. To see how futures markets work, watch the movie *Trading Places*, specifically the scene near the end when futures on frozen concentrated orange juice are being traded. Unless you need a futures contract to insure a price for an asset you need to buy or sell, leave them alone.

Hedge Funds – These private investment funds fall outside the scope of many investment regulations. Hedge funds tend to use a lot of leverage (borrowing) to increase their positions and magnify gains (which also magnifies losses). They also make frequent use of short selling, which is selling a stock you don't own now and replacing it later with stock you buy after the price has dropped. It's a bet that prices will decline. Hedge funds have limited liquidity, so it's hard to pull money out if things turn bad. Hedge fund managers are typically paid a performance fee based on the return of the portfolio, which can lead them to take on much more risk. They gain if the risk succeeds, but don't suffer if it fails. To illustrate this ridiculous compensation structure, the top five hedge fund managers in terms of compensation each personally earned more than $1 *billion* in 2007.

Limited Partnerships – These investments are not as common as they were in the 1980's, in part because they fell out of favor when so many people lost money in them. Limited partnerships pool investors' money and acquire assets like real estate, industrial equipment or gas and oil leases. The investors are known as limited partners because their liability is limited to their investment in the partnership. They hire a general partner who actually runs the operation. Limited partnerships are usually set up for a period of years, and there is very limited liquidity during that time. Historically, limited partnerships have paid attractive dividends during the term of the partnership, but these were offset by little or no return of principal at the end and by tax savings that never materialized as they were supposed to.

Viaticals – For someone with a terminal illness and large medical expenses, a viatical settlement can be a good thing. A viatical settlement is the purchase of a life insurance policy for cash, in exchange for becoming the beneficiary. They became known in the 1980's during the AIDS epidemic, when young AIDS victims needed money and their life insurance was the only source. The amount paid to the policyholder is discounted, based on the life expectancy of that person. The return for the investor in a viatical depends on how long the ill person actually lives. The longer they live, the lower the return for the investor. Medical advances have made it harder to accurately predict how long seriously ill patients will live, which increases the risk to an investor in viaticals. There is also a ghoulish aspect to investing in viaticals. Your return is a direct product of the seller's longevity; the longer they live, the less you make. This condition can't help but create the investor's urge for the terminally ill person to just go ahead and die already. Any investment that would spawn such an inhumane attitude should be avoided. No investment return is worth the sale of your soul.

And in rebuttal, what a MONEY MORON recommends you do:

- **Transfer wealth whenever you can.** Have you any idea how much work it is to create wealth? There's the earning, the delayed gratification, the discipline, the long-term perspective...AARRGGHHH!! If I have the chance to transfer someone else's wealth to me, I'm grabbing it. I realize the wealth can go the other way too, but no risk, no reward is what I say.
- **Don't make your investments work; just make them look pretty.** The goal of an investment is to sell it for more than you paid for it. You want to find someone who is a bigger sap than you, and there must be thousands of people who fall in that category. Don't just put lipstick on that pig, use mascara, blush, perfume and a little black dress.
- **Go for the big score.** Overnight is better than over time, so don't be afraid to be impatient with your investments. If I buy 20 stocks, and 19 of them do nothing but one of them doubles in a year, I had a return on the portfolio of - 5%? Wait, that can't be right....
- **Make your investments give it up.** Total return doesn't do me any good now. Keeping profits and reinvesting them is not what I want my investments to do. Yield, baby, yield. I want the fruits now, even if I'm eating a lot of seeds, too.
- **Time the market.** It's a 50-50 shot, which is way better than the odds when you buy a lottery ticket. It's very simple, really – after the market goes up a while, it comes down; after it goes down a while, it goes back up. Just peg the turning points, and you are in the money.
- **Trading beats investing, so be a trader.** Just look at the names – E*trade, Scottrade, TD Ameritrade, Firstrade. See a pattern? It's also called the trading floor of the New York Stock Exchange. What more evidence do you need that you should be an active trader?
- **Don't dollar-cost-average.** I believe that an investment strategy is successful in direct proportion to how complicated it is. Something as simple as dollar-cost-averaging can't possibly work. Even I am able to understand and implement dollar-cost-averaging, and if I can understand it, it can't possibly be any good.
- **Judge bonds on yield only.** A bond that pays 8% is better than a bond

that pays 6% - end of discussion. I don't care about time to maturity because I don't plan on keeping it that long. And the credit rating doesn't matter – no one ever defaults on a debt. And I can't understand those ratings anyway.

- **Buy the stock, not the company.** Give me a hot stock in a lousy company over a boring stock in a solid company any day. I don't care about how the company does, only how the stock does. It takes time for the market to realize a company is good and the stock is undervalued. I'd rather get a high-flyer with nothing in the company to justify the price, and then unload it before it inevitably tanks.
- **Use mutual funds only if you're weak.** I'm not falling for any of that strength in numbers, economies of scale drivel. I'm not going to pool my money with people afraid to make their own investment decisions. I'm the lone wolf making my own decisions, and I don't need some professional holding my hand, protecting me from myself.
- **Never annuitize.** Even if everyone in your family lives to be 100 and even if you're scared to death at the thought of being old and penniless, don't give in to fear and annuitize. It's the kiss of death, trust me. A month after you trade in that lump sum for a guaranteed income, you'll choke on a chicken bone at the local KFC.
- **Keep flipping those houses.** Investing short-term in real estate is like trading stocks, and you know my opinion about that. Flipping houses is a lot harder than flipping stocks because they're expensive to buy; credit is now tight; they require maintenance and repair, and the resale market has dried up. On the other hand, there's a lot less competition than there was a couple of years ago.
- **Be open to alternative investments.** Are you telling me my complete collection of the works of Menudo isn't a solid gold investment? And if a hedge fund manager was paid $2 billion last year, it was for a very good reason – he earned it! And I don't have a problem with viaticals, either. While I may benefit from someone's early demise, I ease my risk and my conscience by making a counter bet with the guys in the office. No reason they shouldn't get a piece of the action, too.

A HOME FIRST

A HOUSE SECOND

Facade *n.* **1**. *Architecture*. The face of a building, especially the principal face. **2.** An artificial or deceptive front.

In the last twenty years or so, it has become very common in house construction to have an impressive facade on the front of the house. It may be aged brick, stucco, stacked stone or some combination of such materials. Very often, in a move to reduce construction costs, the remaining sides of the house are of a much cheaper material, like masonite siding. The goal of such construction is to impress passersby, rather than impress the eventual owner.

The facade and the entire design of the modern house is based on a theory espoused by builders, developers and realtors – the theory of the "Ten Minute House." Because houses change hands more frequently than ever, it is considered ever more important that a house be marketable and appeal to as many buyers as possible. The theory states that most people will make up their mind, if they like or dislike a house within ten minutes of seeing it. This theory is why curb appeal is so important, which makes an impressive facade so important. It is also why you see impressive two-story foyers, great rooms etc. upon entering these modern homes. If the house doesn't impress a potential buyer within ten minutes, a sale is unlikely to materialize.

It is probably not surprising that houses are now constructed and marketed in such a way. Our ever-shrinking attention spans make it harder to properly deliberate major decisions. The need to grab someone's attention has led to the triumph of style over substance. As a result, potential house buyers look at dozens of houses; they compare all the features and prices; they look at the SAT scores of the local schools; they analyze data like property tax millage rates and resale values. However, they often forget to ask the most important question – Is this house the best place to make a home?

Let me make a distinction here. I refer to the building as a house. It is not a home until people occupy it and imbue the dwelling with the characteristics that humans seek in a home and that only humans can provide: love, peace, security, warmth and a sense of belonging. The person who built the house is not a home builder. That title must be earned by those who reside within.

If you get nothing else from this chapter, I hope that it will remind you that a house can be a tool in helping you make a home for you and your family, but it is nothing more than a tool. The house should help in easing the strains that families must endure; it should not add to them. A large mortgage is not a substitute for a 401k or a college fund. An entertainment room is not a substitute for family time together. A front porch doesn't make you a neighbor. The only need a house provides for is shelter from the elements. All other needs must be provided by the residents within. The house should make it easier, not harder, to meet those needs.

Not Necessarily the Best Investment

Conventional wisdom holds that your home is the best investment you can make. At first glance, such thinking would make sense. You have to live somewhere, so it makes sense to own, rather than rent. Housing prices rise over time, so you would be buying an asset that appreciates while you own it. Each month part of your mortgage payment is applied to paying off the principal, so you build equity through a sort of forced savings. And lastly, you receive a tax deduction for the mortgage interest you pay.

Let's look briefly at each of these arguments for the home as investment. First, there is the comparison of owning vs. renting. Ownership trumps renting if the additional expense of owning vs. renting is more than offset by the increase in equity in the property. However, many homeowners don't consider all aspects of expense. The incomplete analysis might compare rent payments with mortgage payments only. For example, the rent on a 2,500 square foot house might be $1,500 per month. A 30-year fixed-rate mortgage for $250,000 at 6% interest is $1,498.88 per month. The principal payments on the mortgage average about $300 per month over the first six years. The principal payments would increase the equity about $3,500 per year in the early years.

If the house appreciates 3% per year, that would come to $7,500 per year on average in the early years. The interest payments come to about $14,500 per year in the early years. Someone in a 20% tax bracket would see their income taxes reduced almost $3,000 per year. So far, we have appreciation of $7,500 per year, principal paydown of $3,500 per year, and tax reduction of $3,000 per year, for a total advantage of owning over renting of $14,000 per year.

Now we have to look at the factors that whittle down that advantage. Property taxes vary widely by area, but if we assume property taxes of $4,000 per year and the same 20% tax bracket, the net cost of the property tax is $3,200. Then there is the cost of insurance. Both renters and owners need insurance, but the cost of a homeowners policy would be higher, by maybe $500 per year. The cost of maintenance is probably one of the highest costs and can be difficult to gauge. Some maintenance items like roof replacement are infrequent, but expensive. These costs should be annualized to get an accurate picture of ownership costs. Other items like lawn maintenance are small, but constant. If you do much of the maintenance yourself, it is necessary to attach a cost to your own labor, even if it isn't an out-of-pocket expense. For our purposes, we will assume maintenance costs that average 20% of the mortgage payment, or $3600 per year.

The items that are listed in the previous paragraph total $7,300 per year. When you subtract that figure from the $14,000 annual gain, you are left with a net gain of $6,700 per year. That is still a significant amount and a strong argument for home ownership. But, it's important to recognize that the additional expenses of owning over renting in this example ate up over half the advantage of owning over renting.

The frequency of moves can have a big effect on the advantage of owning over renting. The average American family moves every seven years. When you take closing costs and moving costs into account, that could reduce the net gain of owning over renting by another $1,000 or more per year. Frequent moves also increase the chance that you will not see the kind of appreciation in values that are more predictable in the long-term. For someone who bought a house near the peak of the real estate bubble, it may take ten to fifteen years to get the value of their house back up to what they paid for it.

Most people who live in a home for more than five years will make some kind of improvement to it. From a return on investment perspective, kitchen and bathroom remodeling tend to do best, with about 80-90% of the amount spent showing up in increased market value. Other improvements, such as a swimming pool, may not increase value at all and may actually decrease value, since more people may consider a pool to be a liability rather than an asset. Prudent spending is also a key to getting a return on any home improvement expenditures. An $80,000 kitchen renovation will not return even a small fraction of its cost if it is done in a $250,000 house. So, there is likely to be a loss rather than a profit on almost all home improvement projects, which will further reduce the net gain of ownership over renting.

Most of our investments are bought strictly as investments. You don't ask your mutual fund to do anything more than make money for you. Your primary residence has a very different primary task – it is the physical structure where you make your home. It should be selected with that role as the primary reason for selecting one house over another. Your home's ability to act as an investment is secondary. If you buy a well-built house in a good neighborhood, pay a reasonable price for it, maintain it consistently, make improvements judiciously, finance it with a low-interest, fixed-rate mortgage, and live there for at least a decade, it would be hard not to realize a net gain over renting a comparable house over the same period of time. But a house is also an illiquid, highly leveraged investment that can have its value affected by such arbitrary things as the local school's SAT rankings or a local youth's penchant for graffiti. When you consider the expense in blood, sweat, tears and aggravation that a home can entail, there are definitely easier ways to make money.

Percent Change in House Prices as of 6/30/08

(Estimates use all-transactions House Price Index which includes purchase and refinance mortgages)

State	Rank*	1-Yr.	Qtr.	5-Yr.	Since 1980
Oklahoma	1	4.93	1.28	26.52	113.24
Wyoming	2	4.36	1.12	60.56	192.45
South Dakota	3	3.77	0.60	32.01	199.30
North Carolina	4	3.59	0.63	31.60	248.59
North Dakota	5	3.56	0.66	38.15	162.11
Texas	6	3.55	0.72	25.30	132.02
West Virginia	7	3.44	0.73	32.76	138.14
Montana	8	3.38	0.14	57.56	295.20
South Carolina	9	3.28	0.44	32.56	230.22
Alabama	10	3.13	0.30	31.54	197.83
Kentucky	11	3.05	0.62	22.31	197.43
Mississippi	12	3.02	0.27	30.97	166.73
Louisiana	13	2.68	0.27	37.49	155.03
Tennessee	14	2.66	0.30	30.28	215.58
Maine	15	2.20	-0.73	41.19	417.62
Utah	16	1.87	-0.80	51.08	287.75
Iowa	17	1.83	0.13	20.57	155.97
Colorado	18	1.82	0.32	17.72	273.71
Indiana	19	1.77	-0.08	14.17	163.09
New Mexico	20	1.69	-0.57	50.92	240.74
Vermont	21	1.60	-0.52	52.02	373.84
Nebraska	22	1.42	0.39	17.87	162.05
Pennsylvania	23	1.36	-0.35	44.19	314.94
Kansas	24	1.26	0.03	20.19	149.49
Idaho	25	1.18	-0.70	57.54	252.25
Georgia	26	1.11	-0.35	22.85	235.51
Arkansas	27	1.04	0.32	29.10	163.08
Wisconsin	28	1.04	-0.54	28.20	233.90
Missouri	29	0.89	-0.30	25.00	205.48
Washington	30	0.56	-0.90	61.40	405.49
Alaska	31	-0.18	0.05	47.33	184.23
Ohio	32	-0.28	-1.00	9.46	168.46
Illinois	33	-0.37	-0.83	31.18	279.29
Oregon	34	-0.53	-1.07	61.33	364.01

State	Rank*	1-Yr.	Qtr.	5-Yr.	Since 1980
New York	35	-0.81	-1.25	42.27	553.94
Delaware	36	-1.25	-1.00	50.89	407.71
Connecticut	37	-1.44	-1.53	36.56	369.04
United States**	**N/A**	**-1.71**	**-1.44**	**34.84**	**280.82**
New Hampshire	38	-2.11	-1.64	27.80	388.99
Minnesota	39	-2.22	-1.86	23.36	260.42
Virginia	40	-2.60	-1.91	56.76	363.09
Hawaii	41	-2.88	-1.52	81.02	433.01
New Jersey	42	-2.92	-1.96	47.13	459.85
Massachusetts	43	-2.92	-2.32	19.84	585.61
Dist. Columbia	44	-3.38	-1.77	72.27	534.48
Maryland	45	-4.02	-2.15	66.14	418.49
Michigan	46	-4.66	-2.91	0.94	196.60
Rhode Island	47	-4.85	-3.33	37.22	459.82
Arizona	48	-9.18	-4.40	62.68	288.70
Florida	49	-12.41	-5.33	54.03	321.17
Nevada	50	-14.12	-5.57	50.81	245.79
California	51	-15.80	-6.89	41.81	426.04

* Note: Rankings based on annual percent change.
** Note: United States figures based on weighted division average.

For the nation as a whole, house prices have averaged a 6.2% annual increase over the last five years and a 5.0% annual increase since 1980. In 1980, the S&P 500 ended the year at 129.55. To equal the average annual house price increase, the S&P 500 would need to stand at 500 today. If you check its value now, it is likely much higher than 500. It's also important to remember that the size and features of houses have increased substantially since 1980, and those are major factors in house price increases. It is unlikely that the average new house in 1980 is up 280% unless there have been considerable (and costly) upgrades to it in the interim.

The bottom line is this – you should buy the home you need, but don't buy more home than you need, unless you are already financially secure. The money you spend on more home than you need would do a much better job of increasing your net worth if it were invested in stock mutual funds, especially through your 401k. In addition to diversification, liquidity and historically superior returns, you don't have to paint or repair a mutual fund.

The average American millionaire owns a house with a market value equal to approximately 1/10th of his/her total net worth. Millionaires move infrequently, and they rarely buy a bigger house just because they can afford it. They also pay it off ASAP, because they don't like debt. Are you a millionaire? What does your house value/net worth ratio look like? Know now that wealth will not come from lavish digs with large mortgages.

It's Not an ATM

Let's say you live in the great Northwest. House prices in that part of the country have climbed 60% or more in the last five years and have not retrenched like California and other states that had a true real estate bubble. You bought a house in that area in 2002 and paid $300,000, with 10% down. The value of the house is currently between $450,000 and $500,000. Last year you received a solicitation for a no-closing-cost home equity line of credit (HELOC) for $100,000. The loan has a reasonable, variable interest rate (currently 7%), and a ten-year repayment period. You go ahead and get the $100,000 line of credit and use it for the following:

- $35,000 for a new hybrid SUV
- $10,000 for a family vacation to Hawaii
- $40,000 for home improvements
- $15,000 for daughter's college expenses

The typical thought process for someone who takes out a loan in these circumstances is they are tapping $100,000 of the new $175,000 equity. Even though they have additional debt, they still have $75,000 of additional equity in the house that wasn't there when they bought it. The problem with such a thought process is that it ends there, in part because to look more thoroughly at all the consequences might cause them to decline the loan (Goodbye, new car, Hawaii, granite countertops).

If the first mortgage is a 30-year fixed at 5.5% for $270,000, the monthly principal and interest payment is $1,533. In the six years since closing, they have paid down about $25,000 of the principal. The monthly payment on a $100,000 HELOC for 10 years at 7% is $1,161. Let's assume that this household has no other debt, and that household income has risen 4% per year since they moved in; it was $65,000 then, it is $82,000 now. Here's the whole story with regard to the addition of this new debt:

- Their debt-to-income ratio was 4.15/1 when they bought the house; it is 4.21/1 now.
- Their debt-to-equity ratio was 9/1 when they bought the house; it is 2.76/1 now.
- Their debt-to-market-value ratio was .90 when they bought the house; it is .73 now.
- Their monthly debt service as a percentage of income was 28.3% when they bought the house; it is 39.4% now.

The first three statistics are the rationalization for getting the HELOC. The last statistic is the only one that matters because it is the only one that has meaning in the month-to-month struggle to pay the bills and keep the house.

When a family builds equity slowly over time by paying down the mortgage month by month, there is little temptation to pull that equity out and spend it. That equity has been earned with sweat, sacrifice and time, and it is not thought of as something to be spent frivolously. When equity comes as the result of above-average price appreciation, there is a tendency to treat it as "found money", along the lines of a lottery winning or an unexpected inheritance. Such dollars weren't earned, weren't sacrificed for and therefore have less value (psychologically, anyway) than equity built by paying down the principal. It is very easy to pull this new-found money out of the house.

Here lies one of two problems with the abnormal run-up in real estate prices. First, it caused people to pull equity from their homes, which increased their debt load. The other problem is these people are going to end up giving much of that increased value back. Real estate inflation in recent years was the result of a lot of loose money being pumped into the system. But real estate prices can climb in the long term only as much as household incomes climb. When prices get too far ahead of incomes, families get priced out of the market, which causes demand to drop, which causes prices to drop, to get supply and demand back into equilibrium. This has been going on since late 2006, and will continue for some time to come. Take a look at the list of states and their house price changes. The four states with the largest one-year price declines (California, Nevada, Florida, and Arizona) also averaged price increases of 65.2% over the previous five-year period. When prices are climbing 12% per year while incomes are only climbing 4%, people get squeezed out of the market. The market then contracts to bring them back in. If you ever wanted a perfect example of regression-to-the-mean, here you go.

The increased debt burden assumed when borrowing against your home value is the biggest reason to avoid doing it, but it isn't the only reason. For many of the people who borrowed against rapidly rising house values, the adjustment downward in those values is leaving them with negative equity in their homes; in other words, they're upside-down. What do you think happens when someone has a monthly debt service that is almost impossible to cover, and the debt is on an asset that is now worth less than what is owed on it? It's simple – they walk away. High debt service on an asset that you are upside-down on is almost guaranteed to result in default of the loan and foreclosure. The seemingly innocent act of pulling equity from your home can lead to behavior you might not have imagined yourself doing. You end up sticking the lender with the property, packing up your loved ones and your possessions and slinking off in the dead of night like the Colts leaving Baltimore for Indianapolis.

It Starts With the Numbers

Before you begin looking at potential houses to buy, it is important to get some preliminary work taken care of. The first item of business is to determine how much house you can afford to buy and to arrange financing for that amount.

The first step in arranging financing is to get a copy of your credit report and credit score and to determine that all the information on the report is accurate and up-to-date. As I said in the chapter on debt, you should check your credit report some three months before seeking financing. If there are errors that lower your credit score (there's about a one in four chance there are), you need to allow time to get the errors corrected before you attempt to get financing.

Assuming your credit report is complete and accurate, you will want to comparison shop for mortgages. My strong advice here is to consider only fixed-rate mortgages. Adjustable-rate mortgages (ARMs) may look tempting because the initial interest rate is lower than a fixed-rate mortgage. However, the borrower has assumed the risk of rising interest rates. You are likely to end up with a mortgage payment that becomes unmanageable if the lender has the ability to move your interest rate when rates climb. The reason many homes have been foreclosed on recently has more to do with rising mortgage payments than with falling prices. An increase from 6% to 9% on a 30-year mortgage raises the monthly payment by some 35%. An increase of that size may make it impossible to meet the obligation.

If you can find the home you want and finance it with a 15-year mortgage, by all means do so. Everything else being equal, a 15-year mortgage usually has an interest rate about ¼ point less than a 30-year mortgage, which is to be expected, since a longer loan term involves a larger risk for the lender. Many people get a 30-year mortgage with the intention of paying it off early. Their goal is to pay off the 30-year mortgage in 15 years, but they don't want to be committed to paying it off in that shorter time frame. There are two problems with such a plan. The first problem is you are paying an unnecessarily high interest rate. If you can and want to pay off the mortgage in fifteen years, why get a 30-year mortgage that charges you a higher interest rate? The other problem with such a plan is that it almost never happens because life happens. There will always be other items and events pulling at your purse. The plan to pay the mortgage off early will never materialize. The only way to pay a mortgage off in fifteen years is to make the legally binding commitment to pay it off in fifteen years. Leaving yourself an out almost guarantees you will use it, and sooner rather than later.

MONTHLY MORTGAGE PAYMENTS FOR EACH $50,000 BORROWED AT VARIOUS INTEREST RATES*

Interest Rate	15-Year Mortgage	Total Repayment	30-Year Mortgage	Total Repayment
4.00%	$369.84	$66,571.20	$238.71	$85,935.60
4.25%	$376.14	$67,705.20	$245.97	$88,549.20
4.50%	$382.50	$68,850.00	$253.34	$91,204.40
4.75%	$388.92	$70,005.60	$260.82	$93,895.20
5.00%	$395.40	$71,172.00	$268.41	$96,627.60
5.25%	$401.94	$72,349.20	$276.10	$99,396.00
5.50%	$408.54	$73,537.20	$283.89	$102,200.40
5.75%	$415.21	$74,737.80	$291.79	$105,044.40
6.00%	$421.93	$75,947.40	$299.78	$107,920.80
6.25%	$428.71	$77,167.80	$307.86	$110,829.60
6.50%	$435.55	$78,399.00	$316.03	$113,770.80
6.75%	$442.45	$79,641.00	$324.30	$116,748.00
7.00%	$449.41	$80,893.80	$332.65	$119.754.00
7.25%	$456.43	$82,157.40	$341.09	$122,792.40
7.50%	$463.51	$83,431.80	$349.61	$125,859.60
7.75%	$470.64	$84,715.20	$358.21	$128,955.60
8.00%	$477.83	$86,009.40	$366.88	$132,076.80
8.25%	$485.07	$87,312.60	$375.63	$135,226.80
8.50%	$492.37	$88,626.60	$384.46	$138,405.60
8.75%	$499.72	$89,949.60	$393.35	$141,606.00
9.00%	$507.13	$91,283.40	$402.31	$144,831.60
9.25%	$514.60	$92,628.00	$411.34	$148,082.40
9.50%	$522.11	$93,979.80	$420.43	$151,354.80
9.75%	$529.68	$95,342.40	$429.58	$154,648.80

*Mortgage payments include principal and interest, but do not include property taxes or insurance. Note that figures are for a loan amount of $50,000. To calculate your mortgage payment, divide your mortgage by $50,000, then use that figure to multiply the numbers in the row for the appropriate interest rate. For example, for a $225,000 mortgage, the multiplier is 4.5 (225,000/50,000). If the mortgage interest rate is 5.75%, the monthly mortgage payment is $1,868.45 for a 15-year mortgage ($415.21 x 4.5).

The average mortgage in the U.S. is around $140,000. Only about 10% of mortgages exceed $250,000. Let's look at how different mortgage options impact a family purchasing a $187,500 house, with 20% down and a $150,000 mortgage.

We will assume a mortgage interest rate of 5.50% for a 15-year fixed-rated mortgage and a 5.75% interest rate for a 30-year fixed-rate mortgage. The monthly payments for the 15-year mortgage are $1,225.62. The monthly payments for the 30-year mortgage are $875.37 or 28.6% less. The total repayment amount on the 15-year mortgage is $220,611.60. The total repayment amount on the 30-year mortgage is $315,133.20 or 42.8% more.

In this example, the shorter mortgage saves some $95,000 in interest costs, which is a strong argument for biting the bullet and taking the 15-year mortgage over the 30-year mortgage. However, under just the right circumstances, the 30-year mortgage could prove more worthwhile.

The difference in the monthly mortgage payments in this example is $350.25. If our buyer selected the 30-year mortgage, and funded the $350.25 difference into a 401k account every month for the next thirty years, and it averaged an 8% return, the balance in that account after thirty years would be $521,998.

If our buyer instead selected the 15-year mortgage, paid nothing into the 401k during those first fifteen years, but funded the 401k with $1,225.62 per month (the monthly mortgage payment he/she no longer pays) from years 16-30 with the same 8% annual return, the balance would be $424,111.

In this comparison, both situations had a monthly outlay of $1,225.62 for thirty years. Using the 30-year mortgage proved better because the return on the money contributed to the 401k was greater than the interest rate on the mortgage. The buyer who took the 15-year mortgage funded much more every month, but because he started fifteen years later, he could not overcome the head start the person with the 30-year mortgage had.

I provide the above illustration to show that it might make sense to choose a longer mortgage. However, I need to make some very important points regarding this illustration. The difference between the two monthly mortgage payments went into a tax-deductible, tax-deferred account without fail every month. (Automatic payroll deductions would help maintain such discipline). There were no lapses and no loans taken from the 401k. The commitment to funding the 401k in this manner must be as strong as the commitment to paying the mortgage every month if this option is going to prove better. Remember, the more variables that get introduced into a plan, the greater the chance that the plan will fail. Committing to a 15-year fixed rate mortgage leaves only the variable of not paying and foreclosure, which increases commitment and reduces the odds of failure.

Things To Look (Out) For

There are so many factors to consider when buying a house that it's hard to list them on a few pages. It is worth buying a book on home buying; the small investment in money and time is nothing compared to what is at stake. If you search Amazon.com for "home buying guides", you will get about 1,700 results, which should get you started.

Use a real estate agent. This advice applies whether you are buying or selling a house. If you are buying a house, bringing in a buying agent can help you avoid costly mistakes, especially if you are new to the process or to the area. The buying agent and the selling agent split the selling commission, so be aware that both agents benefit from a higher selling price. If you are selling a house, the real estate agent will bring more potential buyers, will likely get a higher price to at least offset the commission and will help you avoid mistakes that may cost thousands of dollars while creating a legal mess. Look for an established reputable agent who is familiar with the area where you are looking to buy. Avoid novice and part-time agents. A proven track record is what you want. Ask for referrals from people you know who have bought or sold a home in the last few years.

If you go to realtor.com, you can begin your house search from the comfort of your current home. You can input location, price range, features, etc. and get an idea of what is on the market. You will also get to see who the more prominent agents are in the area you are looking. Here's an observation I've made when looking at realtor.com – if the listing has plenty of pictures, a complete description and maybe even a virtual tour, I'm much more impressed with the selling agent. It doesn't take much extra effort to make a listing on a web site complete and enticing. An agent that doesn't make the effort to market a house with every tool available shouldn't be in the business, and eventually they won't be.

Because you are likely to look at dozens of houses before deciding to make an offer on one, it's a good idea to take a digital camera or even a camcorder when you are looking at houses. If you look at four or five houses in an afternoon, by the time you get to the last one, it's almost impossible to remember the key features of each house. A photographic record can help you remember each house better and can be a valuable tool as you go through the process of listing the pros and cons of each house. You will need to list the pros and cons of each house in order to more objectively assess each one and to be able to rank them as your first, second, third choice, etc.

Any house you plan to buy will need to be inspected before closing. The inspection can turn up potential problems, so it is important to get a qualified, licensed, competent home inspector. But even the best inspectors are likely to miss some things. A house is just too big and the inspection time is just too short to expect any inspector to catch every imperfection. They are trained to focus on major flaws, not on the flaws you yourself may not even notice until you've lived there for several months. For this reason, you should inspect the house yourself prior to closing. You're not likely to spot many of the flaws a trained home inspector would, but you are likely to spot some things the inspector would miss. Since it will be your house (and your money), your critical senses are more readily tuned to spotting problems.

Here are some specifics to consider when evaluating a house and the neighborhood:

- *Location on the street* – The end of a cul-de-sac will be quiet with little traffic. A location in the middle of a long straightaway on a through street will be just the opposite. A house near the entrance of a subdivision will get all the traffic in and out of the subdivision.
- *Adjoining properties* – Being surrounded by other homes in the same subdivision offers the best protection against unwanted change. A large wooded lot next door might be attractive, until they erect a new Wal-Mart on the site.
- *Rented homes nearby* – A neighborhood with a lot of rental houses is usually in a downward transition. Renters also don't take care of a property like an owner would, so appearance suffers.
- *Relativity* – How does the house compare in size, price and style to the surrounding area? Any house that is more expensive or architecturally different from nearby houses will be difficult to sell.
- *Terrain* – A lot that slopes down from the street may be prone to flooding, and street noise will be more pronounced. A lot that slopes up steeply may be hard to traverse in bad weather.
- *Homeowners Association* – Learn what the annual dues are and what the restrictions are, too. The protections offered may not be worth the freedoms you must forfeit.

- *Corner lots* – There is more traffic, and it is difficult to configure the back yard to give the privacy you want.
- *Bedrooms and baths* - A house with fewer than three bedrooms or two baths will have a limited resale market and will resell for less. Factor that into your offer if you are considering a house with fewer than three bedrooms and two baths.
- *Waterfront property* – It is always much more expensive. You pay for a view, but you also get boat noise and traffic, less privacy, and possible expense of seawall maintenance and repair.
- *Mountain property* – You pay for the view again, but you may also get an isolated location with difficult access, especially in bad weather. Some public utilities may also be hard to obtain.
- *HVAC units* – If the house has multiple floors, a separate heating/cooling unit for each floor will be more energy efficient.
- *Septic or sewage* – Public sewage has a higher monthly water bill, but you don't have to maintain a septic system, and expansion of the house does not require a simultaneous expansion of the septic system.
- *Condition* – If a house is poorly maintained in the areas that are visible, you can bet the maintenance is even worse in the less visible areas. Getting a deal on a poorly maintained house rarely ends up being a deal.
- *Convenience* – Notice the proximity to shopping, hospitals, fire and police stations.
- *Landscaping* – Large grass areas need cutting, and some plantings require a lot of watering and trimming. The appearance may not be worth spending every weekend keeping up appearances.
- *Trees* – Mature trees add to the beauty of the property, and help shade the house in summer. Beware of dead trees; you want them removed before you buy.
- *Exterior materials* – Almost every house has some trim work that needs painting and maintenance. Brick is durable and requires little maintenance. Siding needs painting. Synthetic stucco needs annual inspections. Higher maintenance means a lower selling price.
- *Updates* – Some items like cherry vs. oak kitchen cabinets are just trendy, and don't add value over the long-term. Other items like shag carpeting and avocado-colored appliances definitely need to be replaced.
- *Age of mechanicals* – HVAC units, appliances, water heaters, or anything that involves water, gas or electricity will wear out at some point.

- *Age of roof* – Thirty-year shingles may only last twenty years. Have the roof inspected and get an estimate of remaining life. Adjust your offer to reflect anticipated roof replacement.
- *Water spots* –These indicate water leakage somewhere. It may be plumbing, or it may be from the roof. Water can migrate down pipes, so the water spot may be far from the actual source of the problem.
- *Energy bills* – Ask to see the seller's utility bills over the last twelve months, so you know what to expect. The size of the energy bill can be an indicator of the quality of construction, too.
- *Property taxes* – Taxes are as important as the selling price in determining affordability, because you will pay property taxes every year, even after the mortgage is paid off.

One last item that deserves more than casual mention is the local schools. The quality of the local schools is determined in part (but only in part) by the level of funding, which is commonly funded through property taxes. Higher property taxes are not a guarantee of better schools, though abnormally low property taxes will probably yield a lower quality school system.

Even if you will not have any children in the local public schools, their quality does affect property values and the ease of selling your house in the future. For those reasons, everyone who owns property in a school district should be concerned about the quality of those schools.

In addition to average spending per student, one of the other common measurements of school quality is SAT scores. The high school that serves a community is graded by that community in large part by that school's average annual SAT scores and whether the trend is up or down. Property owners worry that below-average SAT scores, or a downward trend in those scores will lead to lower property values. Lower SAT scores = lower quality schools = lower desirability = lower demand = lower property values.

While SAT scores are important and can be an indicator of school quality, they are often overrated by potential buyers. First of all, do high SAT scores lead to higher property values, or do high property values require higher-income (and higher educated) buyers, who are more likely to have children who are more capable of scoring well on the SATs? Which is the cause and which is the effect?

Paying thousands of dollars more for a house because it is in school district with slightly higher SAT scores just doesn't make sense. The scores do not mean that the school is making smarter students than the competition. More importantly, it does not mean that your son or daughter will become smarter, receive a better education, or end up in a better college because you send them to a school with an average SAT score of 1689 instead of a school with an average score of 1670.

By far, the most important factor in a child's success in school is the level of involvement of the parents. In evaluating schools, the level of parent involvement at the school is a better predictor of success than test scores. An above-average school cannot offset the effect of below-average parent involvement. If you buy an overpriced house because of the local school's reputation, you are doing a disservice to your children. The higher mortgage payment will take money away from other obligations like retirement and college funding. The stress of meeting that mortgage payment may impede your ability to spend quality time helping your children with their studies. In such a situation, there is nothing the school can do that can offset what has been lost in the home.

Where Do You Live?

When I was sixteen, our family took a trip to Toronto to visit one of my father's cousins. They lived in a row house that had been built around 1900. The lots were very small, and the homes were modest. The neighborhood was old, but safe. I was comfortable walking alone in that neighborhood at night, in a way that would never have been comfortable in a comparable American city at that time. The neighborhood was ethnically diverse, and people mingled with each other on the streets day and night.

One morning I awoke at dawn and went out on the small front porch. Across the narrow street I saw an old man of about eighty, neatly dressed with jet black hair that hadn't been his natural color for at least twenty years. The man was sweeping in front of his house. He wasn't sweeping his porch, his sidewalk or even the sidewalk in front of his house. He was sweeping the *street* in front of his house. I watched him for a few minutes as he meticulously collected the dust and dirt that I couldn't even spot from across the street. My curiosity finally got the better of me, and I went over to ask him why he was sweeping the street; it certainly wasn't his responsibility, I said. He gave me that smile only wise old men possess, and he told me in his very heavy Italian accent, "I sweep here because I live here."

In that one statement I understood why this was a vibrant neighborhood with safe streets and well-maintained homes, and not a crime-ridden decaying slum like so many of its American counterparts. The residents, old and young alike, took responsibility for where they live. They didn't just maintain their homes, which they did to an astonishingly high degree. They took care of the neighborhood. They swept the streets. If something got broken, they fixed it immediately, without debating whose responsibility it was. It was their neighborhood, so it was their responsibility. Had there been graffiti, it would have been cleaned up before the paint could dry.

I learned on that visit that those row houses had a market value comparable to a new suburban house in the U.S. with three times the square footage and many more amenities. One might argue that those people took good care of their homes and neighborhood because they were valuable. The reality is the neighborhood and the homes therein were valuable because their owners took care of them.

During the years since that Toronto visit, we have built larger and larger houses. We have created magnificent subdivisions with impressive gated entrances and equally impressive names denoting sophistication and culture. Our homes have so much space and so many amenities, we only need to leave the house to shop and maybe to go to work.

What we don't have as a result of all this (over)building is a sense of neighborhood that was common in the past. Of course, you can't have a neighborhood without neighbors, and we have largely forgotten how to be neighbors. We may be friends with a family or two on our street, but for many of us our involvement with our neighbors ends there. When I was a kid in the 60's, I knew at least 90% of the people who lived on my street, and I was not unusual in that respect.

When we buy a house in an exclusive subdivision, we think we are buying into a neighborhood. We aren't. Neighbors and neighborhoods are not the product of geographic closeness; they are the product of human closeness. The only way a subdivision becomes a neighborhood is by the residents making the effort to get to know each other, by finding out what a neighbor needs and helping them, by sharing good times and bad, by letting your neighbors be a part of your life and by offering to be a part of theirs.

We worry so much about things beyond our control that may affect our property values and enjoyment of our home. We worry about zoning rules, property tax rates, school redistricting, demographics, foreclosure rates and who can be corralled onto the homeowners' association board this year. If instead we simply walked through our neighborhoods regularly (the exercise couldn't hurt), if we stopped to talk to people we saw on those walks, if we introduced ourselves and offered to be a neighbor, if we noted things that needed fixing in the neighborhood and volunteered to fix them, if we made our neighborhoods the kinds of places that everyone would want to move into and that no one would want to move out of, the demand would be so much greater than the supply you would never again have to worry about the value of your home.

And in rebuttal, what a MONEY MORON recommends you do:

- **Buy the most house you can.** It's an investment. The more expensive the house, the bigger the investment. Hasn't the author been telling you how important it is to invest? Here's a sure-fire way to do it. If you fail to pay the mortgage, you're out on the street. If that's not incentive, what is?
- **Buy the biggest house in the neighborhood, too.** This isn't about resale potential. It's about being Lord of the Realm, King of the County, etc. It's easy to look down on neighbors from the biggest crib in the commune.
- **Move to California...or Oklahoma.** California had the biggest drop on house prices in the past year. Oklahoma has the lowest price appreciation since 1980. One of them ought to be a bargain.
- **Don't be afraid of an adjustable mortgage.** They have limits on how much they can go up. And they might go down, too. Even if the rates climb outrageously, you'll probably get a raise, and that should cover most of the increase. Anyway, be an optimist!
- **Pull Equity whenever you have it.** I like to think of price appreciation as manna from heaven. Don't just stand and stare at it. Gather it up and use it before it goes away. Besides, if they foreclose on you, the less equity you leave behind, the better.
- **Don't let high interest rates deter you.** Home mortgage interest is tax deductible. The higher the interest, the higher the government subsidy, and who doesn't enjoy a government handout?
- **Don't use a realtor.** I can buy a "For Sale" sign at Home Depot and print some flyers up at Kinko's. I top it off with an ad in the Pennysaver, and wait for the offers to roll in. I'm not paying a 6% commission for that.
- **Don't fix up your house before you sell it.** People act for their own benefit, so how does spending money to fix up a house that I'm moving *out* of benefit me?
- **Don't get neighborly.** Living next door doesn't qualify you to be my friend, or to borrow my stuff, or to ask me to help you find your lost puppy. On the other hand, invite me over for a beer, and we might start something.

THE $2,000,000 BMW

I was going to call this chapter "The Million-Dollar BMW", but after I ran the numbers, it turned out to be a two-million-dollar BMW. More on that later, though.

I'm not sure most of us fully appreciate how far the car has come in the last few decades. I like old cars (though I don't own any), and I enjoy watching the old car auctions on Speed channel and others. It is interesting to watch the attention and comments surrounding the muscle cars of the late 60's and early 70's. These were cars like the GTO, Roadrunner, Mach I and Z/28. As a teen at that time, I lusted for these cars.

The muscle cars were known for straight-line acceleration, due to their large engines and relatively low weight. When muscle cars faded in the early 70's, due to the burdens of high insurance rates and tougher emissions regulations, most believed such powerful cars would never return. They were mistaken.

The performance cars of today come from Europe and Japan, as well as Detroit, and they can match the best muscle cars of the 60's in terms of brute acceleration. These new cars can also handle and stop much better. They require very little maintenance; they have safety features unimaginable forty years ago; they get about twice the gas mileage, and they emit less than 5% of the emissions of those old cars. When old muscle car fans laments that they don't make them like that any more, they're right. They make them a hell of a lot better.

The Civic is a Legend (and more)

Cars have improved tremendously in just the last twenty years. They have improved in performance, but even more importantly, they have improved in value. Let's compare two models by the same manufacturer to show the value of today's car.

Honda created the Acura division in 1986 to sell upscale cars. The top-of-the-line model was the Acura Legend. In 1988, the car retailed for $29,895, the equivalent of $65,700 in 2008, at 4% annual price increases. The Legend was a fine full-size car, and it helped prove that the Japanese could make luxury cars to compete with Europe's best.

Now let's fast-forward twenty years to 2008 and look at the Honda Civic. The most expensive Civic sedan retails for $22,460. The Civic is about a foot shorter than the Legend, and the interior is about 10% smaller. The Legend had one horsepower per 19.3 pounds of car; the Civic has 20.1 pounds per horsepower. The Legend's mileage was 19/24 mpg (city/hwy). The Civic's numbers are 30/38 mpg. The $22,460 Civic EX-L has every luxury and safety feature that was available on the 1988 Acura Legend. In addition, the Civic has the following features the Legend didn't have:

- Anti-lock brakes
- 100,000 mile interval until the first tune-up
- 5-speed automatic transmission (4-speed automatic on the Legend)
- Six airbags (driver's airbag was optional on the most expensive Legend)
- Heated leather seats
- CD player
- Tire-pressure monitor
- Exterior temperature indicator
- Theft-deterrent system
- Satellite-linked navigation system

I apologize if this is sounding like a Honda Civic commercial, and in the interest of full disclosure, my wife and I do own a 2006 Civic. I'm not trying to sell you a car. I'm trying to show you that a car from 20 years ago that was considered a paragon of luxury and value can't hold a candle to an economy car of today, in value or in luxury.

The broader purpose of this comparison is to help you realize that there are very good cars available today that don't cost a lot of money. The Civic of today is a much better car than the 1988 Legend, and costs $7500 less in absolute dollars. In inflation-adjusted dollars, the Civic's cost is barely one-third the Legend's cost.

If cars are so good today that even the basic models can take us anywhere in safety and comfort, why do so many Americans spend money they don't have on cars they don't need?

Mobile Status

Clothes, cars and jewelry rank highest among items that purvey social position. (Lipstick does too, but only among women; men couldn't care less.) What these items have in common is that they are all portable. You take them with you wherever you go. These items are a big part of the statement you make to the world at large. A big house can certainly be a status symbol, but people have to travel to see it. With a car, you can put your status symbol right in front of anyone you seek to impress.

The desire for mobile status is one reason lower-income groups spend disproportionately on transportation. A June 2007 article in the Atlanta Constitution reported on a new business enterprise where people could *rent* flashy rims and tires for their cars. Someone is not financially capable of paying cash, or even buying on credit, a set of 20 inch chrome rims to dress up their ride. However, because there is a market for it, an entrepreneur has opened a shop (60 of them, actually) where you can rent those rims. The article interviewed a house painter making $2,000 a month, renting a set of wheels and tires that cost over $2,400 to go on his 8 year old truck.

"Ego is fueling the buying spree, said Larry Sutton, the president of Rent-n-Roll, a 60-store chain that claims to be the biggest of its kind. "We want to feel good about the way we look: ***'I don't want to wait for that. I don't want to save for that. I just want it.'*** *"*

"With the cultural shift we are going through, there is a have-it-your-way mentality," said Peter MacGillivray of the Specialty Equipment Market Association. "For a lot of people, their vehicle is a reflection of their personalities."

Before becoming too judgmental about the people who rent rims, it would help to look at some of the options more well-heeled buyers pay big money for:

- Corvette buyers can pay $3,500 extra for a center console trim plate and slightly upgraded leather interior.
- Lexus ES350 buyers pay $5,000 for the Lexus badges. Under the skin, the ES350 is the same car as the Camry XLE, but costs $5,000 more.
- A Lincoln Navigator is a dressed-up Ford Expedition, but you can get a fully dressed Expedition for about $7,000 less than a Navigator.
- Cadillac CTS buyers can pay $28,000 for a 550 horsepower engine, in case the standard 304 horsepower engine isn't enough.
- Mercedes-Benz SL buyers can pay $94,800 for a 604 horsepower engine, in case the standard 382 horsepower engine isn't enough.

These are just a few examples – there are hundreds available.

There is no practical reason for much of the extra spending Americans do when it comes to cars. Lincolns and Lexuses have more status (we assume) than Fords and Toyotas, and we are willing to pay a lot for that status. We pay, on average the cost of a year's tuition at a public university for nothing more than the opportunity to tool around town, feeling superior to those with "inferior" rides.

The Real Cost of Your Car

There are an awful lot of people out there driving BMWs who should be driving Hondas. It's not that they can't make the monthly payments (more on that trap later). The problem is they don't realize how much that BMW is really costing them, and they don't yet realize how badly they are going to need that money in the future.

Edmunds.com is a website with tons of information on buying a car, and the attendant costs. One of their best features is called True Cost to Own (TCO). It estimates the five-year costs of buying and owning a vehicle. Edmunds is thorough, and includes items like insurance, financing, depreciation, fuel and even taxes. I encourage you to use this tool before buying your next car, to avoid being unpleasantly surprised.

I used TCO to compare the true cost to own two vehicles, a 2008 BMW 328i, and a 2008 Honda Civic EX-L (the same model that was compared to the Acura Legend). The cash price of the BMW with typical options is $43,405. The true cost to own this BMW for five years is $59, 210. The cash price of the Honda is $24,776. The true cost to own this Honda for five years is $37,858. We've only just begun, though.

The cost differential for these two vehicles is $21,352, a difference of $4,270 per year. However, this purchase decision could have a $2,000,000 impact on the buyer's future financial security. Here's how it works.

Let's say our hypothetical BMW buyer is in his mid 20's, settling into his first decent-paying job. If he works 40 years, and gets a new car every 5 years, that's 8 new cars in his working life. If his first car purchase is a BMW instead of a Honda, he will likely continue in that pattern. (People only "trade down" cars when they have to.) So we'll have a 40-year pattern of buying more car than is needed. The differential in the true cost to own between what he buys and what he should buy will increase 4% per year, which is just the normal inflationary increase. Relatively speaking, he never gets more carried away than he did with his first car purchase.

If our hypothetical BMW buyer always bought a Honda Civic instead of a BMW and invested the difference at an 8.5% average annual return, by the time he retired, that extra money that didn't go to the BMW would have grown to over *two million dollars*. That number is significant on its own. When you read the chapter "You-At 82" and see what retirement will cost, you begin to realize the folly of spending more on transportation than is practical and necessary. The following chart shows the growth of the money over the years.

COST DIFFERENTIAL BETWEEN BMW AND HONDA AND ITS ACCUMULATED VALUE WHEN INVESTED @ 8.5% ANNUAL GROWTH

	Annual Difference	Accumulated Value		Annual Difference	Accumulated Value
YEAR 1	**$3,942**	**$4,277**	YEAR 21	**$8,637**	**$310,592**
YEAR 2	**$4,100**	**$9,089**	YEAR 22	**$8,983**	**$346,738**
YEAR 3	**$4,264**	**$14,487**	YEAR 23	**$9,342**	**$386,347**
YEAR 4	**$4,434**	**$20,530**	YEAR 24	**$9,716**	**$429,729**
YEAR 5	**$4,612**	**$27,279**	YEAR 25	**$10,105**	**$477,219**
YEAR 6	**$4,796**	**$34,801**	YEAR 26	**$10,509**	**$529,185**
YEAR 7	**$4,988**	**$43,171**	YEAR 27	**$10,929**	**$586,023**
YEAR 8	**$5,187**	**$52,469**	YEAR 28	**$11,366**	**$648,168**
YEAR 9	**$5,395**	**$62,782**	YEAR 29	**$11,821**	**$716,087**
YEAR 10	**$5,611**	**$74,206**	YEAR 30	**$12,294**	**$790,294**
YEAR 11	**$5,835**	**$86,845**	YEAR 31	**$12,785**	**$871,341**
YEAR 12	**$6,069**	**$100,811**	YEAR 32	**$13,297**	**$959,832**
YEAR 13	**$6,311**	**$116,228**	YEAR 33	**$13,829**	**$1,056,422**
YEAR 14	**$6,564**	**$133,229**	YEAR 34	**$14,382**	**$1,161,822**
YEAR 15	**$6,826**	**$151,959**	YEAR 35	**$14,957**	**$1,276,806**
YEAR 16	**$7,099**	**$172,579**	YEAR 36	**$15,555**	**$1,402,212**
YEAR 17	**$7,383**	**$195,259**	YEAR 37	**$16,178**	**$1,538,952**
YEAR 18	**$7,679**	**$220,187**	YEAR 38	**$16,825**	**$1,688,018**
YEAR 19	**$7,986**	**$247,568**	YEAR 39	**$17,498**	**$1,850,485**
YEAR 20	**$8,305**	**$277,622**	YEAR 40	**$18,198**	**$2,027,521**

There are probably millions of Americans right now who are driving a status symbol, but who are not saving nearly enough for retirement. In their defense, they are probably blissfully ignorant about the harm they are doing to themselves. As of right now, you are no longer among their ranks. You now realize that owning an expensive car, while neglecting basic retirement funding (or college funding, insurance funding, or any other obligation you have), is hurtful to yourself and to your loved ones on a massive scale.

Back in the 80's, I saw a bumper sticker on a car (not coincidentally, a BMW) that said, "He who dies with the most toys wins." Even if that philosophy were true (and it couldn't be further from the truth), that BMW driver won't be dying with the most toys. The guy down the street, driving a 5-year-old Ford (the preferred brand of millionaires, by the way), who is quietly, consistently investing what he doesn't spend on cars, will be able to buy more toys than the BMW driver can imagine. Of course, if the unassuming millionaire buys any toys, they will likely be Toys-for-Tots.

Do Your Homework

The most important thing you can do to make sure you get the right car at the right price is to do some research before you ever leave the house to look at cars. It is so easy to get the information you need on the internet. A couple of hours of homework can easily save thousands of dollars.

Internet research gives you the opportunity to collect data on several different models of cars. You can do side-by-side comparisons on impartial sites like edmunds.com, and you can even do side-by-side comparisons on many manufacturers' web sites. You can access road test reviews and consumer ratings for cars that interest you.

You can also research financing options on line. You may first need to find out your current credit score, as that will greatly affect your interest rate. You can look up current rates on different financing packages, and even get pre-qualified for a loan.

The best feature of internet research is that you are doing it on your turf and on your terms. When you are at the car dealer, you are on their turf, and you are largely under their control. When you are trying to determine what cars fit your needs and budget and what kind of financing and terms are best for you, the last thing you need is the distraction of aggressive sales people or even the distraction of the car itself, with its gleaming paint and intoxicating new car smell.

You should always consider models from more than one manufacturer. Even if you have a clear first choice, you give yourself greater leverage in negotiations if you are considering different makes as well as models. If a Honda dealer only has to compete with other Honda dealers, he is less motivated to come down on price than if he has to also compete with the Toyota dealer, the Ford dealer and the Volkswagen dealer. Whichever dealer you are talking to, let them know you are considering other models and that the model they sell is not currently your first choice (even if it is).

Learning about the cars you are considering will help you when talking face-to-face with a salesperson. By demonstrating you have done research beforehand, you will be sized up as a savvy consumer, and you are more likely to be treated with the respect you deserve.

Every model that you consider must fit your needs (not wants) and your budget. Fitting your budget is a function of the car's price; everything else is a product of that number, so that's the number you have to set a firm limit on.

The Question You Must Never Answer

"So, how much were you looking to spend per month?" This question, asked by every car salesman within the first five minutes of meeting every prospective customer, is designed to set you up and take you down. Most people willingly answer this question, too. They answer it not because they are ignorant of the process (though almost all are), nor do they answer it because they don't wish to appear rude. Most people answer this question because the monthly payment number is the only number they focused on when determining how much car they could afford. The monthly payment number is the only one they know, which is the problem.

Ultimately, if you are financing a car purchase or leasing a car, you will want to know what the monthly payment will be. You will have looked at your household income and expenses, and you will have set an upper limit on what that monthly payment can be. Yet, you need to know what generates that monthly payment number. The monthly payment is determined by:

- the amount financed, which should be the purchase price less the down payment/trade-in
- the interest rate on the loan
- the number of months of the loan

For a leased vehicle, the amount financed would be the initial price of the vehicle less the down payment and less the residual value of the vehicle at the end of the lease (more on leasing vs. buying later).

When you answer the question, "How much per month were you looking to spend?", you quickly lose control of the negotiations. That number you gave them is a box into which they can pack extra payments and hide the real cost of the car. Also, whatever number you give them, they will quickly raise it. If you say $400 a month, they will reply, "Up to?" leading to state a number higher than $400, say $450. Then they will come back saying they can put you in that car you want for $500 a month.

It's easy to manipulate the variables that determine the monthly payment to hit the number the customer is hoping for. When you are focused only on the monthly payment, you tend to ignore two of the variables that affect that payment the most – the interest rate and the duration of the loan. The following chart shows how the monthly payments for a $20,000 loan can vary widely, depending on interest payments and length of loan. The car dealer can tweak these variables to get you a monthly payment you will agree to (though not necessarily the number you gave them), while still setting the loan up to maximize their profit.

Loan Amount	Interest Rate	Length of Loan	Monthly Payment	Total Repayment
$20,000	8%	48 months	$488.26	$23,436.48
$20,000	10%	48 months	$507.25	$24,348.00
$20,000	12%	48 months	$526.68	$25,280.64
$20,000	14%	48 months	$546.53	$26,233.44
$20,000	8%	60 months	$405.53	$24,331.80
$20,000	10%	60 months	$424.94	$25,496.40
$20,000	12%	60 months	$444.89	$26,693.40
$20,000	14%	60 months	$465.37	$27,922.20
$20,000	8%	72 months	$350.66	$25,247.52
$20,000	10%	72 months	$370.52	$26,677.44
$20,000	12%	72 months	$391.00	$28,152.00
$20,000	14%	72 months	$412.11	$29,671.92

Our hypothetical customer had a monthly payment figure of $400 in mind. He/she could do about that with a 60 month loan at 8% ($405.53). However, if the customer doesn't know how the numbers are calculated, he/she can be swayed into a 72 month loan at 12%, which has monthly payments of only $391. The dealer actually made the dream car a reality for less per month than was planned for a lesser car! Of course, if you look at the far right column, the amount of all the payments combined, you see that our hypothetical customer will end up paying $3,820.80 more with the 72 month loan than with the 60 month loan.

The Gauntlet

If you've ever bought a car from a dealership, you're familiar with the three main characters you have to deal with: the salesman, the sales manager and the Finance & Insurance (F&I) manager. No deal is complete until you meet with all of them, and jump through the various hoops.

The salesman may be the person you are most concerned about, though he (almost all of them are male) is likely to be the least of your troubles. The sales manager has to approve any deal, and the salesman is answerable to the sales manager. The sales manager looks at every deal to maximize profit; that is his role.

The sales manager isn't usually seen by the customer until the tail end of the negotiation. In a typical negotiation, the salesman yo-yos between the customer and the sales manager, relaying offers and counter-offers. While the sales manager is gathering additional information about the customer during this process (including their fatigue level), the customer is still clueless about the person with whom he/she is actually negotiating. Only when the deal is close to consummation (or about to be lost), does the sales manager appear to show you how close you are to getting the car of your dreams. You only have to go a little farther…

Once you come to terms with the sales manager, you will be sent to the F&I manager, even if you are paying cash for the car. The F&I manager handles all the paperwork, so meeting with him is unavoidable.

It is at this point that your good deal can slip away. You are likely to have been at the dealership for several hours, and you are probably worn to a frazzle. You want to move through this mountain of paperwork ASAP and get out of there. It's not likely to happen, though.

If you are financing, you will be presented with a dizzying array of options. Here is where knowing your credit score and the interest rate you qualify for are critical for you. You may qualify for a 7% interest rate; the F&I manager may tell you the best they can do is 10%. If you don't know for what rate you qualify (the best way is to get pre-qualified before you even go to the dealership), you will almost certainly end up with a higher rate.

Dealers prefer in-house financing because that is a profit-maker for them, too. Even if they offer low-interest financing (through third parties), they want you to use them to finance the vehicle purchase. Low-interest rate financing typically comes with strings attached. They may require the purchase of add-ons, extended warranties, service contracts, etc. If the dealer isn't offering stand-alone low-interest financing, it is better to decline it than be surprised by the high cost of the add-ons.

For Heaven's sake, note the length of the loan. You may have gone through the entire negotiation on the assumption (perhaps created by the sales manager) that the monthly payments were based on one loan term (say 48 months). Then the F&I manager prints out the loan agreement, and the term of the loan is 60 months, or 72 months. Even if you plan to keep the car that long (people also rarely keep a car as long as they planned to when purchased) you don't want to be making payments a year or two longer than planned. Also, since so many people are focused on the monthly payment figure only, they cave in and accept the longer loan term, just so they can take their car and go home. Paying too long for a car is another way of paying too much for the car. You just don't feel the pain until you find yourself making payments on a car that should have been paid off by now.

One of the best ways to know if the figures on the documents match the figures you were quoted is to look at each line carefully, and double-check the math for any number that is the product of another number on the page. The sum total is an obvious example. You should also be able to calculate how the monthly payment was calculated. Bring a calculator with you, especially one that has functions for calculating loan payments. If using such a device intimidates you, then make a copy of this page with the following chart, and you can at least get a very close estimate of what your monthly loan payments should be.

FOR EVERY $1,000 FINANCED,
THE MONTHLY LOAN REPAYMENT IS:

Loan term	Interest Rate								
in months	5%	6%	7%	8%	9%	10%	11%	12%	13%
24	$43.87	$44.32	$44.77	$45.23	$45.68	$46.14	$46.61	$47.07	$47.54
36	$29.97	$30.42	$30.88	$31.34	$31.80	$32.27	$32.74	$33.21	$33.69
48	$23.03	$23.49	$23.95	$24.41	$24.89	$25.36	$25.85	$26.33	$26.83
60	$18.87	$19.33	$19.80	$20.28	$20.76	$21.25	$21.74	$22.24	$22.75
72	$16.10	$16.57	$17.05	$17.53	$18.03	$18.53	$19.03	$19.55	$20.07
84	$14.13	$14.61	$15.09	$15.59	$16.09	$16.60	$17.12	$17.65	$18.19

You'll see in the chart that the longer the repayment period, the less each additional year reduces the monthly payment. Stretching the repayment period beyond 60 months is a point of rapidly diminishing returns. Longer repayment periods also have higher interest rates. There is greater uncertainty over how interest rates will change over a longer period, and that greater uncertainty is compensated by higher rates.

Notice one other aspect. A person with a 48 month loan at 5% interest has almost the same monthly payment as a person with a 60 month loan at 13% interest. A person with a 72 month loan at 13% interest has the about the same monthly payment as a person with a 60 month loan at 8% interest. And a person with an 84 month loan at 13% interest has about the same monthly payment as a person with a 72 month loan at 9% interest or a person with a 60 month loan at 4% interest (not shown on table).

This illustrates the importance of good credit and the ability to qualify for lower interest rates. It also illustrates the need to know your credit score and the interest rate for which you qualify. Having good credit and knowing what you can get for it doesn't just mean a lower interest rate. It can mean you can pay off your car loan a year or two sooner than you otherwise could, without increasing the monthly payment.

The extended warranty offered by the dealership is a waste of your money. Every automaker offers at least a 3-year/36 month warranty, with longer periods covering the powertrain. Some manufacturers are now offering 100,000 mile warranties. If having to pay for major repairs concerns you, look at vehicles from those manufacturers offering 100,000 mile warranties. If you are thinking of the extended warranty because of complicated mechanical/electronic options, consider a more basic model to eliminate options that are expensive to repair. If you are afraid your selected make and model is likely to have major problems as soon as the warranty expires, you should be selecting a different make and model.

F&I managers will also try to sell you packages that bundled high-profit items. These packages include things like paint sealant, fabric protection, VIN etching, Lojack, "free" tire replacement, etc. You don't likely need anything the F&I manager is trying to sell you, and if you do, you can almost certainly find it cheaper elsewhere. By adding the cost of these items to the finance package, they get to charge more because the real cost is spread out over years of payments.

After surviving the back-and-forth of the negotiations with the salesman and his manager, it's easy to let down one's guard when they go to the F&I manager's office. You think the worst is over, and there are just a few papers to sign. Yet, the F&I manager is just another salesman, and he has three advantages over you in this meeting: the element of surprise (You weren't expecting *more* sales pitches), control (The deal's not done until he says it's done), and your fatigue (By now you've been at that dealership how many hours?).

If you're going to a car dealership with even the slightest possibility you may strike a deal that day, allow yourself plenty of time. Get rest the night before. Eat and drink sufficiently before and during the visit. Walk around and clear your head occasionally. In addition, when you get too tired to think straight, *leave*. If they are upset that you are leaving before everything is done, calmly point out that you have been at the dealership now for X hours, and that is long enough for one day. Let them know when you can be back to finish everything.

When you know how the process works before you begin, when you do your homework on the cars and the financing and when you keep your emotions in check, buying a car can actually be an enjoyable experience. The playing field will never be completely even. You buy a car every few years. They sell dozens of cars a week. A knowledgeable consumer is a respected consumer, and when you prepare properly before going to the dealership, you are much more likely to be treated fairly and with respect. It's the best way to make buying a car a win-win transaction.

The Pitfalls of Leasing

There are many valid reasons for leasing. Unfortunately, most of those reasons don't apply to the millions of people who lease vehicles. The main reason people lease a car is because they get to drive a more expensive car compared to what they could afford to buy. So, let me state a guideline for leasing – If you can't afford to buy it, don't lease it.

It isn't surprising that most of the leased vehicles are high-end models, or that 80% or more of luxury models like Mercedes and Lexus are leased. The people driving them couldn't afford to drive them if they had to buy them. Since leasing a car builds no equity in the vehicle, the monthly payment on a lease will always be less than a comparable purchase.

When someone is shopping for an expensive car, they probably already know they will be leasing whatever car they get. Often though, a person who was planning to buy a car ends up leasing one instead, though it isn't the car he/she had planned on getting.

For example, someone goes into the Nissan dealership planning to buy an economical Sentra. His target payment is $300 a month. The dealer is quoting $350 a month on a purchase. The dealer then points out that if $300 a month is a firm number, they are having a special where you can lease an Altima, a step above the Sentra, for $299 a month. The customer sees it only as more car for less money per month. How can he resist?

Car dealers like leases because the numbers get very fuzzy. You see ads all the time touting a particular car for X dollars a month. The fine print will show the length of the lease and required down payment, but that's all you know. How did they get that monthly lease payment number?

The lease payment has to cover two basic costs – the depreciation of the vehicle during the lease period and the interest rate during the lease period. Depreciation is the difference between the car's value when new and its value at the end of the lease.

The dealer states the car's value when new as nothing less than sticker price. They state the value at the end of the lease as the low end of trade-in value. Such value assessments make the gap between those two figures wide, justifying a higher lease payment. Interest rates will also be quoted on the high side, as it is to the dealer's benefit. In order to know if you are getting a good deal on a lease compared to a purchase, you would need to know what you could purchase the car for in a negotiated deal, what the car's trade-in value will be at the end of the lease (quite speculative) and your qualifying interest rate.

As you can see, it is more difficult to determine if you are getting a good deal on a lease, as compared to a straight purchase. Most people also don't realize that lease rates are not carved in stone – they are negotiable, just like the purchase price is negotiable. You can negotiate the beginning price (You wouldn't pay sticker price, would you?), the car's value at the end of the lease (You'd negotiate your owned car's trade-in value, wouldn't you?) and the assumed interest rate. Everything you haggle about in purchasing a car needs to be haggled about when you lease a car, too.

After a lower monthly payment, the other appealing feature of the lease is you can just turn the car in at the end of the lease period. There's no hassling or haggling. But, there are two potential problems – the car's mileage and its condition. The lease contract has a mileage allowance, and any mileage above that number at the end of the lease creates a penalty of X cents per mile. This clause is part of the lease agreement, and there's no getting around it. By the way, if you return the car with fewer miles than the allowance, you don't get any refund.

The other problem is the car's condition. Even though normal wear and tear is expected, your definition of normal wear and tear and the dealer's definition will never be the same. Expect to incur charges for minor things like stone chips in the paint. Major damage will cost you an arm and a leg.

At least when you have a trade-in, you have the ability to negotiate the car's value, and you have the option of not trading in the car at all. The only way out of paying mileage or damage penalties at the end of a lease is to buy the car, at the figure the dealer has determined. If the car has high mileage or damage, you may not want anything more to do with it, but you may be stuck with it as the least expensive option.

Leasing can still make sense under these conditions:

- You are getting a sensible car that you could afford to buy.
- You are putting the difference between the lease payment and the purchase payment into savings.
- You are unlikely to drive over the mileage limit and very likely to drive right up to the mileage limit.
- You will be maintaining the car as well or better than if you bought it.
- You negotiated your lease deal, just as you would a purchase deal.
- You have gap insurance to cover the difference between the car's value and what is owed on it, in the event the car is stolen or wrecked.
- You won't have to change cars during the lease period (i.e. – Sports cars and newborn babies don't mix.)

No Insurance Surprises, Please

For most people, the second largest cost of a car, after the monthly payment, is the insurance premium. For some, it can even exceed the monthly payment. For those unfortunate few, the cost of insurance on the chosen car probably came as a severe shock. An unexpectedly high insurance premium may force you into having to sell the car because you can't afford both the monthly payment and the insurance premium. That can present a real problem if you are driving a leased vehicle, as you are contractually obligated to make the monthly payments for the entire lease period.

It is important to shop for car insurance in concert with shopping for the car itself. If you shop for insurance after you've purchased the car, you may be able to do no better than choose the best of a bad situation. When establishing your new car budget, you need to know the numbers for the two biggest components before you sign anything.

While you are online researching cars, you can do the same thing for insurance. Web sites like insurance.com can give you quotes from several different companies. You have the ability not only to compare the premiums for different companies, but also compare the premiums for different makes and models of cars.

For older drivers with clean records, the make and model of vehicle will have less of an effect on the insurance premium than it will for a young driver, especially if that young driver has any driving record. As a 50-55 year old with a clean record, my rates are low. A 21 year old male with one minor speeding ticket pays, on average, three times what I pay to insure the same car. He needs to know what those numbers look like.

Age and driving record are major factors in determining rates. The type of car plays a big part, too. The previously-mentioned 21-year old can expect to pay about 40% more for insurance on a fast Ford Mustang GT, compared to a tame Honda Civic EX. The car alone is responsible for that 40% jump.

Often, the cheaper car to purchase is not the cheaper car to own, when other costs, especially insurance are factored in. By learning beforehand the cost of insuring a car, you may find the car that was the more expensive becomes cheaper when all the costs are calculated. More important, doing your homework on the insurance costs will keep from ending up in a position where you have to sell the car of your dreams because the only way you can afford to keep it is to move into it.

And in rebuttal, what a MONEY MORON recommends you do:

- **Don't skimp on your wheels.** Your car represents *you* to the rest of the world. Do you want a car that says *"I have my priorities right."*? Of course not. You want a car that says – no, that screams *"I've made it, baby! I'm rich, I'm successful, I'm sexy, and I'm better than you in every way!"* You are what you drive. Or to put it another way, without your car, you're nothing.
- **Think of your car as an investment.** Even though it loses half its value before it's half paid for, your car makes it up to you in other ways. It demonstrates your good taste and sophistication, attracting members of the opposite sex and making you more attractive to employers. The potential for a better job and a better mate can easily offset the $2,000,000+ these cars will cost you over the years.
- **Go with your gut.** When you see a car you like, in a commercial or on the street and it's calling to you, heed the call. This is a Zen, Yin-Yang emotional kinda thing, and thinking about it will just ruin the experience. Besides, the car you want does not abide pencil-pushing, number-crunching weenies, so if you want to prove yourself worthy of this fine machine, stop analyzing and go for it.
- **Make the monthlies work.** If you can swing the monthly payment, the car is yours – simple as that. Trust the dealer to work his magic to get your monthly payments in a range you can afford. Let him help you attain that dream car; that's his dream for you, too.
- **Don't sweat the details.** By details I mean things like length of loan, interest rates, fees and licenses, taxes, insurance premiums, fuel economy, residual value, theft potential and maintenance costs. Details can be deal-breakers. If you don't think about them before the deal, they won't keep you from making the deal.
- **Don't be cheap.** The cheapest car you can own is the one you already own. If a new car says positive things about you, your old car is dissing you every day. Don't put up with those insults. Unload that traitorous embarrassment now, before it damages your reputation any further.

MONEY MORONS: THE NEXT GENERATION

News Item:

In a 50-question survey on financial literacy administered to over 4,000 high school seniors throughout the country, the average correct score on the survey was 50.2%, a grade of F.

News Item:

A college student in the U.S. has an average of four credit cards, and an average balance on those cards totaling over $3,000. One in five students has a balance exceeding $7,000, which is on top of an average student loan balance of $23,600.

Recipe for Disaster

When you compare our level of knowledge on a subject to the importance of that subject in our lives, no subject has a worse imbalance than personal financial management. In an economic system like ours, the importance of financial competence is immeasurable. Yet, our mastery of what we need to know about personal financial management is abysmal. You are reading this book because you have recognized this disparity in your own life and want to correct it. But you're an exception, not the norm.

For young people today, this imbalance of knowledge to importance is even more dangerous. Adults may be ignorant on the subject, but young people are both ignorant and naïve. The problem has become dangerous because young people, especially college students, have unprecedented access to credit now. Part of the freshman orientation ritual now includes numerous applications for pre-approved credit cards and private student loans that have high limits and low requirements. Providing such large sums to untrained youth just because they can sign the application form is akin to giving a loaded handgun to a chimp and assuming that because it has opposable thumbs it knows how to safely operate a firearm.

One of the ironies of credit-to-kids is that it is easier for an unemployed college senior to get a credit card than it is for that same person to get a credit card one year later, when they have graduated and are gainfully employed. A first reaction to that fact should be that the credit card companies are fools. However, what the credit card companies recognize is that the college student is likely still under the protective umbrella of the parents. By that I mean that if the college student gets jammed up with credit card debt, the credit card company knows with a reasonable degree of certainty that the parents will bail out their child to keep his/her credit history from being ruined before it ever even gets started.

Once the child has graduated, creditors are not likely to extend new credit because they cannot assume that the protective umbrella of the parents is still there. Creditors assume that upon graduation the parents feel it's time their child learns the ways of the world, which includes learning the consequences of poor financial management. There are only two problems with such a parental approach. The parents are allowing those important lessons to be learned by trial and error, or to put it more philosophically, wisdom is learned through suffering. The other problem is the parents are allowing the financial education to begin about eight years too late.

When I was a college student in the early seventies, there was no way anyone this side of a loan shark was going to extend credit to me. Credit had to be earned over several years by being a productive and reliable part of the economic system. Also, my generation was less the target of marketing. Certainly, we were larger consumers than our parents were at that age. There were more of us, and we had greater monetary abundance than our parents' generation had when they were young. But any money we had was the product of work already done, either by us or by our parents. There was no money based on a future promise to pay, a dollar of which has much less value than a dollar already earned and in hand.

Children today are marketed to in ways that were unimaginable just a generation ago (more on that later). Money is viewed in a much different context with young people today. In the late sixties, Frank Zappa and the Mothers of Invention released an album called *We're Only in It for the Money*. It was very tongue-in-cheek, a parody of many trends of the time. Kids today listen to 50 Cent's *Get Rich or Die Tryin'*, and he is dead serious (pardon the pun).

This combination of marketing saturation bombing, no financial education, easy credit and a still-developing brain is a toxic mix, a recipe for disaster. For today's generation of young people, if they aren't able to get these forces under control, and themselves as well, it won't matter how well they do in school, how great a job they get or how much money they make. Whatever it is, it won't be enough.

Ten is the New Twenty

It's hard to know what age you are any more. Sixty is the new forty. Fifty is the new thirty. Pop phrases like these imply that we are not aging as fast as we used to. Since life expectancies have increased markedly over the last century, there is some truth to such statements. Yet, as we are growing old more slowly, we are at the same time growing up too quickly.

As a ten-year-old boy, about the only brand names I cared about were Schwinn, P.F. Flyers and Dubble Bubble. There were certainly commercials back then on Saturday mornings aimed at me and my peers, but they were for items like cereal, BB guns and Barbie dolls. There were no high-ticket items, and status was definitely not a part of the marketing message.

The average ten-year-old today has memorized 300 to 400 brands. This trend means that for typical ten-year-olds, five to ten percent of their vocabulary is composed of brand names. The average 8-13 year old spends 3½ hours a day watching TV. Over a one year period, they will watch some 40,000 commercials. Add in advertising from the internet, radio, billboards, product placement in movies and TV, magazines, etc., and it's no wonder they are so brand-conscious and so primed to spend money.

Although the word was coined in the 1940's by jazz musicians, *Cool* has a meaning that carries across generations. The importance of being *Cool* is no less relevant to today's youth than it was to their grandfathers doing their best James Dean impersonation. Everyone wants to be *Cool*, especially the young and insecure.

Everyone can't be *Cool*. Part of being *Cool* is being different from the herd. *Cool* requires a certain social exclusivity. One of the easiest ways to create that exclusivity is to price the majority out of the market. To that extent, being *Cool* tends to be expensive. *Cool* is also a moving target. Once something is deemed *Cool*, the masses will flock to it, cheap knock-offs will appear, and something new must be declared *Cool*. Young people develop many of their spending habits in the pursuit of *Cool*. It is expensive, it is frustrating, and it is the pattern far too many continue for decades into adulthood.

One of the most effective ways to be *Cool* is to appear older than you are. Marketers are keenly aware of this. Products designed for older kids are marketed to younger and younger groups, a trend known as age compression. What was originally intended for 16-year-olds gets touted to 13-year-olds, then 11-year-olds. It's one of the main reasons you have 4th grade girls tarted up like extras in a hip-hop video. They want to appear older than they are, in order to be *Cool*.

Young people today are more concerned about image, status and being *Cool* than any previous generation. They also become concerned about it at a much younger age. Adolescence used to be the beginning of such concerns; now it starts as soon as the kids begin school – elementary school.

Young people (as well as the rest of us) are exposed to over 100,000 marketing messages a year. A great many of these messages to youth equate their worth as a human being with the products they buy. These messages are also being received by youth at a time in their lives when they are full of self-doubts and have a very fragile self-esteem.

Young people are told through marketing messages that an expensive product makes them more exclusive; makes them *Cool;* makes them better than those who do not buy this product. Early adaptors buy the latest expensive status symbol as an offensive weapon, to separate themselves from the herd. The herd ends up buying the product as a defensive weapon; they don't dare be the last one on the block without it.

The average teenager today will earn over $5 million over his/her working life. Today's teens will also need to accumulate $3-4 million during that working life before they can retire. Based on what most of them have learned about money in their youth, and more importantly, what they haven't learned, they will waste a large portion of that $5 million and will never come close to ever retiring.

Learning About Compounds, Not Compound Interest

We send our kids to school for a dozen years or more so they can get good jobs and make good money. But money is the one subject we don't teach them in school. This moronic behavior may top them all.

In the fourth grade, I remember spending what seemed like half a year studying Bolivia; I have no idea why. I have never met a Bolivian. I don't remember the last time I heard Bolivia mentioned in the news. I will likely visit Bolivia only if my plane is hijacked to La Paz.

It's no different in schools today. A lot of time is spent studying nice-to-know subjects, and not enough spent on need-to-know subjects, like financial management.

I think there are two basic reasons why we do not offer comprehensive financial education in our public schools. The first reason is a practical one – there isn't a free minute on the schedule. There are so many required subjects already and there are so many mandates to be met that adding anything to the curriculum seems an impossibility. Colleges do not require any financial education as a prerequisite for admission. Also, most public school curricula are based on a college preparatory model. As long as State U. is more interested in foreign languages than financial management, that is where the public schools will focus their attention.

Public schools today are swamped with standardized testing. Much of it is mandated by the federal government through programs like No Child Left Behind. Much of it is mandated on the state and local levels, as an accountability tool to measure performance of schools and school systems.

Regardless of who mandates it, the average public school student spends at least thirty days per school year preparing for and taking standardized tests, which is one school day out of six. Incidentally, no test sections deal with financial topics, except as a tangent to a math or social studies question.

Time to teach financial management in public schools could be made, if it became a priority. The subjects that currently fill the curriculum enjoy incumbent status, and schools are slower than most institutions when it comes to embracing serious change. As an example, schools still have an extended summer vacation, even though it's been over a century since students needed the summer off to work on the family farm. Extended periods away from school lead to deterioration of learned material and of learning skills, and every school superintendent knows this fact. However, they maintain the status quo because it is the status quo. The same is true of the required curriculum – it's easier to keep things as they are.

The other basic reason why financial education isn't part of the curriculum is more subtle. It has to do with misperceptions about money. The biggest misperception is that studying money elevates money's status. By making a subject part of the curriculum, we are saying that subject is important.

Educators are not generally a materialistic lot. Their choice of profession is testament to that. Teaching young people about money can make educators feel like they are endorsing materialism. After all, a science teacher should have a love of science. A history teacher should have a love of history. A financial management teacher should have a love of... money?

A good financial management teacher would not have a love of money; that would actually be a disqualifier. A financial management teacher should have a respect for money, and the role it plays in our lives. The importance of money in our lives is precisely the reason why it should be taught in schools.

When you study a subject, you demystify it, and you gain a better perspective on that subject. Intensely studying the stars enabled man to realize we are not the center of the universe. Studying money and finance is the first step in realizing that money is not the center of our personal universe. Immersing our children in a comprehensive understanding of money is the only way to teach them about money's limitations, about all the things that money *can't* buy. It's the only antidote to the 3,000 daily messages they receive urging them to spend, to be ever more materialistic.

Why Not the Parents?

I am a former public school teacher. My wife has been a public school teacher for over thirty years. Our daughter is a product of the public schools. My evaluations in this area are based on first-hand observations and no small amount of experience, as an educator, as the spouse of an educator, and as a parent.

One of the biggest trends in public schools over the last three decades is the transferring of responsibilities from the parents to the schools with regard to students' welfare and instruction. This trend is not what the schools want. They already have too many responsibilities with regard to students. The schools are constantly pressured from two sides; by administration that demands improving numbers (test scores, attendance, graduation rates, etc.) and by parents who, intentionally or not keep shifting many parental responsibilities on to the schools. To wit: your public schools shouldn't have to provide free breakfasts to first-graders; they shouldn't have to conduct weapons searches in middle schools; they shouldn't have to teach tenth-graders how to use a condom. Public schools end up shouldering such responsibilities when parents can't or won't shoulder such responsibilities themselves.

I am the first one to advocate that the best teacher for a child is that child's parents. Good parents can offset bad teachers more than good teachers can offset bad parents. The best way for young people to learn about financial management is from their parents, in the home. The home also provides the best real-life example of how financial management works, its benefits and its consequences when mishandled. A child has a vested interest in the family's financial affairs, and nothing generates commitment like an equity stake in the outcome.

Here is the ugly truth – most parents would be embarrassed to have their child learn how the family's finances are being handled. The family's finances would demonstrate that the parents know little more about financial management than their kids do. No parent would choose to be put in such an awkward position.

The news item at the beginning of this chapter cited a financial literacy survey where students scored 50.2%. The parents of those students were also surveyed with the same questions. The parents' average score was 57%. In light of that piece of information, the students' low scores are understand-able. The acorn doesn't fall far from the tree.

In fairness to the parents, how could they be expected to score much higher than what they did? They had no formal training in financial management. Their own parents probably never discussed family finances with them, and the only advice they probably ever received was along the lines of "Save your money for a rainy day", which is meaningless when you're a teenager. Expecting today's parents to score well on a financial literacy test is like expecting them to score well on a Spanish test because they eat at a Mexican restaurant once a week.

Parents could take a crash-course on financial management, but there are several impediments. The first is time; few parents would carve out the time to learn financial management. Second, learning financial management doesn't automatically mean the parents will transfer that knowledge to their children. Finally, it may be difficult to find a worthwhile class to take.

On the subject of the latter, let me digress a moment to tell you that if you want to improve your own financial management skills as well as your financial situation, you should look into Dave Ramsey's Financial Peace University. I have taught the class for a few years now, and it is comprehensive without being overwhelming. It is also entertaining, and it will help you get a proper perspective of money in your life. You can learn more about the class and find classes being held in your area by going to www.daveramsey.com/fpu.

Parents know how important it is for their children to receive a basic financial education. They also know their own limitations in this area. It is natural that parents would welcome the schools instructing their children in this area. Parents may also be uncomfortable about the prospect of their son or daughter becoming more financially astute than they are. It's one thing if your child knows more about chemistry than you do. It's quite another when they begin to question your abilities in a key area like finances. For the good of the child, it's important for the parents to swallow their pride and accept that some of their shortcomings may come to light. On the plus side, there's no reason the child can't teach the parent or thing or two about money.

What's Available Now

Internet searches for "financial education in schools" turns up almost nothing. There are a lot of hits for articles related to financing education, the financial crisis in education, etc. The emphasis is on the education system and their needs, not on the students and their needs. If you go to the home page for the U.S. Dept. of Treasury Office of Financial Education, its purpose seems to be to teach you about the Treasury Dept., but not about finance. Here is their exact copy:

Message to Students and Teachers

We are pleased to welcome you to Treasury's Learning Vault, where you can learn all about the history of the Treasury Department, its role in the Federal government, and its mission to serve you.

The Department of Education web site had a five year old press release announcing a joint grant by the Departments of Treasury and Education to "help educate the nation's schoolchildren about personal finance". The amount of the grant - $250,000, or less than half-a-cent per child. In short, there is not a lot going on at the federal level pertaining to financial education in schools.

Have you ever heard of NEFE, or the Jump$tart Coalition? Probably not, even though they are two of the most prominent players in financial education for our youth. NEFE is the National Endowment for Financial Education. It is a non-profit organization "dedicated to helping all Americans acquire the information and gain the skills necessary to take control of their personal finances". NEFE's high school financial planning program was introduced in 1984, and has been taken by approximately 4 million students in the last quarter-century. However, it is taught within the context of existing courses, and involves as little as ten hours of classroom instruction.

The Jump$tart Coalition for Personal Financial Literacy was started in 1995. Their objective is "to encourage curriculum enrichment to ensure that basic financial management skills are attained during the K-12 educational experience". Jump$tart serves as a clearinghouse of personal finance materials for educational use.

As welcome as NEFE's and Jump$tart's efforts are, they don't have the reach or the resources to properly address the need for financial education in schools. Anything that might be classified as financial education is almost never taught in a class labeled as such. Typically, any financial education is incorporated into classes in math, economics, business or social studies. If these classes are subject to standardized testing, the schools are inclined to focus only on the material to be tested, which rarely includes much on financial management.

Finally, it takes a dedicated teacher to utilize anything offered by NEFE or Jump$tart. It takes the curriculum out of the box, which means more work for the teacher, usually without any additional support from the administration. The students and their parents may appreciate the teacher's efforts to teach a new subject, but if these students' test scores in other subjects decline, administrators will pull the plug. This result is inevitable when test scores, rather than learning are the focus of education.

A 2% Solution

By the time students graduate from high school, they have been attending school for thirteen years. They have averaged six classes per day. (In early years they may not be broken down into separate classes, but they have spent the same amount of time in class and studied a variety of subjects.) They typically have had two semesters to a school year. By graduation day, the student has had approximately 150 semester-length classes. If their curriculum were revised to include three one-semester financial education classes (in 8th, 10th and 12th grades), these classes would consume only 2% of the total time the student spends in the classroom.

The average student currently spends over 15% of their total class time preparing for and taking standardized tests. Such tests teach nothing and mostly measure a student's ability to regurgitate data on command. The time required for financial education classes could easily come from this time block, without compromising the school's ability to measure students' progress.

As students move into higher grades, their elective classes increase. Most schools require a minimum number of credits in math, science, language arts and social studies. But, through middle and high school, students typically have 25% or more of their schedule made up of non-required classes. I won't contend that the subject of financial management is more important than the required areas of study. Yet, I defy any educator to show me any elective subject area that is more important to a child's future than learning about managing the $5 million they will make or the six million minutes they will spend making it.

Elective classes are typically offered in areas like music, the arts, physical education and career track courses. Such classes offer valuable exposure to subjects that can broaden a student's frame of reference. However, students choose an elective because they already have an interest in that area. They don't need much encouragement to study that subject. The curriculum in grades K-12 should be based on subjects a) that the students will have to know with a minimum competency level as soon as they graduate and b) that the minimum competency level is unlikely to be reached without formal classroom training before the student graduates. By these criteria, financial management classes rank just behind reading and math in importance. (Math and reading competence, by the way, would be a prerequisite to successfully completing any financial management class, and many other classes, too.)

On the following pages are my suggested curricula for the one-semester financial management classes for 8th, 10th and 12th grades:

Eighth-Grade Financial Management Curriculum

- *The Importance of Financial Management in Our Lives*
  Explanation of why the students are taking this class, how it can help them in their future and the consequences if they enter adulthood without this base of knowledge.
- *Money – Its History, and its Purpose in Our Lives Today*
  Money has an interesting history, not just in how it developed, but why it developed. Money is one of the most important influences in our lives, even as it evolves from the tangible to the digital.
- *Understanding What Money Cannot Do*
  Early in their financial education, students need to develop a respect for money's power, but must also recognize its limitations. In this developmental stage, they need to know what money cannot do for them, so they can accept what they must do for themselves.
- *Marketing in America*
  Because they are the targets of some 100,000 marketing messages every year, students need to know how to handle such non-stop bombardment. Far too many of these messages encourage behavior detrimental to the student's long-term psychological and financial well-being. They need to learn how to respond to these messages.
- *Share / Save / Spend*
  The cornerstone to a healthy relationship with money is recognizing the importance of using material wealth to help those in need, as well as the importance of taking care of yourself in the future by saving for that future. Learning to do these things, in the right order and in the right proportion is a cornerstone of financial management.
- *How Wealth is Created*
  Students will learn that wealth is not finite and that their wealth does not come at someone else's expense. They will also learn that wealth is the product of work, delayed gratification and taking a few calculated risks along the way.
- *Becoming a Smarter Consumer*
  This topic is broad, and can cover topics ranging from how to understand a contract, how to compare products and alternatives and how to use negotiation techniques to get a better deal. The goal of this topic is to teach students how to get more for less or at least to enable them get what they are paying for.

Tenth-Grade Financial Management Curriculum

- *Review of Eighth Grade Curriculum*
  Because of the two-year interval between financial management classes, it is important to have a refresher at the beginning of tenth grade to remind students of what they have already studied and why.
- *Getting a Job & Making a Career*
  Since work will be the primary source of income for almost everyone, students need to learn what they must give on the job to get the most from the job. What they learn about jobs can be for the present; what they learn about careers is for their future.
- *Car Ownership*
  The first major purchase for these students is probably a car, and young people especially are likely to make expensive mistakes in their choice of car and how to pay for it.
- *Understanding the Pitfalls of Debt*
  Since many students will begin accumulating debt while still in high school, they need to learn now how it can harm them and how to avoid it. These lessons can also encourage students to work and save for college, rather than assuming they will borrow their way through it.
- *Saving and Investing*
  While work provides the raw material for wealth creation, saving and investing is where money is converted into wealth. Students will learn how to save for the short-term and invest for the long-term. They will also learn about stocks, bonds, mutual funds and the other investment vehicles, these instruments that will generate much of their wealth during their lives.
- *Stewardship*
  We enter the world with nothing; we take nothing when we leave. Just as we teach students about being good stewards of the earth, we must also teach them to be good stewards of mankind's creations. Businesses rise and fall, as do family fortunes. Whether they rise or fall depends on the quality of stewardship more than anything else.

Twelfth-Grade Financial Management Curriculum

- *Review of Eighth and Tenth Grade Curriculum*
  Before students can be educated on new topics, it is important to remind them of what they have already learned. It reinforces the base and makes learning new topics easier.
- *Personal Financial Statements*
  Students will learn how to prepare a household budget, the items that make up a budget and how to reconcile budget and reality. They will also learn how to prepare personal income statements and balance sheets, so they can measure where they are and their progress financially.
- *Home Ownership*
  Most students aspire to own their own home one day, and it will be the largest investment many of them will make. Learning to buy the right home and finance it in the right way will enable them to live better and have more money to reach other financial goals.
- *Risk Management/Insurance*
  It is important for students to understand that there is an offense and a defense in the world of financial management. They need to learn the defensive tools, their purposes and their costs. Learning the cost of auto insurance alone should have immediate benefits by changing some behaviors for the better.
- *Retirement*
  Seventeen-year olds have a hard time imagining themselves as old and retired. They need to learn that such a time will come. These students need to know that they must take care of themselves when they are old and that they can only do so if they begin learning now what must be done.
- *In Summary*
  The class will tie all the lessons learned in the three grades into a comprehensive view of financial management, and will empower the students to begin adulthood with the information they need to make the right decisions about money for the rest of their lives.

Time to Get the Ball Rolling

Please look once again at the topics to be studied in these proposed classes. I have never taught a financial management class to adults (which includes the same topics as in the proposed classes) where at least one adult didn't say to me at the conclusion, "God, I wish someone had taught this to me when I was young!" For them, it's better late than never. For our children, it's better now than later.

Imagine how much better your financial position would be today if you had had the opportunity to study a curriculum like this one when you were in high school. Imagine how much better off today's students would be if they could begin their working/earning/spending/saving lives armed with this kind of knowledge. Imagine how much more fiscally responsible business and government leaders would have to be if they knew that the public could no longer be scammed because the public now knew how to identify and stop such abuses.

The previous pages offer just a broad outline of the topics that should be considered at each grade level of financial management. Textbooks appropriate for each class level can easily be assembled from existing materials. Textbook publishers would fall over themselves to service this need, once they knew there was going to be a need and market for such materials.

Like most worthwhile change, this one will have to be from the bottom up, rather than from the top down. No congressman or school superintendent who reads this is likely to initiate any action. That action will be up to us. At the end of this chapter, I have prepared two draft letters; one to send to your local school superintendent and one that can go to a congressman, senator or high state education official. Feel free to copy verbatim or slice and dice them as you feel appropriate to say what you want on the subject.

Only when politicians and education administrators recognize that *we* recognize the necessity of formal financial management in schools will something be done to implement such programs. We all have an interest in a financially astute and fiscally responsible population. Taxes can be lower. Productivity can be higher. Debt can be lower. Savings and investing can be higher. Stress can be lower. Bankruptcy can be lower. Divorce rates can be lower. Financial independence and security can be higher. Also, as a result of all of the above, personal serenity and happiness can be higher. Can any other school subject offer all these benefits?

And in rebuttal, what a MONEY MORON recommends you do:

- **Don't support financial education in schools.** If schools start teaching this stuff, Money Morons will soon be extinct. Don't live with that guilt. Save us! Save us!
- **Get your kid a credit card ASAP.** How did you teach your kid to ride a bike? You propped him on the seat, gave a good push, and told him to pedal like crazy. Same principle here. No training wheels, either. The quicker your kid gets bloodied by the credit card, the quicker he'll learn how to use it.
- **Support materialism in your child.** Don't you know this economy is consumer driven? Only commies discourage materialism. Besides, if your kid can find happiness in some toy or video game, he won't waste your time trying to find it with you.
- **Encourage Age Compression.** Let your 13-year old get what the 16-year-olds are getting. They'll grow up faster and then won't be a burden to you any more. Some things your 13-year old gets that 16-year olds get can really help them grow up fast (like a positive pregnancy test).
- **Be Brand Savvy.** Nothing helps your child's self-esteem like knowing all the cool brands. It impresses their peers, and it's way cooler than knowing the state capitals or other nerdy displays of knowledge.
- **Be Cool, at all costs.** If it takes $100 sneakers to be cool, so be it. It's unlikely your kid would spend $100 of his own hard-earned money for such an item, so it's up to you to step in to shore up your kid's fragile self-esteem. Unless of course you don't love your kid and you think that saving for your retirement is more important, you selfish jerk!
- **Teach your kids about financial management yourself.** All you need is the time to teach them, the desire to do so, their full attention, their desire to learn, a solid base of knowledge, information and experience, a solid track record of astute financial management, a willingness to show them the family finances and how you manage them….hey, where'd you go?!?

You can write to your representative in Congress by going to this web site: https://forms.house.gov/wyr/welcome.shtml, entering your information, and then you can email your representative directly.

You can write to your senators by going to this web site: http://www.senate.gov/general/contact_information/senators_cfm.cfm, and selecting the senators from your state.

State education governing bodies vary by name. To find the contacts in your state try Googling (your state) school superintendent, or (your state) board of education, or (your state) department of education. You should be able to find the web site for the appropriate organization, along with contact info.

Sample Letter to any of the above parties follows below:

Dear :

I read with interest a book called *Money Morons*, and a chapter called *Money Morons – The Next Generation* really caught my attention. It talks about the dangers our young people face because of their financial ignorance, and how these dangers could be addressed with three one-semester classes in 8th, 10th and 12th grades. The chapter even included a proposed curriculum for each year.

I know that the local school curriculum is largely controlled at the state and federal level. This situation is due to the requirements of accountability, which results in standardized testing consuming 15% of the school year. The financial management curriculum would consume 2% of a student's class time from K-12. It would seem a far better investment to shift some of that time, energy and money from testing to financial education.

Our students go to school in large part to get good jobs and make good money. Shouldn't we also be teaching them how to manage that money as well? Shouldn't we be teaching them how to become better stewards and managers, which will make them more productive citizens? Won't more productive citizens earn more and therefore be capable of paying more taxes while still keeping more for themselves? It seems like a classic win-win situation for everyone.

I encourage you to work to make financial education a part of every child's public school education. The young citizens who benefit will make our nation even stronger in the future.

Local school superintendents can initiate changes in curriculum, but they are still answerable to state and federal officials. You can find contact information on local school systems by Googling (blank) school system, or (blank) board of education, or (blank) public schools, or (blank) school superintendent.

Sample letter to a school superintendent follows below:

Dear :

I know you spend a lot of time between a rock and a hard place – state and federal officials demanding accountability on one side and parents and students on the other side demanding most everything else. I know you have a tough job and I thank you for your efforts to give our children a quality education.

I read with interest a book called *Money Morons*, and a chapter called *Money Morons – The Next Generation* really caught my attention. It talks about the dangers our young people face because of their financial ignorance and how these dangers could be addressed with three one-semester classes in 8th, 10th and 12th grades. The chapter even included a proposed curriculum for each year.

I understand many of the limitations you face when adding anything new to the school curriculum. I know you face battles with state and federal officials, which is why I have also written to my congressman (woman), my U.S. senators, and the state school board (superintendent) expressing my support for financial education in schools and asking for their support as well.

I know you face resistance from inside the schools, because it may seem to them to be one more burden to bear. But our children go to school in large part to get good jobs and make good money. Shouldn't we also be teaching them how to manage that money as well? A comprehensive financial management curriculum would require 2% of a student's total time from K-12, which seems a small investment for the dividends it would pay.

Please know that you have my full support in your attempts to move this curriculum forward. I know it will take time and effort, but any worthwhile change always does. Thank you for your support of our children.

YOU

AT 82

A Longer Life – Blessing and Burden

We have been given the gift of an extra generation. In 1900 a newborn American had a life expectancy of 47.3 years. By 1950, a newborn American had a life expectancy of 68.2 years. By 2000, that number was up to 77.0 years. In the elapsed time of four generations, we have made the average lifespan more than a generation longer.

If you were born a century ago, your lifespan was almost 40% shorter than it is today. Childhood diseases and injuries were your biggest obstacles. If you made it to adulthood, your prospects for a long life got better. In 1900, just three infectious diseases accounted for half of all deaths. Those three diseases were tuberculosis, pneumonia and diarrhea, which rarely kill today.

Childhood back then was abbreviated, because life spans were shorter, and children were a financial liability. Families were larger then, and the sooner a child went from financial liability to financial asset, the better. If you were a male, you would likely be working full-time by age 16. If you were female, you were likely to be married by that same age. A shorter lifespan meant a compressed lifespan. Adulthood and its responsibilities arrived a lot earlier than it does now.

Up until about sixty years ago, your children were your security in your old age. People had more children then for several reasons. Infant mortality might claim some, and some might never become productive citizens. The law of large numbers says that the more children you have, the more likely at least one of them will be in a position to care for you in your old age.

A century ago, retirement was an unknown concept. You tended to work until you were no longer able. However, with 60-hour workweeks and dangerous working conditions, work-related death or disability was a serious prospect. Few people were in a position to save much toward a retirement fund. Also, the idea of not working while you were still capable of doing so ran counter to the Protestant work ethic pervading at the time.

In 1900, as today, the first quarter of your life was childhood. Childhood was shorter as well as harder back then. In 1900, childhood was over by age 15, evidenced by the fact that 90% of children did not go to high school. Today, childhood often extends into our twenties, as college delays true adulthood for an ever-increasing percentage of the population.

In 1900, as today, a person could expect to spend about 40 years in the workforce. Back then, though, the average workweek was 60 hours, there were no benefits packages and by the time you were in your mid-fifties, you were used up. If you stopped working, it wasn't usually by your choice or on your terms.

Those extra years of life we've gained in the last century are mostly being spent as retirees. They are being spent at the time in our lives when our expenses are at their highest (mostly due to inflation); we don't have others to support us (as in our childhood), and we are generating no income.

In 1935, when The Social Security Act was made into law, the selected retirement age was set at 65, in part because only half of the nation's workers lived that long. Those workers who made it to age 65 collected Social Security for only five years on average before they died. They basically worked ten years for each year spent in retirement.

Today, college graduates start work around age 22. Their goal typically is to retire at age 62, currently the earliest age to collect social security retirement benefits. A 62-year-old today can expect to live 23 more years, on average. Forty years from now, when that 22-year-old is 62, he/she can expect about 30 more years of life.

Understand what this data means. On the day these graduates begin full-time work, they have 70 years of life left. They plan to only work the first 40 years, and then live off their accumulated savings for the last 30 years. What a huge change from two or three generations ago when people worked 50 years with the hope they could retire for the last 5 years. The ratio of work to retirement has gone from 50:5 to 40:30.

The Burden Has Shifted

As I write this, my parents are in their 81st and 82nd years. They are still married after 58 years, they enjoy good health for their age, and they are financially secure and comfortable, though hardly wealthy.

We should all be as fortunate at age 82 as Tony and Jean DiGiovanni. Most of the current U.S. population will likely live to see age 82. Unfortunately, most of the current U.S. population will likely not live as well as my parents at age 82.

My parents are not exceptional for their generation. Most of them married once and stayed that way. Nothing helps financial stability like marital stability. They lived below their means, while raising and educating four children. My father was a firefighter in Rochester, NY; my mother was a housewife and part-time secretary. They've only lived in two different houses since 1960. They've never lived in a house younger than they were.

My parents have one advantage in their old age that most of the readers of this book will not enjoy. They have a pension. After thirty-five years in the fire department, my dad gets a monthly pension check that continues until both my parents pass away. It also has annual cost of living adjustments that help to keep them (somewhat) even with inflation.

My dad's employer provided what is technically known as a defined benefit retirement plan. A defined benefit plan usually means the retiree receives a monthly check – a pension. The benefits to the retiree are defined; the cost to the employer is not. Hence the name, defined benefit plan.

Employers are not fond of this type of plan. Not surprisingly, employees rather like it. Employers don't like it because while the benefits are defined, the cost is not. The employer is obligated to provide the stated benefits, regardless of the cost. Employees like it because they know exactly what they will receive in retirement, and they can't outlive their benefit.

While you might think an employer could accurately calculate the cost of a defined benefit plan and plan accordingly, the two factors most affecting the cost of such a plan are beyond an employer's control.

The first factor is the cost of living increase, which is based on the inflation rate. No one can know from one year to the next what inflation will be like that year. An employer can cap the annual cost of living increases at a fixed percentage, but that's only a partial solution and can adversely affect the retiree.

The other factor is the life expectancy of the retiree. Constant advances in medicine keep increasing our life expectancy. Calculations based on current data and technology can be rendered obsolete in a few years by unexpected breakthroughs.

For example, if an employer estimates a new retiree will live 15 more years and the cost of living increase will average 3% per year, while the reality is that the retiree lives 17 more years and the cost of living increase averages 4% per year, that retiree will cost the employer 27.4% more in benefits than was anticipated. Small differences between estimates and reality lead to big differences in the cost for an employer, which is why employers don't like defined benefit plans and why they're becoming extinct.

In the private sector, about the only place you still find defined benefit plans are in union-controlled jobs. Moreover, many of these jobs are being eliminated as lower-priced competition, free from the burden of a defined benefit plan, moves in. The costs of funding such retirement plans can be passed on to the customer only as long as everyone in the industry has to do it. Once someone breaks ranks, as overseas automakers did several years ago, an employer can no longer fund such a program and remain competitive.

The only place that the defined benefit plan is likely to remain in place for much longer is in the public sector, which includes most government jobs, teachers, anyone whose wage is paid by tax revenues. There are a couple of reasons for this continuation. A defined benefit retirement plan is seen as a way of attracting and retaining quality employees in jobs that may not have a competitive salary to the private sector. In public sector jobs, generous retirement benefits are less prone to public disapproval than are high salaries. Also, stewards in the public sector are answerable to taxpayers, as opposed to their counterparts in the private sector, who are answerable to stockholders. Of those two groups, stockholders are much more cohesive, scrutinizing and bottom-line oriented than taxpayers.

In most corporations, the defined benefit retirement plan has been replaced by the defined contribution retirement plan. The defined contribution plan eliminates the cost uncertainties for employers, which is why they love it. The employer defines the *contribution* they will make each year to an employee's retirement account, rather than defining the *benefit* the employee will receive at retirement. The contribution an employer makes can be based on any number of formulas. The contribution calculation typically involves a percentage of the employee's salary, and/or a contribution based on the company's profitability that year. The latter is commonly known as a profit-sharing plan.

It is important to know how this change in retirement funding affects you. First, and most importantly, you must understand that the safety net of a guaranteed income at retirement is gone. The employer meets its obligation to your retirement funding during your employment, not during your retirement.

Analysis Risks Paralysis

I must confess that calculating what it takes for someone to retire comfortably can be frustrating and depressing, for me and for them. It's actually easy to run the numbers – it's what the numbers say that can lead to frustration and depression.

Part of my frustration stems from the disconnect most people have between the retirement they envision, and what it will actually take to get there. It reminds me of the British visitor we had one time, who wanted to take a weekend car trip to the Grand Canyon. We live in Atlanta. You can't get there from here, at least not in that time frame with that mode of transportation. Since they were unfamiliar with the vastness of the U.S.

compared to Britain, their perceptions were distorted. Unfamiliarity about the costs of retirement can lead to distortions about what is possible.

It's important to make people aware of the need to save for retirement, and to give them guidance as to what exactly it will take. However, there is a very real risk that being blunt with the numbers will shock and depress the person to the point that he/she will go into complete denial and do nothing to prepare for retirement. The situation will have been made worse, not better.

Here is an example. A 45 year old making $50,000 a year, with $50,000 saved for retirement, wants to know how much of their salary they need to save in order to retire at 62. I crunch the numbers and reply matter-of-factly, "About half of your salary". I have not helped this person. I may have provided an answer, but this person needs solutions, not just answers.

It is more important to find what is in the realm of possibility, make retirement projections based on what can be done and then get this person to actually do what they are capable of doing. By the way, if this example sounds like you, don't panic. You can't do the impossible. You can and should do the doable, and then estimate how far that will take you.

Rather than insert extensive charts in the middle of this chapter about required contributions for retirement, I have given some examples at the end of the chapter. Right now I want you to read and comprehend and not become numb from an avalanche of data. Among the examples given later, it's unlikely any one of the charts would accurately reflect your particular situation. I strongly encourage you to run your own set of numbers. You can go to my web site, www.marathon-forthelongrun.com and click Retirement Calculators. (On the gatekeeper page, click *Yes I am a Resident* to access the site.) You can also Google Retirement Calculators and get dozens of web sites with calculators.

It seems that almost without exception, every calculation I make for any person of any age in any situation indicates that person should be saving *at least* 10% of their income for retirement. Even a brand new college graduate, with forty-five years of work ahead of him/her, should be saving 10% of every paycheck in order to retire properly around sixty-seven.

Before you start thinking of reasons why you can't save 10%, take a different perspective. If your employer told you tomorrow that, in order to stay in business, every employee had to take a 10% pay cut, what would you do? Unless you knew you could immediately get another job at your old salary, you would accept the 10% pay cut and make the necessary adjustments in spending. If you could make those changes when they are externally imposed, couldn't you also make them when they are internally imposed and when the sole beneficiary of those changes is you? My task here is to educate you and motivate you, and you will then be capable of much more than you were before.

Self-Preservation is not Selfish

We've all heard the advice of "Pay Yourself First." That advice is simple, yet profound. It could also be rephrased to "Take Care of Yourself First.", which may initially seem like a selfish perspective; it is anything but.

We all know the parable of the Good Samaritan. We would all like to emulate him. To be called a Good Samaritan by someone is high praise indeed. But when you read the parable (Luke 10:25-37), there's something interesting we tend to overlook. The Samaritan takes the injured man to an inn, pays for his lodging and care, tells the innkeeper he will make a final settlement upon his return and then continues on his journey.

He continues on his journey. The Good Samaritan offers help, but he does not make a sacrifice that impedes his ability to help in the future. The Good Samaritan probably had business he needed to attend to, and he knew that changing his plans would affect that business, hence his ability to make a final settlement with the innkeeper or to help others in the future who might need it.

When you take care of yourself first by paying yourself first, you accomplish two things: you enable yourself to remain independent and not be a burden to others, and you maintain your ability to help others on a long-term basis.

It is important to understand this concept in the context of planning for your old age. There are many reasons why so many people enter retirement unprepared financially. One of the biggest reasons people are unprepared is that they have sacrificed their own preparedness by well-intentioned, but misguided, financial support to loved ones.

In the best-selling book, *The Millionaire Next Door*, one of the six chapters that tell how millionaires become millionaires is titled *Economic Outpatient Care*. The chapter deals with providing financial support to others, primarily adult children. Here are some of its key points:

- Adult children who receive financial support have less wealth than those children who receive no support.
- Adult children who receive financial support are less productive.
- Adult children who receive financial support have higher levels of consumption and lower levels of saving and investing.
- Adult children who receive financial support have more debt.

- Teaching your children to live on their own is the best gift you can give them.

One of the messages of this chapter of *The Millionaire Next Door* is that if you think that helping your children now will enable them to help you in the future, you are mistaken. Your Economic Outpatient Care may weaken your own financial situation to the point where you will have to rely on others for support in your old age. Just as important, those to whom you have provided the Economic Outpatient Care will be less capable of helping you financially than if they had had no help from you in the first place.

Once your children reach adulthood, it is necessary that they become financially self-sufficient. The only exception should be the adult child who is unable to be financially productive because of a disability. (Disability in this case should be defined by an objective professional or agency, not by you or by your child.) Even if you are a millionaire, you aren't doing a capable adult child any favors by providing financial subsidies.

Even before your children reach adulthood, it is important to make them understand you are not a bottomless financial well. One common mistake I see made is when parents forego saving for retirement (or withdraw money from a retirement account) in order to pay for a child's higher education.

Budgeting, and paying yourself first become so important here. Whatever financial support you provide for your children's higher education must come after you have made the necessary periodic contribution to your retirement account. There is really no other alternative to funding your retirement than for you to do it yourself. There are alternatives to funding your child's education, rather than for you to do it yourself.

I believe that taking large student loans should be avoided if at all possible. Yet, I also believe it is better to graduate with a large student loan than to have your parents reach old age with little or nothing saved. Your young adult child may not agree with that statement at the moment. Your child will hopefully agree with it when he/she is a little older and has accumulated more wisdom. Your child will definitely agree with it when you are living with him/her because it's the only affordable option.

A college degree does not have to be a financial back-breaker. A year of tuition, books and fees at most state universities averages about $6,000. A student working a minimum-wage job 20 hours a week will earn enough to cover these expenses. A college degree is attainable without sacrificing your retirement fund and without being deep in debt upon graduation. If you're worried about how work will affect your child's grades, numerous studies over the decades have shown that students with part-time jobs have higher GPAs than students who don't work. In addition to being more organized and disciplined, these students also have a vested interest in their success.

If you can afford to send your kid to Harvard without jeopardizing your own long-term financial security, go for it. For the other 99% of us, some boundaries are recommended. I've already stated my opposition to funding a child's education at the expense of your long-term financial security. When you are sending your child to an expensive private school because that's the only place that would accept him/her, and you're shortchanging your retirement fund in the process, I am adamantly opposed to that.

I realize that in many cultures, paying fully for a child's education is considered a primary parental responsibility, and I respect that. These same cultures also place great emphasis on caring for elderly parents. In many of these cultures, it is expected that elderly parents live with and are supported by their children. These cultures emphasize reciprocity – parents take care of the children now; the children take care of the parents later. Unfortunately, these are not the cultural norms of broader America today. A culture of individuality and mobility has weakened the parent-child bond, leaving more and more elderly Americans to fend for themselves, which is the sad reality, and it's important that we not be in denial about it.

Having What It Takes

If you look at the FAQ's below straight from the Social Security web site (www.socialsecurity.gov) it should be clear that prudent people should not be relying on Social Security for much of their retirement income. My quick and dirty advice is that prudent planning for retirement should assume that Social Security will provide no more than 20% of your retirement income. Coincidentally (or not) that 20% figure is what is about what you'll pay in taxes.

Q. I'm 35 years old in 2007. If nothing is done to change Social Security, what can I expect to receive in retirement benefits from the program?

A. Unless changes are made, at age 69 in 2041 your scheduled benefits could be reduced by 22 percent and could continue to be reduced every year thereafter from presently scheduled levels.

Q. I'm 26 years old in 2007. If nothing is done to change Social Security, what can I expect to receive in retirement benefits from the program?

A. Unless changes are made, when you reach age 60 in 2041, benefits for all retirees could be cut by 22 percent and could continue to be reduced every year thereafter. If you lived to be 101 years old in 2082 (which will be more common by then), your scheduled benefits could be reduced by 25 percent from today's scheduled levels.

Q. I hear that Social Security has a big financial problem? Why?

A. Social Security's financing problems are long term and will not affect today's retirees and near-retirees for many years, but they are very large and serious. People are living longer, the first baby boomers are nearing retirement, and the birth rate is lower than in the past. The result is that the worker-to-beneficiary ratio has fallen from 16.5-to-1 in 1950 to 3.3-to-1 today. Within 40 years it will be 2-to-1. At this ratio there will not be enough workers to pay scheduled benefits at current tax rates.

Q. Should I count on Social Security for all my retirement income?

A. No. Social Security was never meant to be the sole source of income in retirement. It is often said that a comfortable retirement is based on a "three-legged stool" of Social Security, pensions and savings. American workers should be saving for their retirement on a personal basis and through employer-sponsored or other retirement plans.

Historically, people have been told that they would need approximately 75% of their pre-retirement income in retirement to continue the same standard of living. Obviously, that is a very generic number, and an individual's requirements could vary widely from that estimate. The ability to maintain a standard of living with a 25% income reduction is predicated on several assumptions.

First, there is an assumption that one's mortgage gets paid off prior to retirement. If that can be accomplished, it's probably easy to maintain your standard of living despite an income reduction of 25%. For many if not most families, the mortgage eats up 25% or more of net income. However, since people move more frequently than ever before and since real estate appreciation over the last two or three decades has prompted many people to pull equity out of their homes, a smaller percentage of the population is likely to be in a position to enter retirement with no mortgage. Of course, downsizing the home at retirement may enable you to avoid having a mortgage, but downsizing also implies a reduction in your standard of living.

Second, it is assumed that there will be employment-related expenses that will cease at retirement. The cost of commuting to work and the cost of maintaining a business wardrobe will stop, but these won't amount to 25% of anyone's income. You may drive your car less, which will enable you to lower the annual cost of transportation. However, the expense of transportation won't go away; it may actually change very little in retirement.

Once you reach age 65, you can get covered under Medicare, which would allow for a reduction in health insurance premiums. Although, if you retire before age 65, you will need to maintain private health insurance until Medicare eligibility kicks in. There is no guarantee that the eligibility age for Medicare won't rise in the future. Considering the gloomy predictions about the system's financial stability in the future, we are likely to see some sort of increase in the eligibility age for both Social Security and Medicare in the years to come. Also, medical expenses, including health insurance premiums are increasing much faster than the rate of inflation. Even if you begin retirement on Medicare and see an initial reduction in your health insurance premiums, that reduction may not be there for long. Within a very few years, you could be paying more for health insurance premiums in retirement than you were prior to retirement.

Unless you are within five years of retirement, it can be difficult to accurately predict the amount of your expenses in retirement. You may be able to recognize which expenses will disappear at retirement and which ones will remain. The expenses in your last year of work may carry over fairly intact into the early years of retirement.

Since people like to pursue new activities in retirement that they were unable to pursue while working full-time, new expenses may show up in retirement, especially in the early years when you are still active and in good health. The most common item in this category is an increase in travel expenses. International travel, cruises and extended vacations are on most retirees' to-do list, and these items aren't cheap.

Other new expenses in retirement include personal growth. These expenses may be traditional items like country club dues, but they may also include expenses like tuition for continuing education, museum member-ships, and other expenses that enable you to grow as a person and fill the hours that used to be filled with work.

The result of this review of likely monthly expenses in retirement is that there may not be much of a reduction in expenses once retirement begins. My gut feeling is that many new retirees will find they need 90% or more of their pre-retirement income to maintain their standard of living.

For most retirees in the future, most of their retirement income will be coming from qualified retirement accounts (401ks, IRAs, SEPs, company pensions, etc.) Any money received from these sources is taxed as regular income. If we assume a federal tax rate of 15%, and a state tax rate of 5%, that would require an additional 20% of income. Thus, if you need $5,000 per month in retirement to meet expenses, you would also need another $1,000 per month to cover income taxes. What you need to live on annually in this case isn't $60,000, it is $72,000.

Let's sum up to this point. Calculating the necessary size of your retirement fund when you begin retirement requires you to consider the following:

- The level of income you will need in retirement compared to your income just before retirement (75-90% is the probable ratio).
- What your income will likely be in those last few years of work. (If your income grows 3.5-4% per year, it will double in 20 years.)
- How long you will be retired. (The earlier you retire, the longer the retirement.)

Twenty times - when asked how much money someone needs to save for retirement, a standard answer is twenty times the required income in the first year of retirement. The second part of the standard answer is that you will draw 5% of the value of the investments as income in the first year of retirement.

If you are 40 years old now and you make $50,000 per year, if you want to retire at age 65 and if you anticipate 4% annual raises between now and retirement, then you will be making $128,000 the last year you are working. If you need 85% of this income in retirement, then you will need a retirement income of $109,000. If your retirement fund needs to be twenty times $109,000, then you will need a retirement fund of $2,180,000.

There are a lot of "If's" in the preceding paragraph. That is an important point. If/Then equations are the cornerstone to retirement planning. If the "If" part of the equation creates an impossible "Then", you need to change the "If" part of the equation.

Don't feel bad if you realize you are not going to be able to achieve your idealized retirement. For a great many people, an idealized retirement means retiring in their mid-50's with an income equal to or greater than the income they had while working. To achieve that goal, a person would have to save over 20% of their income beginning with their first paycheck, and that money would have to earn a 10% return every year until they died at age 90. The level of foresight and self-denial required to meet an idealized retirement goal is beyond most of us. Instead, we need to tweak both ends of the equation, the "If" and the "Then" and find where they can meet.

The worst thing you can do is to do nothing. Today may be the first time you've given serious thought to exactly how expensive retirement will be. The reality of the situation may feel overwhelming to you right now. Do not give in to those feelings and enter a state of denial. The future penalty of inaction is just too serious. Denial and procrastination do more than reduce comfort in your old age; they greatly increase your misery. You owe it to yourself to do what is necessary now to minimize actual hardship in retirement.

You can't do much about the circumstances. You can do a lot in terms of your response to the circumstances. Your first goal should be simply to do better. If you're doing nothing to save for retirement, it's time to start. Even if you start by setting aside a mere 1% of your pay into a 401k plan, it is the biggest single step you will take to your financial security. If you just get started, all subsequent steps will be easier by comparison. Increasing your savings from 1% to 5% is easier than going from 0% to 1%, just as increasing a car's speed from 10 mph to 50 mph is easier than going from a dead stop to 10 mph. Inertia is your enemy – fight it.

Vehicles Into Your Future

Hopefully, your employer is trying to help you save for retirement by offering a qualified retirement plan to enable you to save. The most common plan is the 401k, used in for-profit organizations or 403b, used in non-profits. We'll refer to the 401k only, for simplicity. Unless you work for a very generous employer, 60% to 80% of the money that goes into your retirement account will have to come from *you*, most typically through salary deferrals into your 401k plan.

The 401k has many features to help you save for retirement. First, you can defer some of your income (currently up to about $15,500) to go into the 401k. That money is withheld from your paycheck and goes directly into your 401k account. The contributions you make to your 401k reduce your taxable income dollar for dollar, which means that, if you have an income tax rate of 20%, putting $10,000 into your 401k will reduce your tax bill by $2,000. What this really means is that you came up with $8,000 out of your paycheck, but ended up with $10,000 in your 401k. Turning $8,000 into $10,000 is an automatic 25% return on your money. And that money hasn't even been put to work yet.

Most of the money that is in your retirement account on the day you retire will have come from the growth of the investments in the account, not from contributions to the account. That is not to say that contributions to the account are not important; the contributions are the seeds – the investments create the fruit. A person who contributes to their 401k for 35 years will only have about 20% of the final amount come from contributions; the rest will come from the growth of the investments, assuming the investments aren't too conservative and grow about 8% per year on average, which is why your investment selections within your retirement account are so important. The performance of the investments in your retirement account, as well as your level of contributions to your retirement account, will determine if you get to retire at 62 – or 82.

In the 401k, you have investment options, typically mutual funds that invest in various asset classes. You choose how you want your money to be invested. The longer you have until retirement, the more aggressive your investments can be. Being too conservative reduces the likely return on your investments and will require you to save more and/or work longer.

Every 401k may have a slightly different contribution formula, and you need to find out what your employer offers. If your company offers matching contributions at all, your first goal is to immediately increase your contributions to your 401k to get every penny of company match. So, if your company offers a 50% match on contributions up to 6% of your salary, get your contributions to 6%. If you are at 0% now, increase the contributions 1% per month for the next six months. A steady increase will make the reduction in take-home pay a little easier to take. If increasing your contributions means canceling HBO and developing a taste for home-made grilled cheese sandwiches, do it anyway.

Think about your sacrifice in positive terms. If you defer $200 a month into a 401k, the tax deduction for that deferral comes to around $40. That means a $200 contribution really only cost you $160 in take-home pay – the difference was covered by reduced tax withholdings. In addition, if the company matches your $200 with another $100, you now have $300 in your 401k, but you only sacrificed $160 to get $300. That's a gain on your money of 87.5% immediately and with no risk. Then all that money gets invested so that it can grow tax-deferred until you need it at retirement, which may be decades from now. Why wouldn't you make the necessary adjustments to take advantage of this opportunity? This is the "deal of a lifetime" you've always dreamed about. Do you see it now?

Let me give you one more subtle reason for taking full advantage of the company match to your 401k. The 401k match is a test. Your company is using the 401k plan to see who in the company possesses the following traits:

- Vision, demonstrated by imagining yourself at age 82
- Self-discipline, demonstrated by not spending all your paycheck
- Self-interest, demonstrated by "paying yourself first"
- Selflessness, demonstrated by not wanting to burden others in the future
- Shrewdness, demonstrated by knowing a great deal when you see one

If a promotion is in the offing and it comes down to you and one other person, wouldn't you want to have these traits listed on your side? Wouldn't you have an advantage over a competitor if you demonstrated these traits by your 401k contributions, especially if that competitor couldn't do the same? Everything else being equal, I would promote the person in the 401k plan. There's more involved than money. The opportunity for career advancement could be a little-recognized, but very important benefit to participating in your 401k.

Your Biggest Enemy in Retirement

Inflation will make the last thirty years of your life your most expensive. Even if you reduce your expenses going into retirement, inflation will soon have your expenses back to their old level, and they will keep increasing each year.

Inflation is the most misunderstood and the most insidious enemy of retirees. Inflation is simply a decline in purchasing power as a result of rising prices. Retirees often have little discretionary income. They also often have little if any ability to increase their income in retirement. They are between the rock and a hard place.

The average annual inflation rate in the U.S. is about 4% per year, measured over the last several decades. That number does not move in a straight line, though. There have been periods, such as in the late 1970's, when annual inflation was in the 10-15% range. When inflation averages 4%, you need to double your income every eighteen years just to stay in the same place regarding your purchasing power. It also means that, if you plan on a 30-year retirement, you will need over three times the income in your last year of retirement that you needed in your first year, unless you are willing to accept a decline in your standard of living.

A long-term national average inflation rate may not seem to have much bearing on an individual. What really matters is one's own personal inflation rate. If you have your home paid for by the time you retire, then any increase in housing prices won't have much of an effect on your personal inflation rate. But, even if you retire with no debt and few obligations other than the normal monthly expenses (food, transportation, medical, utilities, etc.), you are still subject to inflation. Your personal inflation rate may also be higher than the national average.

Consider medical expenses. These costs include items like prescription drugs, insurance premiums and deductibles and other expenses connected to maintaining health. For decades, medical expenses have risen faster than inflation - about 8% per year. As we age, we also increase our use of medical products and services. If our use of medical products and services increases 5% per year during retirement and the cost of those services increases 8% per year from inflation, that's a personal medical inflation rate of 13%. At that rate of increase, someone who spends $5,000 per year for medical expenses at age 65 will be spending over $57,000 for medical expenses at age 85. By age 90, that figure would climb to over $100,000 per year.

When you consider that as we get older we see more different doctors on a more frequent basis, we require more prescriptions and our hospital stays become more frequent and of longer duration, a double-digit personal medical inflation rate is hard to avoid, unless we are willing to jeopardize our health by cutting back in some areas.

When you consider the likelihood of a high personal medical inflation rate in retirement, it almost doesn't matter if all our other expenses remain flat. You at age 82 may be paying eight times as much for medical expenses as you were at age 65. No pension, annuity or social security payment is going to keep up with an increase of that magnitude. These increased expenses can only be covered out of your personal savings.

To illustrate how inflation increases the income we need to maintain the status quo, look at the following chart. It shows a 65-year old new retiree starting retirement with an annual income of $50,000. As time goes on and inflation keeps working, our retiree needs a higher and higher income just to stay where he started.

INCOME NEEDED AT THESE ANNUAL INFLATION RATES

AGE	3%	4%	5%	6%	7%	8%
65	$50,000	$50,000	$50,000	$50,000	$50,000	$50,000
66	$51,500	$52,000	$52,500	$53,000	$53,500	$54,000
67	$53,045	$54,080	$55,125	$56,180	$57,245	$58,320
68	$54,636	$56,243	$57,881	$59,551	$61,252	$62,986
69	$56,275	$58,493	$60,775	$63,124	$65,540	$68,024
70	$57,964	$60,833	$63,814	$66,911	$70,128	$73,466
71	$59,703	$63,266	$67,005	$70,926	$75,037	$79,344
72	$61,494	$65,797	$70,355	$75,182	$80,289	$85,691
73	$63,339	$68,428	$73,873	$79,692	$85,909	$92,547
74	$65,239	$71,166	$77,566	$84,474	$91,923	$99,950
75	$67,196	$74,012	$81,445	$89,542	$98,358	$107,946
76	$69,212	$76,973	$85,517	$94,915	$105,243	$116,582
77	$71,288	$80,052	$89,793	$100,610	$112,610	$125,909
78	$73,427	$83,254	$94,282	$106,646	$120,492	$135,981
79	$75,629	$86,584	$98,997	$113,045	$128,927	$146,860
80	$77,898	$90,047	$103,946	$119,828	$137,952	$158,608
81	$80,235	$93,649	$109,144	$127,018	$147,608	$171,297
82	$82,642	$97,395	$114,601	$134,639	$157,941	$185,001
83	$85,122	$101,291	$120,331	$142,717	$168,997	$199,801
84	$87,675	$105,342	$126,348	$151,280	$180,826	$215,785
85	$90,306	$109,556	$132,665	$160,357	$193,484	$233,048
86	$93,015	$113,938	$139,298	$169,978	$207,028	$251,692
87	$95,805	$118,496	$146,263	$180,177	$221,520	$271,827
88	$98,679	$123,236	$153,576	$190,987	$237,026	$293,573
89	$101,640	$128,165	$161,255	$202,447	$253,618	$317,059
90	$104,689	$133,292	$169,318	$214,594	$271,372	$342,424

Don't Forget Your Spouse

It may be hard to imagine yourself living to age 90, but you're probably not alone on this trip. If you have a spouse, then the retirement fund has to cover both your lives, which is actually longer than either of your lives. It makes sense statistically (if no other way).

The IRS establishes distribution schedules for qualified retirement plans. It's interesting to look at the life expectancy schedules they use to calculate the required minimum distributions from retirement accounts. Here's how it breaks down for selected ages:

Age	Male Only	Female Only	Joint Life Expectancy
50	28.5 years	32.3 years	40.4 years
55	24.3 years	27.9 years	35.6 years
60	20.4 years	23.7 years	30.9 years
65	16.8 years	19.7 years	26.2 years
70	13.4 years	15.9 years	21.8 years
75	10.5 years	12.5 years	17.6 years
80	7.9 years	9.5 years	13.8 years
85	5.9 years	7.0 years	10.5 years
90	4.3 years	5.0 years	7.8 years

Did you notice that the joint life expectancy number is significantly higher than the female life expectancy, which is always higher than the male? One would assume that the female's life expectancy and the joint life expectancy would be the same, since the female usually outlives the male. Here's why they vary. The numbers for male-only and female-only life expectancies are calculating how long any one person in that group can be expected to live. Any one 50-year-old male can expect to live 28.5 more years. The joint life expectancy number is calculating how long before *every one in a group* dies. Even if that group consists of only two people, it will take longer for everyone to die than for any one to die.

Did you notice one other thing? The joint life expectancy is never less than 90 years, if you both make it to age 50, which means that there's at least a 50-50 chance that either you or your spouse will get the opportunity to blow out 90 birthday candles. These statistics are the reason all the tables in this chapter go to age 90. Future editions will probably have to go to 100.

If you will be getting a traditional pension at retirement, you will have choices on what benefit your surviving spouse will receive. Since living expenses don't change dramatically when one spouse dies, the income shouldn't change much either. Generally speaking, any surviving spouse benefit that's less than 75% of the joint benefit will likely create some financial stress for the survivor. It's better to take a smaller benefit while the two of you are alive than to risk financial hardship for the surviving spouse.

If the person receiving the pension has a permanent life insurance policy that pays the surviving spouse a substantial death benefit, then a smaller survivor benefit can be considered. In this case, the insurance proceeds can supplement the reduced income from the pension. Two things, though – make sure it's permanent insurance that can't be canceled and make sure the death benefit will be enough to offset the lower income for the rest of the surviving spouse's life.

Whipsawed By Our Own Emotions

As you know, fear and greed are the two human weaknesses that do the most to destroy one's finances. While it is unlikely that older people are more prone to fear and greed than younger people, they can suffer from the effects of fear and greed more. When you are young, you may still overcome damage done to your finances by fear or greed because you have more time, and you are still earning an income. An older person has neither of those luxuries.

Greed is probably the easier emotion to understand and recognize (at least in others). We aren't talking about the over-the-top-CEO-type greed that makes headlines. The more common greed is the type that lures us into buying an investment that we don't understand, that doesn't seem right to an objective observer, but that just looks too hot to pass up. We deny the risk because we are so tempted by the reward.

If you are thirty years old, and you permanently lose 20% of your portfolio because the too-good-to-be-true investment turned out to be just that, you still have plenty of time to make up that loss. If you are seventy years old and you lose 20% of your portfolio, you may soon be donning a blue Wal-Mart vest as penance.

Please note that I said *permanently* lose. Even a well-diversified portfolio has its ups and downs. During a bear market, it is possible to see the value of your portfolio drop by 20, 30 or even 40%, which is volatility, not loss. The investments are still intact, and will rebound with the market. You only lose in that situation if you give in to fear and sell good investments just because they are temporarily down.

Permanent loss involves an individual investment that has sunk and isn't coming back. If you buy stock in a company that goes out of business, that stock is likely to become worthless, which is permanent loss. If you buy a stock that had a fantastic run up to $100 per share (which is what you paid for it), but that stock is now at $4 per share (because the market finally figured out that $4 per share is its real value), that too is permanent loss.

Greed can ruin a retiree's investment portfolio and consequently, ruin their retirement, too. However, greed doesn't impact as many retirees as its counterpart, fear. We tend to become more cautious and conservative as we age; we fear losing what has taken a lifetime to accumulate, which is normal, and mostly a good thing – it's part of our survival mechanism.

Yet, fear that makes us too cautious and conservative in our retirement investing can end up guaranteeing the scenario we most fear – outliving our money.

Only those people who have managed to accumulate a large stockpile of assets can afford to have a risk-free portfolio in retirement. A risk-free portfolio consisting of CD's, treasury bonds and similar guaranteed investments isn't likely to provide a return sufficient to keep you even with inflation, much less keep you ahead of it. If your investment portfolio has the same return as the inflation rate and if you increase your income each year by the inflation rate, in order to survive a thirty-year retirement, you need *thirty times* your first year's retirement income in that account on Retirement Day One.

Let me restate the above with an example to help you understand. You want to retire with an income of $50,000 per year, and you want to be able to increase that income 4% per year to offset 4% annual inflation. Your investment portfolio earns a 4% annual return. The return exactly matches the inflation rate – it never outperforms or underperforms it. In this example, you will need to have $1,500,000 on your first day of retirement. And, at the end of the thirtieth year of retirement, almost all the money will be gone. The numbers are on the following chart:

	Beginning Account Value	Withdrawal for Income	Investment Return	Ending Account Value
Year 1	$1,500,000	$50,000	4.0%	$1,509,000
Year 2	$1,509,000	$52,000	4.0%	$1,516,320
Year 3	$1,516,320	$54,080	4.0%	$1,521,811
Year 4	$1,521,811	$56,243	4.0%	$1,525,316
Year 5	$1,525,316	$58,493	4.0%	$1,526,665
Year 6	$1,526,665	$60,833	4.0%	$1,525,683
Year 7	$1,525,683	$63,266	4.0%	$1,522,179
Year 8	$1,522,179	$65,797	4.0%	$1,515,953
Year 9	$1,515,953	$68,428	4.0%	$1,506,795
Year 10	$1,506,795	$71,166	4.0%	$1,494,477
Year 11	$1,494,477	$74,012	4.0%	$1,478,764
Year 12	$1,478,764	$76,973	4.0%	$1,459,402
Year 13	$1,459,402	$80,052	4.0%	$1,436,126
Year 14	$1,436,126	$83,254	4.0%	$1,408,652
Year 15	$1,408,652	$86,584	4.0%	$1,376,683
Year 16	$1,376,683	$90,047	4.0%	$1,339,902
Year 17	$1,339,902	$93,649	4.0%	$1,297,976
Year 18	$1,297,976	$97,395	4.0%	$1,250,552
Year 19	$1,250,552	$101,291	4.0%	$1,197,258
Year 20	$1,197,258	$105,342	4.0%	$1,137,699
Year 21	$1,137,699	$109,556	4.0%	$1,071,459
Year 22	$1,071,459	$113,938	4.0%	$998,100
Year 23	$998,100	$118,496	4.0%	$917,159
Year 24	$917,159	$123,236	4.0%	$828,144
Year 25	$828,144	$128,165	4.0%	$730,542
Year 26	$730,542	$133,292	4.0%	$623,806
Year 27	$623,806	$138,623	4.0%	$507,362
Year 28	$507,362	$144,168	4.0%	$380,605
Year 29	$380,605	$149,935	4.0%	$242,895
Year 30	$242,895	$155,933	4.0%	$93,560

It doesn't matter what the inflation/investment return numbers are. If your investment returns only match inflation and if your income keeps up with inflation, you will need thirty times your first year's income at the beginning of retirement, and all the money will be gone after 30 years. Most people can't accumulate that thirty-times figure. They also don't want to see it all gone by the thirtieth year.

This predicament is the price of fear in retirement. You will have to accumulate a lot of wealth in order to be able to own only "safe" investments during retirement. Paradoxically, one of the few ways to accumulate such wealth is by making "risky" investments during the accumulation period. By risky, I don't mean that high-flying stock that ends up crashing. I mean equities – a balanced portfolio of stocks (preferably through mutual funds) that will enable you to accumulate sufficient wealth to retire comfortably and on schedule.

Let's look at how having a figure of twenty times income might work out. If you started with $1,000,000 at retirement, you could have an income of $50,000 (5% of the total) in the first year. If you wanted to increase your income 4% per year to offset inflation, you would need an annual return of 7% during thirty years of retirement. You would have to get that 7% return every single year of your retirement, and the account would still run dry about halfway through Year Thirty-one. The following chart gives the details:

	Beginning Account Value	Withdrawal for Income	Investment Return	Ending Account Value
Year 1	$1,000,000	$50,000	7.0%	$1,018,250
Year 2	$1,018,250	$52,000	7.0%	$1,035,708
Year 3	$1,035,708	$54,080	7.0%	$1,052,234
Year 4	$1,052,234	$56,243	7.0%	$1,067,679
Year 5	$1,067,679	$58,493	7.0%	$1,081,876
Year 6	$1,081,876	$60,833	7.0%	$1,094,646
Year 7	$1,094,646	$63,266	7.0%	$1,105,791
Year 8	$1,105,791	$65,797	7.0%	$1,115,097
Year 9	$1,115,097	$68,428	7.0%	$1,122,330
Year 10	$1,122,330	$71,166	7.0%	$1,127,237
Year 11	$1,127,237	$74,012	7.0%	$1,129,541
Year 12	$1,129,541	$76,973	7.0%	$1,128,942
Year 13	$1,128,942	$80,052	7.0%	$1,125,114
Year 14	$1,125,114	$83,254	7.0%	$1,117,705
Year 15	$1,117,705	$86,584	7.0%	$1,106,330
Year 16	$1,106,330	$90,047	7.0%	$1,090,574
Year 17	$1,090,574	$93,649	7.0%	$1,069,987
Year 18	$1,069,987	$97,395	7.0%	$1,044,083
Year 19	$1,044,083	$101,291	7.0%	$1,012,332
Year 20	$1,012,332	$105,342	7.0%	$974,166
Year 21	$974,166	$109,556	7.0%	$928,967
Year 22	$928,967	$113,938	7.0%	$876,069
Year 23	$876,069	$118,496	7.0%	$814,750
Year 24	$814,750	$123,236	7.0%	$744,234
Year 25	$744,234	$128,165	7.0%	$663,679
Year 26	$663,679	$133,292	7.0%	$572,180
Year 27	$572,180	$138,623	7.0%	$468,757
Year 28	$468,757	$144,168	7.0%	$352,355
Year 29	$352,355	$149,935	7.0%	$221,837
Year 30	$221,837	$155,933	7.0%	$75,976

Despite having a large nest-egg to begin with and despite good, consistent returns, the money is still gone after about thirty years. In this example, the rate of return on the portfolio was 3% above the inflation rate, every single year. Regardless of how high or low inflation may be, your investments need to earn 3% above the inflation rate, just to make it to Year Thirty.

So, what do the previous two charts tell us? First, if you want a "risk-free" investment portfolio when you're retired, you need to save like crazy during your working years. Also, you can't assume you'll be leaving anything in that portfolio for your heirs.

Second, if you plan to "only" accumulate twenty times your income in your retirement portfolio, you need a return that's a consistent 3% above the inflation rate. And again, you can't assume you'll be leaving anything in that portfolio for your heirs.

Based on the above information, how is it that millions of retirees still manage to retire with that twenty-times figure, live comfortably and still leave a sizable chunk of that portfolio to their heirs? One reason is that those retirees tend not to increase their incomes in direct proportion to inflation. They often look for cheaper alternatives, take advantage of sales or cut back slightly. If their personal inflation rate is 4%, they often increase their income only 3%. In the previous two examples, reducing the income increases from 4% per year to 3% enables the accounts to still have between $600,000 and $900,000 in them after thirty years. Minor adjustments can make major differences, over time.

The last 30 years have also been an excellent time to be a retiree with an investment portfolio. Despite the ups and downs of the stock market, the S&P 500 index has grown at an average annual rate of 7.6% over the last thirty years, excluding dividends. During the period 1979 through 2008, the S&P 500 has been up more than 35% in its best year, and down more than 35% in its worst.

Despite the volatility of the stock market, if someone had retired in 1979 with $500,000, invested it all in the S&P 500 (not recommended), took $25,000 (5%) out of the account the first year, and increased their income from the account 4% per year, do you know what they'd have now? Over $1,400,000. The following chart shows how these numbers could be:

Year	Beginning Value	Income	Return of S & P 500	Ending Value
1979	$500,000	$25,000	14.2%	$542,450
1980	$542,450	$26,000	13.5%	$586,171
1981	$586,171	$27,040	-7.1%	$519,432
1982	$519,432	$28,122	20.7%	$593,012
1983	$593,012	$29,246	12.5%	$634,236
1984	$634,236	$30,416	9.9%	$663,598
1985	$663,598	$31,633	17.9%	$745,087
1986	$745,087	$32,898	29.4%	$921,572
1987	$921,572	$34,214	-6.2%	$832,342
1988	$832,342	$35,583	15.7%	$921,850
1989	$921,850	$37,006	10.6%	$978,638
1990	$978,638	$38,486	4.5%	$982,458
1991	$982,458	$40,026	18.8%	$1,119,610
1992	$1,119,610	$41,627	7.3%	$1,156,676
1993	$1,156,676	$43,292	9.8%	$1,222,495
1994	$1,222,495	$45,024	-2.3%	$1,150,390
1995	$1,150,390	$46,825	35.2%	$1,492,020
1996	$1,492,020	$48,698	23.6%	$1,783,947
1997	$1,783,947	$50,645	24.7%	$2,161,427
1998	$2,161,427	$52,671	30.5%	$2,751,926
1999	$2,751,926	$54,778	9.0%	$2,939,892
2000	$2,939,892	$56,969	-2.0%	$2,825,264
2001	$2,825,264	$59,248	-17.3%	$2,287,495
2002	$2,287,495	$61,618	-24.3%	$1,684,989
2003	$1,684,989	$64,083	32.2%	$2,142,838
2004	$2,142,838	$66,646	4.4%	$2,167,545
2005	$2,167,545	$69,312	8.4%	$2,274,485
2006	$2,274,485	$72,084	10.8%	$2,440,260
2007	$2,440,260	$74,968	3.5%	$2,448,078
2008	$2,448,078	$77,966	-38.7%	$1,452,878

At this point, you may be looking at the first and last lines of this chart. You may be noticing that this retiree has more than tripled his income over the last thirty years, while the value of his/her investments has more than quadrupled. You may be deciding that if the S&P 500 by itself was good enough then, it's good enough for you now.

You might also go back to the paragraph above this chart, see the words "not recommended", and conclude that this book is not only about Money Morons, but has been written by the Master Money Moron himself. Bear with me. I have two strong reasons for not recommending this strategy for a retiree. They are Human Nature and Luck.

The previous chart represents a hypothetical investor, not a real person. In addition, we have the benefit of 20-20 hindsight to know that this scenario worked out. In reality, our hypothetical retired investor would probably have stayed with the S&P 500 through about 1997. However, then the internet bubble would have been heating up, and the 25% annual gains of the S&P 500 would have seemed paltry compared to the internet stocks that were doubling by the week. Greed would likely have caused this investor to move at least some of his/her assets to those risky tech stocks. And we know what happened to most of them around 2000.

Worse, look what happened to the S&P 500 between 2000 and 2003. It was the worst bear market since the Great Depression (at least until 2008-2009). Our hypothetical retired investor lost more than 40% of his/her account value in those three years. Just as greed would have motivated a move out of the S&P 500 in the late 90's, fear would have really motivated a move out after a drop of 40%, and the inevitable rebound would have been missed.

Greed, Fear, and our tendency to take the immediate past and extrapolate it out into the indefinite future are the very human characteristics that would have (and did) cause more than 80% of such investors to stray form their original investment plan during this volatile period.

Now for the Luck part. Over the long term, stocks have exhibited a fairly predictable, steady upward climb. Yet, as we can see from the S&P 500, it is impossible to know what the markets will do in the short term. Out of curiosity, I made a simple change in the circumstances of our retired investor. I reversed the order of the S&P 500 returns over the thirty-year period (2008, became 1979, 2007 became 1980, etc.). The average annual return was surprisingly unchanged – it was 7.6% in either direction. Yet, the reversal's change on our retiree's portfolio was astounding – see the following chart:

	Beginning Value	Income	Return of S & P 500	Ending Value
Year 1	$500,000	$25,000	-38.7%	$291,175
Year 2	$291,175	$26,000	3.5%	$274,456
Year 3	$274,456	$27,040	10.8%	$274,137
Year 4	$274,137	$28,122	8.4%	$266,681
Year 5	$266,681	$29,246	4.4%	$247,881
Year 6	$247,881	$30,416	32.2%	$287,489
Year 7	$287,489	$31,633	-24.3%	$193,683
Year 8	$193,683	$32,898	-17.3%	$132,969
Year 9	$132,969	$34,214	-2.0%	$96,780
Year 10	$96,780	$35,583	9.0%	$66,704
Year 11	$66,704	$37,006	30.5%	$38,756
Year 12	$38,756	$38,486	24.7%	$337
Year 13	$337	$40,026	N/A	-$39,689
Year 14	-$39,689	$41,627	N/A	-$81,316
Year 15	-$81,316	$43,292	N/A	-$124,608
Year 16	-$124,608	$45,024	N/A	-$169,631
Year 17	-$169,631	$46,825	N/A	-$216,456
Year 18	-$216,456	$48,698	N/A	-$265,154
Year 19	-$265,154	$50,645	N/A	-$315,799
Year 20	-$315,799	$52,671	N/A	-$368,470
Year 21	-$368,470	$54,778	N/A	-$423,248
Year 22	-$423,248	$56,969	N/A	-$480,217
Year 23	-$480,217	$59,248	N/A	-$539,465
Year 24	-$539,465	$61,618	N/A	-$601,083
Year 25	-$601,083	$64,083	N/A	-$665,166
Year 26	-$665,166	$66,646	N/A	-$731,812
Year 27	-$731,812	$69,312	N/A	-$801,124
Year 28	-$801,124	$72,084	N/A	-$873,208
Year 29	-$873,208	$74,968	N/A	-$948,175
Year 30	-$948,175	$77,966	N/A	-$1,026,142

How can this discrepancy be? The average annual return of the S&P 500 was still 7.6% over this thirty-year period. How does our retired investor go from a surplus of over $1.4 million to a deficit of over $1 million? Luck.

If you look at the chart of the actual returns of the S&P 500, you will see that it had a lot of good years early on. There were only two down years in the first fifteen, and they were small drops in the 6-7% range. The worst years were in the second half, when our retired investor had already seen a sizable increase in his/her wealth. That's good luck.

When you reverse the order, our retiree is taking it on the chin early. By year five, the account is at half of its starting value; by year thirteen, it's all gone. (I list N/A for returns after Year 13 because, if you have no money left, the return of the S&P 500 is moot. Also note the income needs don't go away just because the income source did.)

Does this illustration mean that luck is what will determine if we get to live like a Prince or a Pauper in our retirement? No, unless you leave yourself exposed to the uncertainties of a small investment universe.

The goal of a successful retirement portfolio is to provide returns that will enable you to stay ahead of inflation, while at the same time smoothing out volatility as much as possible, which is the purpose of diversification. If your money is spread out over not just several assets, but several different asset classes, you are much more likely to get returns that will enable you to maintain your standard of living and also keep the portfolio from having the kind of down years that are difficult to recover from.

Diversification means you have positions in large U.S. companies, small growing U.S. companies, established overseas companies and developing overseas companies. You also have some bond holdings and some cash in money market funds.

How much you have in each asset class is a topic of much discussion. Your asset/income ratio as well as your personal tolerance for risk and volatility will be large factors in the actual asset allocation. I will make some general recommendations.

First, whatever amount you plan to draw from the retirement account over the next 18-24 months should be in nothing riskier than a money market fund. Even if that money market fund is paying a low interest rate, you need to know that the value won't be dropping. When you are looking at having to use that money to pay a bill within a year or two, it is the return *of* the money, not the return *on* the money that is of greatest importance.

Next, whatever amount you plan to draw from the account over three to four more years should be in short-term and intermediate-term high quality bonds. These bonds tend to pay a better interest rate than money market funds, with lower volatility than stocks.

By having five to six years of income in something other than stocks, you are able to ride out the worst bear markets. After peaking in early 2000, the S&P 500 dropped more than 40%. It didn't fully recover for about six years. By having six years' income in bonds and cash, there would have been no need to sell a stock holding when it was down so substantially. You would have had the cushion of time to enable that part of your portfolio to recover, which it ultimately did.

For a retiree drawing about 5% per year from the portfolio for income, the money market/bond part of the portfolio represents 1/4 to 1/3 of the total portfolio. This part of the portfolio dampens volatility – it trims the peaks and troughs of your portfolio's performance. More importantly, it can reduce stress. When you know you can go five years without having to sell any stock holding, you are no longer worried about the daily gyrations of the stock market. The talking heads on CNBC become irrelevant. You are able to turn off the TV and go relax in your garden.

The remainder of your investment portfolio is going to do the long-term heavy lifting, which is the 2/3 to 3/4 that will be devoted to stocks. Only stocks have shown the ability to generate long-term returns that will keep the portfolio growing well ahead of the inflation rate. While stocks may comprise 2/3 to 3/4 of your portfolio, they will be responsible for 90% or more of the income and appreciation generated by the portfolio.

As a very general guide, a retiree should have at least 50% of their stock holdings invested in large U.S. companies, the kind of companies that you find in the S&P 500 and similar large company indexes. These companies offer stability, as well as historically good returns. They may fluctuate in value, but they rarely go out of business.

The remainder of a retiree's stock holdings should be divided between small U.S. companies, large foreign companies and developing markets. The small U.S. companies are small only in comparison to the Fortune 500 companies. Many companies with a market value of $5 billion are classified as small companies. These companies are typically on the cutting edge of new markets and technologies. Among them lurks the next Microsoft, and those kinds of companies have the potential to get very big very fast.

Large foreign companies offer stability and the opportunity to diversify beyond the U.S. economy. Many of these companies are familiar to Americans. They include names like Toyota, Nestle, BP and Sony. These companies are less affected by adverse economic conditions in the U.S. than companies that are strictly domestic.

Lastly, developing markets offer excellent long-term growth potential. These markets include countries like Hungary, Thailand and India. We are referring here to countries with established infrastructures, representative governments and transparent accounting. Since this asset class has a larger risk to go along with its larger potential reward, only established mutual funds should be used as an investment vehicle.

Each year, money for income will come out of the money market fund. When it comes time to replacing that money each year, the investment categories that have done the best in the previous year will be sold down to provide the cash. In most years, creating cash for income will mean selling some of the various stock holdings. This strategy does two things – it disciplines you to sell when the asset is high, and it rebalances the portfolio at the same time. The chart below shows an example of how the portfolio could change in a year and what steps would be taken to rebalance the portfolio and prepare for the coming year.

Asset Class	Value on 1/1x1	Value on 12/31/x1	Return	Amount Sold	Value on 1/1/x2
Money Market	$100,000	$52,000	3%*	$0	$102,000
Bonds	$200,000	$208,000	4%	$5,000	$203,000
U.S. Large Stocks	$400,000	$424,000	6%	$22,000	$402,000
U.S. Small Stocks	$100,000	$110,000	10%	$10,000	$100,000
Foreign Large Stocks	$100,000	$98,000	-2%	$0	$98,000
Developing Markets	$100,000	$113,000	13%	$13,000	$100,000
Total	$1,000,000	$1,005,000	5.5%**	$50,000	$1,005,000

*Average balance in money market is about $75,000; 3% return adds about $2,000.
**Overall portfolio return was 5.5%; $50,000 was withdrawn from money market as income.

The numbers in the above chart are not designed to reflect anticipated performance for any category, or for the portfolio as a whole. They are simply to illustrate how a portfolio can change in a year and what steps are then taken to provide funds for the coming year and rebalance the portfolio at the same time.

One last piece of advice – The easiest way to avoid a financial crisis in retirement is to avoid retirement. The easiest way to avoid retirement is to find work you love. If you find work you love, it will never seem like work, and the idea of retiring from it will seem crazy to you. The happiest 80-year olds I know are ones who are still working at what they love. Physical decline may eventually force you into retirement, but doing work you love will almost certainly postpone that day. If you want help on finding work you can love forever, I encourage you to read *6,000,000 Minutes on the Clock* by yours truly.

And in rebuttal, what a MONEY MORON recommends you do:

- **Work a job you hate.** You'll have less worry about money because you'll have less money. People who hate what they do don't do it well and aren't burdened by large salaries. You'll also have lots to complain about every day.
- **Look only at salary.** If you start considering other things like a company's 401k plan, you'll only get confused. The company probably only contributes to your 401k plan to get you to work harder, and who wants to do that? The only money that matters is the money they give you now.
- **Count heavily on Social Security.** It hasn't gone broke yet, right? It's money from the government, and the government can get all the money it needs from taxes. Besides, old people collect Social Security and old people vote, so politicians wouldn't dare mess with Social Security.
- **Lean on your kids.** When you're old and can't support yourself, you know your kids will be there for you. They'll be happy to have you move in with them. They'll gladly rearrange their lives to revolve around your needs. And you'll be right there to help them deal with their own childrens' "issues".
- **Start late, leave early.** Don't join the workforce until you absolutely have to. Travel, join a commune, go to grad school. The sooner you go to work, the sooner people will expect you to act like an adult, and do things like plan for your old age. Also, hope to retire as young as possible. You can join AARP at Fifty. Anybody who works longer than that is a chump.
- **Don't sweat inflation.** A dollar bill looks the same size that it always has. Inflation's probably some kind of government conspiracy anyway. How else can prices double every 20-25 years? Besides, in the 1930's, there was actually Deflation. Maybe we'll get lucky and have one of those depressions like they had back then.
- **~~Procastr~~ ~~pocatrinate~~ Drag your feet.** The sooner you start thinking about retirement and saving for it, the sooner it will get here. Since old people retire, the sooner you retire, the sooner you'll be old. Do you really want to do something that makes you older faster? Delay acting

like an adult, so you can stay young forever, like Peter Pan or Michael Jackson.

- **Don't get professional advice.** Just because someone studies for many years and then has many years of experience, it doesn't mean they're qualified to give you advice that conflicts with your desires. Besides, if these professionals are so smart, why aren't *they* retired?
- **If you can't do it all, don't even start.** If you want to retire at 60, but it looks like the best you can do is retire at 70, don't waste your time and money saving for retirement. You have high standards, and if you can't have the best retirement, don't settle for less. You may get lucky and not even make it to 70.
- **Pay yourself last.** These "Pay Yourself First" fanatics aren't fooling anyone. If you pay yourself first, you will have less money for fun stuff, like a bigger house, a fancier car, or season passes for pro wrestling. More for the future means less for the present, and don't you live in the present?
- **Fear not greed.** Investing is a competitive sport, and you don't want someone else getting a better return than you. Sure, you gotta take risks, but you don't want your manhood questioned, even if you're a woman.
- **Listen to your fears.** When the stock market starts heading down, no one knows where the bottom is - it might go all the way to zero. Waiting for a rebound takes patience and discipline, and those take work. If your portfolio doesn't go up all the time, something's wrong.
- **Abuse yourself.** Smoke; drink; take drugs; eat like a pig; avoid exercise like the plague; have unprotected sex. If you live like there's no tomorrow, you increase the chances there won't be. The best way to avoid a retirement funding crisis is to die long before you get there.

On the following pages are some tables showing various cost-of-retirement projections. Tables were done for ages 25, 35, 45, and 55. The projections are not intended to illustrate any individual's actual situation. They are an exercise to show how making small changes in assumptions can create large changes in results. Investment returns are intended to be realistic, based on decades of historic returns. Two facts should become evident when looking at these tables – delaying retirement can greatly ease the burden of saving for retirement. Also, even a delayed retirement won't be cheap.

Retirement Cost projections for a 25-year old:

INPUT						
Current Income*	$30,000	$35,000	$40,000	$30,000	$35,000	$40,000
Current Retirement Savings	$10,000	$5,000	$10,000	$5,000	$10,000	$10,000
Projected Retirement Age	55	60	60	65	65	70
Projected Years in Retirement**	35	30	30	25	25	20
Post/Pre-Retirement Income Ratio	80%	85%	80%	90%	85%	85%
Pre-Retirement Investment Return	9.0%	8.5%	8.5%	9.0%	7.0%	8.5%
Post-Retirement Investment Return	7.0%	6.0%	7.0%	7.0%	5.5%	7.0%
RESULTS						
Needed Income - Retirement Year One	$77,800	$117,400	$126,300	$129,600	$142,800	$198,600
Needed Savings at Start of Retirement	$1,701,000	$2,657,000	$2,512,000	$2,287,000	$2,980,000	$2,986,000
Current Savings Alone Will Grow To	$132,700	$86,900	$173,800	$157,000	$149,700	$393,000
Shortfall Without Additional Savings	$1,568,300	$2,570,100	$2,338,200	$2,130,000	$2,830,300	$2,593,000
Percentage of Income that Should Be Saved	23.9%	22.7%	18.1%	12.2%	22.3%	8.0%
For Current Year That Amount Is	$7,200	$7,900	$7,200	$3,700	$7,800	$3,200

* Current income increases 4% per year. ** Everyone lives to age 90.

Retirement Cost projections for a 35-year old:

INPUT						
Current Income*	$30,000	$40,000	$50,000	$60,000	$70,000	$80,000
Current Retirement Savings	$10,000	$10,000	$20,000	$40,000	$10,000	$100,000
Projected Retirement Age	65	60	70	65	65	60
Projected Years in Retirement**	25	30	20	25	25	30
Post/Pre-Retirement Income Ratio	80%	85%	80%	90%	85%	85%
Pre-Retirement Investment Return	9.0%	8.5%	8.5%	9.0%	7.0%	8.5%
Post-Retirement Investment Return	7.0%	6.0%	7.0%	7.0%	5.5%	7.0%
RESULTS						
Needed Income - Retirement Year One	$77,800	$90,600	$157,800	$175,100	$193,000	$181,300
Needed Savings at Start of Retirement	$1,373,000	$2,052,000	$2,374,000	$3,089,000	$4,026,000	$3,607,000
Current Savings Alone Will Grow To	$132,700	$76,900	$347,600	$530,700	$76,100	$768,700
Shortfall Without Additional Savings	$1,240,000	$1,975,000	$2,026,000	$2,559,000	$3,950,000	$2,838,000
Percentage of Income that Should Be Saved	18.9%	40.8%	12.5%	19.5%	36.2%	29.3%
For Current Year That Amount Is	$5,700	$16,300	$6,300	$11,700	$25,300	$23,400

* Current income increases 4% per year. ** Everyone lives to age 90.

Retirement Cost projections for a 45-year old:

INPUT						
Current Income*	$40,000	$60,000	$80,000	$100,000	$125,000	$150,000
Current Retirement Savings	$100,000	$175,000	$220,000	$25,000	$350,000	$1,000,000
Projected Retirement Age	65	60	70	65	65	60
Projected Years in Retirement**	25	30	20	25	25	30
Post/Pre-Retirement Income Ratio	80%	85%	80%	90%	85%	85%
Pre-Retirement Investment Return	9.0%	8.5%	8.5%	9.0%	7.0%	8.5%
Post-Retirement Investment Return	7.0%	6.0%	7.0%	7.0%	5.5%	7.0%
RESULTS						
Needed Income - Retirement Year One	$70,100	$91,800	$170,600	$197,200	$232,800	$229,600
Needed Savings at Start of Retirement	$1,237,000	$2,079,000	$2,566,000	$3,478,000	$4,857,000	$4,568,000
Current Savings Alone Will Grow To	$560,400	$595,000	$1,691,000	$140,100	$1,354,000	$3,400,000
Shortfall Without Additional Savings	$676,300	$1,484,000	$874,500	$3,338,000	$3,503,000	$1,169,000
Percentage of Income that Should Be Saved	22.7%	64.2%	9.0%	44.9%	46.8%	20.2%
For Current Year That Amount Is	$9,100	$38,500	$7,200	$44,900	$58,500	$30,300

* Current income increases 4% per year. ** Everyone lives to age 90.

Retirement Cost projections for a 55-year old:

INPUT						
Current Income*	$50,000	$75,000	$100,000	$125,000	$150,000	$200,000
Current Retirement Savings	$300,000	$350,000	$675,000	$1,100,000	$960,000	$2,450,000
Projected Retirement Age	70	65	70	65	75	60
Projected Years in Retirement**	20	25	20	25	15	30
Post/Pre-Retirement Income Ratio	80%	85%	80%	90%	85%	85%
Pre-Retirement Investment Return	9.0%	8.5%	8.5%	9.0%	7.0%	8.5%
Post-Retirement Investment Return	7.0%	6.0%	7.0%	7.0%	5.5%	7.0%
RESULTS						
Needed Income - Retirement Year One	$72,000	$94,400	144,100	$166,500	$279,400	$206,800
Needed Savings at Start of Retirement	$1,083,000	$1,859,000	$2,167,000	$2,937,000	$3,744,000	$4,115,000
Current Savings Alone Will Grow To	$1,093,000	$791,300	$2,295,000	$2,604,000	$3,715,000	$3,684,000
Shortfall Without Additional Savings	$0	$1,068,000	$0	$333,300	$29,200	$431,200
Percentage of Income that Should Be Saved	0%	15.6%	0%	13.8%	.3%	31.2%
For Current Year That Amount Is	$0	$56,700	$0	$17,200	$500	$62,300

* Current income increases 4% per year. ** Everyone lives to age 90.

DON'T MAKE THIS JOURNEY ALONE

By this point in the book, you should feel smarter than you did on page one. You should also recognize that the path to personal financial success and happiness is fraught with countless pitfalls. No book is sufficient to help you make your journey successfully, in part because your life circumstances, your goals and your personality are all unique to you.

If you've ever used Google maps to get directions, you have probably noticed that the directions they give are not always the ones that are best. Your familiarity with an area lets you know that a route they recommend has delays, more traffic or something else that causes you to modify their directions. Personal knowledge and experience are something you have, but Google doesn't. Google, *Money* magazine, CNBC and even this book have one-size-fits-all limitations that make them insufficient tools on their own.

In this chapter, I want to advise you on what to look for in a financial advisor. However, before I do, I need to advise you on why you should use a financial advisor in the first place. The most basic reason for using a financial advisor, and the only reason you need, is that you will increase your chances of reaching your financial goals, and you will be less stressed about financial matters along the journey. More success and more happiness (at least the probability of them) are all the reasons you need to work with a financial advisor.

Over the years, the reasons I've encountered for people not using a financial advisor really boil down to two reasons. The first reason is a lack of trust. This chapter will help you with criteria to select an advisor who merits your trust, and it pains me to say that there are still too many people who call themselves financial planners and advisors who should not be trusted. Yet, there is a big difference between not trusting *an* advisor and not trusting *any* advisor. If you have interviewed several trustworthy advisors, but you still can't bring yourself to trust any of them, then none of them can help you. This relationship is not unlike marriage, in that there is a lot at stake and requires a measure of trust in your partner, but such a commitment is necessary to receive the benefits of the relationship.

The other reason for people not using a financial advisor is cost – or more accurately, misperceptions about cost. There are three ways financial advisors can justify what you pay them, and any single one of them is likely to more than justify their fee. Your financial advisor will help you do more right things, fewer wrong things and will relieve you of the responsibility of knowing about and acting on all of those right and wrong things.

It's important to understand that the tasks the financial advisor performs are absolutely essential to reaching financial goals. Eschewing the services of a financial advisor means accepting the responsibility of performing these tasks yourself – as well as the responsibility of failing to perform them.

Before someone assumes such responsibilities, they should self-evaluate in three areas – time, training and temperament. Most people who favor do-it-yourself never consider the cost of their time when calculating their "savings." There is only one situation when time spent on your finances has no cost – when there is nothing else you would rather be doing with that time. (If there is nothing you would rather do with your time than work on your finances, you need professional help, but not the kind I provide.) To do for yourself what a financial advisor can do for you will take you much more time than it will them, and certainly a lot more time than you think it will.

What is your training in finance? If it matches that of a financial advisor and if you love spending time working on financial matters, you may want to consider a career change to my profession. The truth is no one amasses the training that a professional financial advisor does unless they are going to make a living at it. The gap between an individual's knowledge and the professional's knowledge is more than large enough to swallow you whole.

Lastly and most importantly, is the issue of temperament. A financial advisor can be objective about your situation and how events affect it. There is no way any of us can be objective about our own situation; not me, not you. Financial advisors earn their keep by doing nothing more than slapping reins on their clients' fear and greed, wrapping those reins in their hands and then yanking those impulses into submission time and time again. The ever-increasing volatility of the stock market is not the result of economic conditions; it is the result of so many people acting on emotion because they have no one to stop them. The fortunes lost from mismanaged corporations and scam artists absolutely pales in comparison to the fortunes lost from unconstrained fear and greed by people like you and me. Financial advisors can't cure this disease, but they can control it.

As I write in the following pages about what to look for in a financial advisor, you may wonder if I'm listing only what applies to me, as a type of self-promotion. In the interest of full disclosure, I do meet all the objective criteria that I discuss. I can't say if I meet the subjective criteria, because that is determined by others, primarily clients and colleagues, but I have put the horse before the cart. I have made the effort to meet these criteria because I firmly believe they are essential to properly serve my clients, my profession and the public. I've met these criteria because they are important; they aren't important because I've met them.

Any financial advisor must first merit your trust before he or she can merit your business. Every client survey I have ever seen always ranks trust as the most important criteria in selecting and retaining an advisor. It is easy to evaluate an advisor's experience and education, which can give you an idea of their level of competence. Measuring their trustworthiness is much more subjective, and harder to do.

The first question you should attempt to ask yourself about any potential advisor is, *Is he/she a missionary or a mercenary?* It's not a question you can ask the advisor directly – you have to glean your answer from other data. By missionary, I mean an advisor who sees what he or she does as more than a way to make money. They see their job as a way to help people develop a better quality of life. That is their driving force, not how much income they make. I'm not saying that money should not be a motivator; it should not be the primary motivator.

Advisors who are more mercenary than missionary are likely to focus on numbers, and primarily numbers with dollar signs in front. One of their first questions to you may be how much money do you have to invest. They may start talking about products early in the conversation, before they have gotten to know you and your situation adequately. They may tout their success in investment selection with their current clients. They may refer to their large number of clients and the large amount of assets under management as proof of their expertise and worthiness to be your advisor. All of these factors may be points for you to consider, but only secondarily.

Advisors who are more missionary than mercenary are likely to focus on the person and qualitative issues before they focus on the money and quantitative issues. The missionary advisor understands that the client drives the money decisions, not the other way around. Until the advisor understands the clients and their situation, it is impossible to devise a financial strategy for them. A missionary advisor will always show greater interest in the client than in the client's money, which is not to say that missionary advisors don't pay attention to the client's money. I contend that they pay greater care and attention to it because missionary advisors are also a steward of the client's assets. They certainly want to make a buck for their clients and themselves, but they are also aware of the dangers of losing a buck, so they are not reckless.

Missionary advisors will also use their expertise in ways that may not generate an income but that raise the profession in the public's eye. They may be active in a professional organization, offer pro bono services to low-income families or speak to church and civic groups without making a sales pitch. Their desire is to help others, especially those who may not be potential clients. Look for evidence of such activities when evaluating advisors.

In the past, the client-advisor relationship was transaction-based. Today it is or should be relationship-based. In the past, the advisor's income came from commissions, which was why the relationship was transaction-based. Today, clients overwhelmingly prefer a fee-based compensation model, which makes long-term relationships more advantageous to both parties.

I have heard financial advisors brag that they have over 800 clients. I have had to hold my tongue and not tell them that they actually have about 100 clients, and about 700 ticked-off customers. Their high number of clients means that none of them are getting the kind of attention that a relationship requires. All advisors have their own upper limit on the number of clients they can serve effectively. You may be reassured by using an advisor who proudly claims that over 500 people have made the smart choice to use him or her. But do you really want to stand in line with 500 other people to talk to your advisor? I don't ever want to have so many clients that I can't return a phone call within 24 hours, or that I might not recognize one of them and know them by name when I see them at the supermarket. If I can't do that, I don't have a relationship.

I believe that the professional financial advisor has three main duties to their clients – steward, teacher and director. The first and most important role is steward. Stewardship here means protecting the assets of another and enabling those assets to grow and be used to meet the desires of the owner. If an advisor is doing something with a client's assets that he or she would never do if those assets belonged to an immediate family member, that advisor is not practicing good stewardship. Stewardship means never putting a client at any risk greater than the minimum needed to reach the client's goals.

Too often when I talk with a new client, they will tell me about a minor incident that is often a reason for their coming to me. They will tell me they called their old advisor with a question or a concern and their advisor replied with a dismissive, "Oh, don't worry about it." Every question from a client merits a proper answer. Every concern from a client merits attention, including concerns that may be based on inadequate or incorrect information. It is the role of the advisor to educate the client by answering questions fully, by validating concerns that have merit and by extinguishing baseless concerns through teaching the truth.

How would you feel about a doctor who asked for your input on the best way to cure an affliction you had? How would you feel about a doctor seeking your approval for any prescribed treatment for that affliction? From my perspective, my confidence in that doctor would be shot. Clients don't want their financial advisor to act that way, either. They want to be told what they need to do. They want someone who is sure enough in their knowledge and strong enough in their convictions to give unambiguous directions.

I like a doctor or an advisor, who will say, "Here is my assessment of the situation. If you do this, here is the likely outcome. If you don't do this, here is the likely outcome. There are no guarantees either way, but my expertise and experience tell me this is what we need to do. Shall we proceed?" Any doctor, advisor or any professional whom I pay for their expertise gains my confidence by such an approach. A professional financial advisor accepts and expects to be the director of your financial plan.

All that I've talked about so far assumes that the financial advisor possesses honesty. By honesty, I mean much more than not stealing from your account. I mean the advisor tells the truth, all the time, even if it hurts the advisor. What a client wants and what a client needs are often diametrically opposed. In conjunction with that conflict, what a client wants to hear and what a client needs to hear are also often at opposites. An advisor who won't tell you something you need to hear just because you don't want to hear it is not earning his/her fee. The truth is the truth whether the client likes it or not, and an advisor worth having won't be afraid to tell you the truth – tactfully, of course.

Professional advisors know what is and isn't within their control, and they make sure the clients know, too. No one can predict what the stock market will do in the short-term, and advisors shouldn't be whipping out a crystal ball just because clients ask them to do so. Making such predictions can lead clients to believe the advisor knows the unknowable, which violates the honesty doctrine. Professional advisors don't take credit when the markets go up, which also means they don't take blame when the markets go down.

When the advisor and the client are well matched, the advisor will have the ability to manage the client's behavior, at least in the sense of keeping the client from behaviors that are detrimental to the client. Long-term financial success has much more to do with investor behavior than it does with investment behavior. The professional advisor knows this difference and focuses more attention on the investor than the investment. This advisor knows what can be controlled, and what is important to control.

Professional advisors don't attempt to dazzle. To that end, they don't use flashy presentations full of jargon. I've seen financial advisors prepare beautiful 100-page financial plans for clients, complete with enough charts, graphs and technical terms to impress – if only the client could understand it. The plan usually ends up in a drawer, unimplemented. I personally prefer to use a legal pad, on which I may write no more than five steps the client needs to take, in order of importance. Some steps, like upping 401k contributions, don't involve me at all. When those steps are completed, we move on. The only good plan is one that gets acted on, and that usually means keeping it easy to understand.

If you are the type that wants to have multiple advisors, you are unlikely to get any who are very good. Some people who favor using multiple advisors argue that it is a method of hedging their bet, protecting against bad advice from any one advisor. They also contend that an advisor who has competition does a better job. However, these people misunderstand the most basic part of the relationship – they aren't paying for the advice; they're paying for the advisor. A good advisor gives good advice, and the more advisors you have, the greater the chance that one of them is giving bad advice. As far as the competition argument, competing advice leads to confusion for the client. Professional advisors know this is a relationship business, and relationships are not based on competition or half-hearted commitment on either side. The professional advisor accepts all of you or none of you and expects you to do the same.

Since there is little or no regulation regarding who can call themselves a financial planner or advisor (the terms are synonymous for our purposes), people call themselves financial planners who are not by any reasonable standard. A stock broker is not a financial planner, nor is an insurance agent, an accountant, nor an attorney. For any of them to call themselves a financial planner implies additional qualifications that misrepresent their actual breadth of knowledge.

To be assured a person has the qualifications to be called a financial planner, they should be a Certified Financial Planner (CFP). The CFP designation has been around for over thirty years, so there has been plenty of time for those in this line of work to earn the designation. The CFP program consists of study and testing in five areas: estate planning, retirement planning, tax planning, investments and insurance. In addition to passing a ten-hour comprehensive exam, a person must have a bachelor's degree plus three years of full-time experience as a planner before they can use the CFP designation.

The lack of a CFP designation should not prompt you to leave an otherwise good financial advisor. However, if you are looking for a financial advisor, one of the first requirements should be that they are a CFP. The requirements to earn and maintain the CFP designation mean that education, experience and ethics standards are enforced that are not enforced on those without the designation. These standards help assure (but don't guarantee) that the CFP you work with will meet your expectations.

All financial advisors expect to be paid, but the manner in which they are paid can vary. Until fairly recently, almost everyone who claimed to be a financial advisor was paid by commissions earned through the selling of a product to the client, such as a stock, mutual fund, annuity or insurance policy. Such an arrangement could cause the solution to be product-driven, rather than needs-driven. Commission-based compensation can also raise a question in a client's mind about the motives for a recommendation – is the advisor recommending a product because it is the best thing for me, or because it pays the best commission? Most recommendations are in fact based on the client's needs, not the advisor's, but the ability to create that doubt in a client's mind means such a compensation system is flawed.

In the last ten to twenty years, more and more advisors have switched to a fee-based model of compensation. Rather than earning commissions for selling products, the fee-based advisor earns an annual fee for the management of the client's assets. The annual fee is much less than the commission would be for the same product, but the fee is an ongoing fee, rather than a one-time commission. While commissions might average 5% of the value of an investment, fees are typically closer to 1% per year. By law, an advisor can earn a commission or a fee, but not both.

There are several advantages to both the client and the advisor for a fee-based compensation structure. The client doesn't have to worry that a product is being recommended based on the size of the commission. Any potential or perceived conflict of interest has been eliminated. The fee is paid for ongoing service and is paid on an ongoing basis. If the client becomes unhappy with the level of service they are receiving, they can move their account, and the advisor loses that revenue. Since the fee is a percentage of the assets under management, the financial fate of the advisor is linked to the financial fate of the client. In order for the advisor's fee to increase, the value of the client's account must first increase. When the value of the client's account drops, the advisor's income drops in direct proportion.

For the advisor, a fee-based compensation structure means a more reliable income. Under a commission structure, advisors have to spend a great deal of time hunting and capturing new clients, which is time they can't spend servicing their existing clients. Focusing on existing clients to maintain the income they provide improves the relationship and makes for a less stressful business environment. Growth of the advisor's business is more predictable and more assured. As new clients are brought onboard and assets under management grow, the advisor's income grows as well. Long-term planning is made easier, and the financial stability and the market value of the business are both improved in a fee-based environment.

In the current marketplace, it is hard to find financial advisors who work on a fee-per-job basis. It is too piecemeal to make an acceptable income, and the advisor has little influence in getting the client to implement his/her recommendations. It is transaction-based business of a different nature, but this one makes it difficult for all but a few advisors to survive in business. Such advisors are Rand McNally when what is needed is Sacajawea.

So far I've talked about what you should expect from your financial advisor. Let's talk now about what your financial advisor should expect from you. Since this is a relationship, there are mutual rights and responsibilities.

Just as you have the right to expect the truth from your advisor, your advisor has the right to expect the truth from you. I'm not referring too much here to misrepresentation by the client; that is rare. I'm talking about letting the advisor know when something changes in your life, like divorce, death, job loss, retirement, anything that might affect the advice they will render. Just as important, you need to talk to your advisor whenever you have a question or a concern. I am never irritated when clients call to ask a question or voice a concern. I only get irritated when they *don't* call. Such inquiries are not an interruption of the advisor's work; they *are* the advisor's work, or they should be. You have the responsibility to talk to your advisor whenever there is something on your mind. They can't solve a problem unless they know it exists.

As a client, you would be crazy to pay for advice you don't intend to follow, which means you have the responsibility to act on the advice you receive, or at least have a meaningful discussion with your advisor on why you can't follow that advice. Advisors put their professional reputation on the line when they render advice. It makes them look bad when the client ignores that advice, and no advisor with an ounce of self-respect will continue to take money from a client who doesn't heed counsel. There is also the matter of liability. A client who insists on self-destructing despite the best efforts of the advisor is also likely to sue that advisor later, rather than placing the blame where it belongs. Don't solicit advice unless you intend to follow it.

Recognize your limitations. The most important of these may be to recognize that your decisions come from the emotional side of your brain, not the logical side. We make our decisions emotionally, then sift through our data banks to extract whatever supports the decision we've made. No one is bad for doing this; it just means we're human. The advisor has a much greater ability to see your situation objectively, dispassionately and logically than you do. Accept that fact, so that you can also accept the advice you receive.

Men, this one is for you. We are known for our refusal to ask directions. This stubbornness applies not just when we navigate highways, but also when we navigate life. We think that needing directions diminishes our self-reliance and our masculinity, which is totally false. Putting our pride before the welfare of our loved ones diminishes our manhood. You don't have to know everything about finances; you only have to know that you don't know. Then go get help for those things you know you need help. We don't have to do it all. We only have to do what we do best, to the best of our ability. For everything else, we should accept help whenever it's available. It's the manly thing to do.

In the movie *Michael Clayton*, George Clooney plays the title character, a lawyer who has a unique specialty. When one of his firm's biggest clients commits a hit-and-run, Clayton goes to his client's home to assess the situation. The distraught client doesn't like the options presented, and berates Clayton for not being the "miracle worker" Clayton's boss said he was sending. Michael Clayton coldly replies, "I'm not a miracle worker. I'm a janitor."

Don't expect your financial advisor to be a miracle worker or a janitor. No financial advisor can enable you to retire in ten years if you've only saved $50,000 to date and you're 50 years old. No financial advisor can obtain life insurance you can afford if you smoke three packs a day. No financial advisor can plan your estate if you don't first accept your mortality. No financial advisor can make college attainable for your son if he refuses to finish high school. No financial advisor can change the past. No financial advisor can change someone who refuses to change. No financial advisor worth a damn ever accepts the role of janitor.

If you are looking for a financial advisor, start first with people you know and respect and find out who they use. Good advisors grow their business mostly by word-of-mouth, and an endorsement of an advisor by someone you respect should carry a lot of weight. You can find Certified Financial Planners in your area through the Financial Planning Association's web site, www.fpanet.org.

MISCELLANEOUS MONEY MUSINGS

The possession of gold has ruined fewer men than the lack of it.
-Thomas Bailey Aldrich

If God would only give me some clear sign! Like making a deposit in my name in a Swiss bank account.
-Woody Allen

Work for your future as if you are going to live forever, for your afterlife as if you are going to die tomorrow.
-Arabian Proverb

One cannot both feast and become rich. *-Ashanti Proverb*

Money, it turned out, was exactly like sex; you thought of nothing else if you didn't have it, and thought of other things if you did.
-James Baldwin

Money is a terrible master but an excellent servant. *-P.T. Barnum*

Interest works day and night in fair weather and in foul. It gnaws at a man's substance with invisible teeth.
-Henry Ward Beecher

Frugality is founded on the principle that all riches have limits.
-Edmund Burke

Cessation of work is not accompanied by cessation of expenses.
-Cato the Elder

If you mean to profit, learn to please. *-Winston Churchill*

It is difficult to set bounds to the price unless you first set bounds to the wish.
-Cicero

He who will not economize will have to agonize. *-Confucius*

There is no dignity quite so impressive and no independence quite so important as living within your means.
-Calvin Coolidge

Mark DiGiovanni

Thousands upon thousands are yearly brought into a state of real poverty by their great anxiety not to be thought poor.

-William Corbett

Plan ahead: it wasn't raining when Noah built the ark.

-Richard Cushing

In prosperity, caution; in adversity, patience. *-Dutch Proverb*

Not everything that can be counted counts. And not everything that counts can be counted.

-Albert Einstein

The first wealth is health. *-Ralph Waldo Emerson*

Poor men seek meat for their stomachs; rich men seek stomachs for their meat.

-English Proverb

The man least indebted to tomorrow meets tomorrow most cheerfully.

-Epicurus

If we don't discipline ourselves the world will do it for us.

-William Feather

What maintains one vice would bring up two children.

-Benjamin Franklin

The sound of your hammer at five in the morning, or eight at night, heard by a creditor, makes him easy six months longer.

-Benjamin Franklin

God provides the nuts, but he does not crack them. *-German Proverb*

Is not dread of thirst when your well is full, the thirst that is unquenchable?

-Kahlil Gibran

I am indeed rich, since my income is superior to my expense, and my expense is equal to my wishes.

-Edward Gibson

This is one of the bitter curses of poverty: it leaves no right to be generous.

-George Gissing

The worst crime against working people is a company which fails to operate at a profit.

-Samuel Gompers

The darkest hour of any man's life is when he sits down to plan how to get money without earning it.

-Horace Greeley

Failure can be bought on easy terms; success must be paid for in advance.

-Cullen Hightower

If a man has money, it is usually a sign too, that he knows how to take care of it. Don't imagine his money is easy to get simply because he has plenty of it.

-Edgar Watson Howe

Lots of folks confuse bad management with destiny. *-Elbert Hubbard*

The future is purchased by the present. *-Samuel Johnson*

No gain is as certain as that which proceeds from the economical use of what you already have.

-Latin Proverb

I don't like money actually, but it quiets my nerves. *-Joe Louis*

For which of you, intending to build a tower, sitteth not down first, and counteth the cost, whether he have sufficient to finish it?

-Luke 14:28

I would rather have people laugh at my economies than weep for my extravagance.

-King Oscar II of Sweden

He that maketh haste to be rich shall not be innocent. *-Proverbs 28:20*

Good times are when people make debts to pay in bad times.

-Robert Quillen

Never invest your money in anything that eats or needs repairing.

-Billy Rose

Don't buy the house; buy the neighborhood. *-Russian Proverb*

Ask thy purse what thou should spend. *-Scottish Proverb*

Economy is too late at the bottom of the purse. *-Seneca*

Neither a borrower nor a lender be
For loan oft loses both itself and friend,
And borrowing dulls the edge of husbandry.
-William Shakespeare, from "Hamlet"

Never measure your generosity by what you give, but rather by what you have left.
-Bishop Fulton J. Sheen

A man is rich in proportion to the things he can afford to let alone.
-Henry David Thoreau

I am opposed to millionaires, but it would be dangerous to offer me the position.
-Mark Twain

Hell is the state in which we are barred from receiving what we truly need because of the value we give to what we merely want.
-Virgil

Work banishes those three great evils, boredom, vice and poverty.
-Voltaire

Make all you can, save all you can, give all you can. *-John Wesley*

APPRECIATIONS

Beth
Mara
Tony & Jean DiGiovanni
Sam Rainwater
Rocco & Concetta DiGiovanni
Ed & Mil Prevost
Gina & Ed Swart
Andrea & John Wheatley
Sam Pettyjohn
Lewis Walker
Michael Smith
Elizabeth Jetton
Nick Murray
Mitch Anthony
Audrey Porter
Hank Ezell
Bill Pittroff
Bud Schooler
Howard B. Stroud Sr.
Dave Ramsey
Dr. Thomas Inzana
St. Augustine School
The Aquinas Institute
SUNY, Oswego
University of Georgia
Kennesaw State University
The Safford Group
FPA
SFA
Rotary
St. Matthews Church

REFERENCES

- Ariely, Dan; *Predictably Irrational;* Harper Books; 2008
- Belsky; Gilovoch; *Why Smart People Make Big Money Mistakes*; Simon & Schuster; 1999
- Brafman; Brafman; *Sway-The Irresistible Pull of Irrational Behavior*; Doubleday; 2008
- Block; Hirt; *Foundations of Financial Management;* Irwin; 1992
- Browne, Harry; *Why the Best-Laid Investment Plans Usually Go Wrong*; Simon & Schuster; 1989
- Clason, George; *The Richest Man in Babylon;* Signet Press; 1926
- Davies, Glyn; *A History of Money from Ancient Times to the Present Day;* University of Wales Press; 2002
- DeGraff; Wann; Naylor; *Affluenza*; Berrett Koehler; 2005
- Dungan, Nathan; *Speaking of Faith: Money and Moral Balance*; 2004
- Easterbrook, Greg; *The Progress Paradox – How Life Gets Better While People Feel Worse*; Random House; 2003
- Eisenberg, Lee; *The Number – A Completely Different Way to Think About the Rest of Your Life*; Free Press; 2006
- Ellis, Charles; *The Investor's Anthology*; John Wiley & Sons; 1997
- Fitzhenry, Robert, Ed.; *The Harper Book of Quotations*; Harper Perennial; 1993
- Gerstein, Ellsberg; *Flirting With Disaster-Why Accidents are Rarely Accidental*; Union Square; 2008
- Gladwell, Malcolm; *The Tipping Point*; Little, Brown & Co.; 2000
- Goldstein; Martin; Cialdini; *Yes!-Proven Ways to Be Persuasive*; Free Press; 2008
- Goodman, Ted, Ed.; *The Forbes Book of Business Quotations*; Black Dog & Leventhal; 1997
- Harford, Tim; *The Logic of Life*; Random House; 2008
- Kasser, Tim; *The High Price of Materialism*; MIT Press; 2002
- Kidder, Rushworth; *How Good People Make Tough Choices*; Harper Collins; 1995
- Kinder, George; *The Seven Stages of Money Maturity*; Delacorte Press; 1999
- Koch, Richard; *The 80/20 Principle*; Doubleday; 1998
- Levitt; Dubner; *Freakonomics*; Penguin Books; 2005
- Littell; Tacchino; Cordell; *Financial Decision Making at Retirement*; The American College; 1995
- MacKay, Charles; *Extraordinary Popular Delusions and the Madness of Crowds*; Three Rivers Press; 1980

- Manning, Robert; *Credit Card Nation*; Basic Books; 2000
- Moore; Simon; *It's Getting Better All the Time – Greatest Trends of the Last 100 Years*; Cato Institute; 2000
- Murray, Nick; *Simple Wealth, Inevitable Wealth*; Nick Murray Inc.; 1999
- Needleman, Jacob; *Money and the Meaning of Life*; Doubleday; 1991
- Pink, Daniel; *A Whole New Mind*; Riverhead Books; 2005
- Piquet, Howard; *The Economic Axioms*; Vantage Press; 1978
- Ramsey, Dave; *Financial Peace Revisited*; Viking Press; 2003
- Rejda, George; *Principles of Risk Management and Insurance*; Harper Collins; 1995
- Sadler; Kreft; *Changing Course – Navigating Life After 50*; Center For Third Age Leadership; 2007
- Simmel, Georg; *The Philosophy of Money*; Routledge; 2003
- Schor, Juliet; *Born to Buy*; Scribner; 2004
- Schor, Juliet; *The Overspent American – Why We Want What We Don't Need*; Harper Perennial; 1998
- Schwartz, Barry; *The Paradox of Choice – Why More is Less*; Harper Collins; 2004
- Sowell, Thomas; *Basic Economics – A Citizen's Guide to the Economy*; Basic Books; 2004
- Stanley; Danko; *The Millionaire Next Door;* Pocket Books; 1996
- Stanley, Thomas; *The Millionaire Mind*; Andrews McNeel Publishing; 2001
- Waud, Roger; *Economics*; Harper & Row; 1980
- Weatherford, Jack; *The History of Money*; Three Rivers Press; 1997
- Wood; Lilly; Malecki; Graves; Rosenbloom; *Personal Risk Management and Insurance*; American Institute; 1989

www.ajc.com
www.cfp.net
www.edmunds.com
www.fairisaac.com
www.forbes.com
www.fpanet.org
www.ftc.gov
www.housebuyingtips.com
www.ircweb.org
www.marathon-forthelongrun.com
www.myfico.com
www.nefe.org
www.nobelprize.org
www.ofheo.gov
www.philanthropy.com
www.socialsecurity.gov
www.ustreas.gov
www.wikipedia.org